"**If you're struggling to figure out your business model, then this book has a lot to offer you.** It gives you an insider's look at how different people created different practice structures to suit who they are and how they want to deliver their services. Somewhere in *In Search of the Perfect Model* is *your* perfect business model; all you need is the book and the courage to follow where it leads you."

BOB VERES
Publisher, *Inside Information*
Author, *The Cutting Edge*

"**This is it!** With this book, Mary Rowland captures the heart and soul of the certified financial planner practitioner. **This is a must-read for the person in search of the essence of financial planning** and the myriad structures and platforms practitioners have constructed to deliver their personal financial advice and financial services."

JOHN T. BLANKINSHIP, CFP®
Partner, Blankinship & Foster

"A unique aspect of the financial planning profession is the non-standardized approach for providing our services. This provides two benefits. First, planners can create the office environment that is most appealing for their work style. Second, consumers have choices concerning how they would like to be served. **Mary Rowland's *In Search of the Perfect Model* provides great insight into the successful, yet different, business styles of our profession.**"

ELAINE E. BEDEL, CFP®
President, Bedel Financial Consulting, Inc.
Past Chair, CFP Board of Standards

"***In Search of the Perfect Model* is like the collected works of the early masters—a terrific rendering of how creative people using innovative ideas constructed financial-advisory practices** whose only commonality is how well they work—both for them and for their clients. Mary Rowland has proved once again that she knows both where and how to mine the nuggets of gold in the provision of financial planning services, and greenhorns and old-timers alike will get a little richer in knowledge by going along on her expedition."

BOB WACKER, CFP®, EA
President, R. E. Wacker Associates, Inc.

In Search of the Perfect Model

Also by
MARY ROWLAND

Best Practices for Financial Advisors

Also available from
BLOOMBERG PRESS

Deena Katz on Practice Management:
For Financial Advisers, Planners, and Wealth Managers
by Deena B. Katz

Deena Katz's Tools and Templates for Your Practice:
For Financial Advisers, Planners, and Wealth Managers
by Deena B. Katz

Virtual Office Tools for a High-Margin Practice:
How Client-Centered Financial Advisers
Can Cut Paperwork, Overhead, and Wasted Hours
by David J. Drucker and Joel P. Bruckenstein

The Financial Planner's Guide to Moving Your Practice Online:
Creating Your Internet Presence and Growing Your Business
by Douglas H. Durrie

Getting Started as a Financial Planner
by Jeffrey H. Rattiner

A complete list of our titles is available at
www.bloomberg.com/books

In Search of the Perfect Model

The Distinctive Business Strategies of
Leading Financial Planners

By

Mary Rowland

Bloomberg PRESS

PRINCETON

First edition published 2004
1 3 5 7 9 10 8 6 4 2

Library of Congress Cataloging-in-Publication Data

In search of the perfect model : the distinctive business strategies of leading financial planners / by Mary Rowland. -- 1st. ed.
        p. cm.
Includes index.
    ISBN 1-57660-125-0 (alk. paper)
    1. Financial planners. 2. Investment advisors. I. Title.
    HG179.5.R69 2004
    332.6'2'092--dc22   2003015790

Edited by Mary Ann McGuigan

Book Design by LAURIE LOHNE / DESIGN IT COMMUNICATIONS

To Mary Ann McGuigan,
for her inspiration and hard work

Contents

Part One

The Quest

Part Two

The Seekers

Part   Three

New Findings

Preface

ONE OF THE THINGS I've come to admire most about the financial planning business is that advisers are continually raising the bar. There seems no limit to how far beyond good enough they're willing to go. But can planners maintain such high standards and still manage to grow a business?

Smart advisers put serving clients first, but not at the cost of survival. No surprise, then, that those on the cutting edge are looking beyond comprehensive client service; they're figuring out how to develop a practice model that attracts the kind of clients they want most and allows their business to grow. A practice model often emerges by happenstance. Keats, Connelly & Associates in Phoenix, Arizona, for example, chose to specialize in dual citizenship because so many Canadian snowbirds had become clients. But all planners at some point must make a decision—serendipitous or not—about their practice model and how they will build on it. It may be time to make yours. Whether your firm is large or small, that means figuring out who you are and what you do best.

No business stands still; it dies or it expands to the point at which you must make choices about the work you love most and how to tackle the growing administrative tasks that get in the way of doing it. Some planners, like Harold Evensky, principal of Evensky, Brown & Katz in Coral Gables, Florida, hire a chief executive officer to run the business, so that they can spend time with clients. Others, like Sheryl Garrett, principal of the Garrett Planning Network in Shawnee, Kansas, free themselves from a 24/7 client obligation by parceling out advice by the hour.

In Search of the Perfect Model introduces you to some of the most creative minds in the industry and takes a look at how each one turned a fledgling practice into a business that offers the very best service to a particular group of clients. The planners presented in this book don't have photocopied success stories. You'll find here many different models that suit different strengths, personalities, businesses, and lifestyles. Clearly, many options are available to you as a financial adviser. But if you want a business that showcases your strengths and taps into your passion, you must evaluate your practice and develop a model that will create it. That's true whether you're:

➤ just starting out and wondering what direction to take;
➤ tied to commissions and want to bring your business to a new professional level;
➤ spending more time at the office and enjoying it less;
➤ losing clients because you're not meeting their expectations;
➤ feeling heat from the competition;
➤ satisfied with your business but perplexed about how to grow it;
➤ debating whether to get more involved in the life-planning trend; or
➤ wondering whether to sell out, merge, buy up firms, or form a network.

Financial planning has grown into a prestigious and lucrative profession, one that can bring much satisfaction to you as a planner. But like so many emerging disciplines eventually do, it has reached a crossroads. And you'll have to choose which direction to go. I offer you a look at the ways some of the most successful planners have structured their firms. Some of these business models are quite innovative, and all reflect the strengths of the advisers who shaped them. If you're looking for a way to grow your business and to meet the higher expectations that clients now have, these models can motivate and even inspire.

So come along. Meet some planners who've paved the way— people who started out from a place much like the one you're in now and arrived at another uniquely their own. Let them show you how to get there from here.

MARY ROWLAND

The Planners

Ginger Applegarth, an honors graduate of Vanderbilt University and president of Applegarth Advisors Group in Boston, used her planning practice as a platform to become a speaker, television personality, and author. She has served as a regular correspondent on the *Today Show,* hosted her own radio show, and appeared several times on *The Oprah Winfrey Show.* Her books, *The Money Diet: Reaping the Rewards of Financial Fitness* (Viking Press) and *Wake Up and Smell the Money* (Viking Press), have been on several bestseller lists.

Applegarth Advisors Group Inc.
10 Mount Vernon Street
Suite 225
Winchester, MA 01890
781-721-5445
www.GingerApplegarth.com

Darcy Garner Bhatia planned to work for the United Nations or Unicef—someplace where she could make a difference—when she was an undergraduate studying psychology, linguistics, and behavioral finance and while getting an M.B.A. in international business. Instead, Bhatia ended up working as a financial adviser to wealthy clients, some of whom have followed her from employer to employer in California and even across the country, when she married and moved to New York. There she set up a multiclient family office practice with three partners in the spring of 2002. Within six months, the new firm, Highmount Capital, had thirty to forty-five client relationships and $500 million in assets under management.

Highmount Capital, LLC
12 East 49th Street
New York, NY 10017
646-274-7454
www.highmountcapital.com
dgarner@hmcap.com

Eleanor Blayney majored in English and French at Mount Holyoke College and Cambridge University before getting an M.B.A. from the

University of Chicago. She is director of portfolio management for Sullivan, Bruyette, Speros & Blayney, a regional planning firm based in McLean, Virginia. From the time of the firm's founding in 1991, the partners began to work out how they might build a business. To keep everyone focused on that goal, they signed an agreement to make the firm their lifework. In the course of ten years, the firm has moved from having a flat organizational structure to six separate teams, each with its own clients. "The team takes ownership of that client," Blayney says. The firm's goal is to be seen as one of the top three financial planning firms by prospective clients in the Washington metro area. [Author's note: Sullivan, Bruyette, Speros & Blayney was purchased by Harris Bank of Chicago in 2003.]

Sullivan, Bruyette, Speros & Blayney
8180 Greensboro Drive
Suite 450
McLean, VA 22102
703-734-9330
www.sbsbinc.com

Janet Briaud was hunting for something to do with her life—something she could feel passionate about—when she happened on financial planning. Briaud, who works with college professors at Texas A&M University, set up her fee-only business in 1986 after earning a master's degree in physical education. A good investor and astute financial planner, Briaud's work has been not just a career but also a personal journey. "You have to look at your own heart first and see what you want to do and what you might love doing," she says. What she really loves is going beyond the nuts and bolts of financial problems to help people see how a flawed approach to money gets in the way of happiness. "I'm always using intuition with clients," she says. "The more you go into yourself, the more you can do that with clients. You peel off one layer after another."

Briaud Financial Planning
4444 Carter Creek Parkway
Suite 110
Bryan, TX
979-260-9771
www.briaud.com

Elissa Buie has been a financial planner since she was a "beer-drinking college student" at the University of Virginia. After graduation, she did temp work and got a job with a broker-dealer, where she was introduced

to financial planning. She earned an M.B.A. and started a financial planning arm for the broker. In 1993 she opened her own financial planning
firm. When Buie attended George Kinder's Seven Stages workshop, it
changed her life as well as her practice. Buie discovered that what she
would regret if she had just twenty-four hours to live was that she hadn't
found her soul mate—a realization that led to her divorce. She used her
new insights to revamp her practice, hiring a business consultant to help
her screen for clients she could get to know well. Buie realized that she
worked best with the clients she was closest to. Her personal experience
led her to see what mattered to her in financial planning. And she found
that soul mate—planner David Yeske.

Financial Planning Group Inc.
510 N. Washington Street, #300
Falls Church, VA 22046
703-538-2116
ebfp@aol.com
www.fpginc.com

Tom Connelly was an exploration geologist who got an M.B.A. from
Arizona State University to find job stability in an unstable field. When
his first job out of graduate school lasted just two weeks, he turned to
financial planning, joining forces with Bob Keats to develop a specialty
in Canadian snowbirds in and around Phoenix, Arizona. Clients with dual
citizenship have special investment, tax, and estate planning problems,
and the company has developed a niche with a solid barrier to entry—so
solid, in fact, that Connelly is often asked to speak on developing a niche
business.

Keats, Connelly and Associates
3336 N. 32nd Street
Suite 100
Phoenix, AZ 85018
602-955-5007
www.keatsconnelly.com

David Diesslin, president of Diesslin & Associates in Fort Worth, Texas,
is a sole practitioner with 250 clients from seventy families and a staff of
fifteen. The firm provides customized services to each client, with the
goal of bringing corporate efficiencies to families while offering individual service. Diesslin's wife, Deena, is a psychologist, and her influence on
his practice is evident. Not only does he seek her advice on client issues;
he also begins his work with each client by looking at Abraham Maslow's

hierarchy of needs: survival, safety, belonging, achievement, and self-actualization. Diesslin's goal is to help clients talk about their own life's vision so that he can develop a plan for them to attain it. A former president of NAPFA, Diesslin founded his firm in 1980. He specializes in estate planning, retirement planning, and charitable giving.

Diesslin & Associates
303 Main Street
Suite 200
Fort Worth, TX 76102
817-332-6122
www.diesslin.com

David Drucker, who received his M.B.A. from American University in Washington, D.C., was a financial analyst with the government and a director of finance in private industry before becoming a financial adviser in 1981. He concentrates in planning for retirement-age couples, widows, and professionals and is recognized in the industry for his innovative approach to creating the virtual, or paperless, office. He pioneered the virtual office when his instincts led him to leave a thriving practice in Maryland and move with his wife and daughter to Albuquerque. He is coauthor, with Joel P. Bruckenstein, of *Virtual-Office Tools for a High-Margin Practice* (Bloomberg Press), editor of the *Virtual Office News* newsletter, and writes regularly on planning issues for professional magazines, including *Bloomberg Wealth Manager.*

Sunset Financial Management, Inc.
8800 Northridge Drive, NE
Albuquerque, NM 87111
505-453-5703
www.daviddrucker.com

Harold Evensky, chairman of Evensky, Brown & Katz in Coral Gables, Florida, and his partner and wife, Deena Katz, are two of the best-known planners in the business today. Evensky wrote *Wealth Management: The Financial Advisor's Guide to Investing and Managing Your Client's Assets* (Irwin Professional Publishing), outlining a curriculum for planners who want to consult with the wealthy and anointing them wealth managers—a name that stuck. Katz is author of *Deena Katz on Practice Management* (Bloomberg Press) and *Deena Katz's Tools and Templates for Your Practice* (Bloomberg Press). The two agree with Mark Hurley that the future of financial planning lies with big firms, and they plan to build their own national firm, the Evensky Group, by starting out small in Florida and growing gradually nationwide. "We need to amortize the costs and spread them over a larger base," Evensky says. The couple's first attempt at building a larger firm failed. But they are not the kind to give up, and they believe the time is right. "The planets are all aligned," Katz says.

Evensky, Brown & Katz
2333 Ponce de Leon Boulevard
Penthouse Suite 1100
Coral Gables, FL 33134
305-448-8882
www.evensky.com

Barry Freedman and his son, Marc, have worked out a hybrid system in which Barry works with established clients and new high-net-worth clients, charging an asset-management fee while Marc brings in younger clients and works with them on a commission basis if that structure is more advantageous to them. The two also offer workshops for families, working with them on succession and estate planning and on dealing with money issues for the next generation. The Freedmans provide the unique perspective of father-and-son planners who have worked out their own succession plan, whereby Barry will hand the business over to Marc. In the meantime, the Freedmans have set up a second office in Florida, where Barry spends stretches of time, realizing a dream of many planners: to stay active in the business and still achieve a personal vision and find balance in life.

Freedman Financial Associates
5 Essex Green Drive
Peabody, MA 01960
978-531-8108
www.freedmanfinancial.com

Sheryl Garrett knew as a teenager that she wanted to help people with investing and money problems but it took her a while to find a model that suited her. She tried working as a commissioned financial planner and as a fee-only wealth manager before landing in her niche—the hourly-fee practice she set up in Shawnee, Kansas, in 1998. Like others who offer advice by the hour, Garrett considers herself a helper and a teacher and enjoys the satisfaction that comes from answering a client's immediate questions and getting him on the right track. She also likes working with people in various income ranges. Because she doesn't manage money, she savors the freedom she has to disappear on camping trips without worrying about the markets. She has franchised her business and works with planners across the country to set up an hourly-fee business based on her model.

Sheryl Garrett
Garrett Planning Network, Inc.
12700 Johnson Drive
Shawnee, KS 66216-1643
866-260-8400
www.garrettplanningnetwork.com

Roger Gibson, president of Gibson Capital Management in Pittsburgh and author of *Asset Allocation: Balancing Financial Risk* (McGraw-Hill) is a favorite speaker at financial planning conferences. He once gave a wonderful speech called "Gibson Unplugged," in which he talked about how his life started to come together just when he thought it was falling apart. The turning point came when he recognized the need for balance. Although almost everyone in the industry knows of Gibson and his work, strictly speaking, he is no longer a financial planner. He does asset allocation and money management for clients but does not do other aspects of planning.

Gibson Capital Management, Ltd.
3200 McKnight East Drive
Suite 3210
Pittsburgh, PA 15237-6423
412-369-9925
www.gibsoncapital.com

Meg Green, founder of Meg Green & Associates in North Miami Beach, Florida, is a good example of someone who successfully implemented what consultant Mark Tibergien calls the "famous person" strategy. Green, who is one of Tibergien's clients, is something of a local celebrity thanks to her television and other media appearances. Her website makes the point that no matter where you turn for financial advice, whether it be the *Miami Herald* or NBC, you'll find Meg. But Green also knows that to grow her firm she must delegate responsibility and move on from the famous-person image. And so her website details the duties of each of her staff members so that new clients won't expect that they'll be spending all their time with Green.

Meg Green & Associates
2627 Ives Dairy Road
Suite 201
North Miami Beach, FL 33180

305-931-1400
www.meggreen.com

Charlie Haines grew up exposed to great wealth and went to elite private schools like Groton and Williams College in the Northeast before going to the University of Virginia, where he picked up a southern drawl while getting his M.B.A. Haines, who heads a multiclient family office in Birmingham, sounds like he's always been in Alabama. A great strategist, Haines went to work for Lynn Hopewell and Don Rembert, two of the top planners in the country, in Falls Church, Virginia. Once he got some training, he set up his own firm and then focused on building a multi-client family office with an on-staff psychologist, a philanthropy center, and special services for family businesses. He also created National Advisors Trust, a trust company owned by more than one hundred advisory firms. The trust can be a custodian of client assets and also serves as a purchasing coop.

Charles D. Haines, LLC
600 University Park Place
Suite 501
Birmingham, AL 35209
866-871-3334
www.charlesdhaines.com

Patti Houlihan, president of Houlihan Financial in Fairfax, Virginia, uses index funds and exchange-traded funds with very low expenses and puts together large-cap stock portfolios herself so that she can offer her wealthy clients a fee of just 1 percent of assets, including the mutual fund fees. Also included in her fee is the management of all investments, financial planning, and even insurance placement, which she offers by arranging no-load policies through TIAA-CREF.

Houlihan Financial Resource Group
4000 Legato Road
Suite 140
Fairfax, VA 22033-4055
703-352-1570
www.houlihanfinancial.com

Bill Howard decided early on that he wanted his Memphis planning practice to specialize in working with doctors. He came from an insurance background and had arranged a good deal of disability coverage for doctors and felt that he understood their needs and could leverage that knowledge. In 1989, he went to the Shelby County Medical Society in Memphis and offered to provide financial planning for the group's doctors. Although his offer was turned down, Howard didn't give up. He offered to write a financial planning article for each issue of the membership's publication. Patience paid off, and he has built a success-ful practice that serves mostly doctors.

William Howard & Co.
6410 Poplar Avenue
Suite 330
Memphis, TN 38119
901-761-5068
www.whcfa.com

Mark Hurley, who has a B.S. degree from West Point and an M.B.A. from Stanford University, ran the Investment Management Industry Group at Goldman Sachs and was managing director in charge of world-wide marketing for Merrill Lynch before setting up the fund company Undiscovered Managers in Dallas in 1997. Hurley has become a key player in the financial planning market, thanks largely to his controversial reports on the industry and the invitation-only conferences he holds for planners each June. His funds are managed, the firm's website states, by "some of the best money managers in the world you've never heard of—until now." One of Hurley's interests is behavioral finance, and his fund managers employ techniques to make use of investor behavior patterns.

Undiscovered Managers
700 N. Pearl Street
Suite 1625
Dallas, TX 75201
888-202-3981
www.undiscoveredmanagers.com

Kermit Johns, president of Christopher Street Financial, together with co-owner Jennifer Hatch, serves the special planning needs of gays and lesbians. The name Christopher Street serves to remind clients of the Stonewall Rebellion in 1969, which became a turning point for gay rights. Johns and Hatch moved their practice in 2003, heading uptown from Wall Street to Fifth Avenue. Hatch, a former trader at J.P. Morgan Chase & Co. and at Bear Stearns Companies, and Johns, who worked in the financial department at Time-Warner Communications, bought Christopher Street Financial in 1997 and expanded the firm's services from investment management to all aspects of financial planning. Christopher Street focuses on the special needs of unmarried couples in estate planning, insurance, titling of property as well as investing. "There is always this affinity that comes into play," Johns says. "Someone has been disenfranchised in some way, and we understand because we've been through the same thing."

Christopher Street Financial
101 Fifth Avenue
Suite 1100
New York, NY 10003
212-242-2800
www.csfin.com

Diana Kahn set up the Financial Pharmacist in her home in Miami in 1997. After working as a planner with Evensky, Brown & Katz, she realized that what she wanted was to be something of a family practitioner for clients' money, including those clients who had very little of it and were merely trying to climb out of debt. Kahn, a certified financial planner, charges by the project—a flat fee of $400 that includes two hours of meeting time.

The Financial Pharmacist, Inc.
3200 NE 211 Terrace
Aventura, FL 33180
305-935-5499
FinPharmInc@aol.com

When **George Kinder** graduated from Harvard, he chose to live as a free spirit, writing, painting, and studying philosophy and religion. But he realized he also needed to make a living, so he took the certified public accountant exam, passed with the third-highest score in the state, and set up a tax-preparation business, which he figured would tie him up only in the first quarter of each year. But his clients' needs were complicated and they weren't getting the right financial advice, so Kinder eventually dived in, becoming a money manager and "life planner." He practices in Cambridge, Massachusetts, and in Maui, Hawaii, and came full circle when he sold off the money-management portion of his firm to Sherman Financial in Philadelphia so that he could concentrate on life planning, which he does for $300 an hour, and on money psychology, which he pursues through the workshops that evolved from his book, *The Seven Stages of Money Maturity: Understanding the Spirit and Value of Money in Your Life* (Dell Books). He is also a Zen Buddhist teacher.

Kinder and Co.
PO Box 1350

Littleton, MA 01460
978-486-8053
www.kinderinstitute.com

Tim Kochis "fell into" the financial advisory business when Continental Bank in Chicago was hiring law grads in the early 1970s, after Kochis got his law degree from the University of Michigan. He worked as a compensation consultant at Hewitt Associates, an employee benefits firm in Chicago, headed the executive financial counseling group at Bank of America, and was national director of personal financial planning at Deloitte & Touche, picking up an M.B.A. from the University of Chicago along the way. No surprise, then, that when Kochis set up an independent firm with Linda Fitz in 1991, the two specialized in executive-compensation issues. The firm has grown in both size and prestige to become a solid regional player from its San Francisco base. The firm's goal is to provide unparalleled service to clients of high net worth and to grow a firm large enough to provide value for the present owners and create value for the next generation of owners.

Kochis Fitz Tracy Fitzhugh & Gott
60 Spear Street
Suite 1100
San Francisco, CA 94105-1599
415-394-6670
www.kochisfitz.com

Nancy Langdon Jones, president of NL Jones Financial Planning, tried her hand at many things—including acting—before turning to financial planning. She got a master's degree in financial planning from the College of Financial Planning and works with clients in Upland, California. A member of the Nazrudin Group, Jones enjoys the softer aspects of planning, especially life planning. She resolved her aversion to money management by farming that out to Michael Ling, an economist with his own planning practice, Berkely Inc. in Boise, Idaho. She has also worked out a succession plan with Ling, who will buy her practice in two or three years. Jones is author of *So You Want to Be a Financial Planner: Your Guide to a New Career* (AdvisorWorks), available on Amazon.com.

NL Jones Financial Planning
2485 Mesa Terrace
Upland, CA 91784
909-985-5550
www.nljones.com

Judy Lau, principal of LauOlmstead LLC, is a nationally recognized certified financial planner, specializing in serving wealthy individuals. In 1985, Judy founded Lau & Associates, Ltd., providing comprehensive financial planning and family-office services to its clients through a team of planning, investing, accounting, and tax professionals. The firm merged in January 2003 with Olmstead & Co., a multifamily office advisory firm owned by John Olmstead. Lau was drawn to planning after a "less than satisfactory" experience with a financial planner who had little time for Lau's questions and whose commission-based compensation structure made her uncomfortable. Judy has been recognized year after year as one of the top financial advisers in the country by such publications as *Worth* magazine and *Medical Economics,* and *Bloomberg Wealth Manager* magazine ranks LauOlmstead among the industry's top independent financial advisory firms. Lau is on the advisory board for the TIAA-CREF Institute, a trustee for the Financial Planning Foundation, and is on several community nonprofit boards.

LauOlmstead LLC
300 Bellevue Parkway
Suite 120
Wilmington, DE 19809
302-792-5955
judylau@lauolmstead.com

Richie Lee, president of Lee Financial in Dallas, serves as mentor to many younger financial planners, who respect him for his creativity, his willingness to take risks, and the fresh approach he brings to planning, even after thirty years in the business. Lee is perhaps best known for his work in alternative investments such as energy, coal mining, rail cars, and other out-of-favor assets. "When things get really, really bad, you can buy something for cash in an amount that would normally serve only as down payment," he says. But Lee is equally well known for his emphasis on preserving and developing a client's human capital, by which he means encouraging the best use of the education, knowledge, and experience that client has acquired.

Lee Financial
12201 Merit Drive
Suite 530
Dallas, TX 75251
972-960-1001
www.leefincorp.com

Ross Levin, past chairman of the IAFP, and one of the most entertaining speakers in the planning business, is president of Accredited Investors in Minneapolis. In 1997, Levin wrote a book called *The Wealth Management Index: The Financial Advisor's System for Assessing and Managing Your Client's Plans and Goals* (Irwin Professional Publishing), detailing his firm's way of categorizing client goals such as asset protection, disability and income protection, debt management, investment and cash flow planning, and estate planning. Within these categories, Levin developed a series of targeted questions and subcategories designed to quantify a client's goals and to measure progress over each year. Levin, a truly innovative thinker, continually pushes himself toward the next level—whether it's in planning, philosophy, the arts, raising his twins, or whatever else he might be doing.

> **Accredited Investors, Inc.**
> 7701 France Avenue, South
> Suite 105
> Edina, MN 55435
> 952-841-2222
> www.accredited.com

James Lowell, a graduate of Harvard University and chairman and chief executive officer of Lowell Blake & Associates, cofounded the firm in 1974 to operate as an "ethical investment adviser." Lowell believes investment ethics must include two key principles: The adviser's fee should be fair (Lowell Blake charges a fixed, flat fee), and the money should be invested in what's now called a "socially responsible" way. Blake, a member of one of Boston's most prestigious families, tells his clients that the wealthy should give something back. Unfortunately, he finds most charities are poorly run and practically worthless. So Lowell sets up his own charitable endeavors for clients, giving them the opportunity to invest in timberland preservation or in the rehabilitation of a working-class neighborhood or in films that promote the preservation of endangered wildlife.

> **Lowell Blake & Associates**
> 141 Tremont Street
> Suite 200
> Boston, MA 02111-1209
> 617-422-0064
> www.lowell-blake.com

Cicily Carson Maton woke up to financial reality when she got a divorce in 1982 and had no job and very little financial knowledge. Once she learned to understand the finances of divorce, she became so intrigued with financial planning that she earned her certified financial planner designation in 1986 and set up her own business. One of her clients that year was a woman going through a divorce, the first of many clients to seek advice in what would quickly become Maton's specialty—the finances of divorce. When her daughter, Michelle, joined the firm after graduating with honors from Stanford University, the two broadened the practice to include life transitions in general. Values—those of staff and those of clients—continue to form the core of Aequus, the Latin word for "equal."

Aequus Wealth Management Resources
303 West Erie Street
Suite 311
Chicago, IL 60610
312-664-4090
www.aequuswealth.com

Cynthia Meyers, a sole practitioner in Sacramento, California, has been one of the hold-outs among top planners in switching from commissions to fees, because she believes that low-load, low-cost investments like those offered by the American Funds are the best option for clients. But Meyers—who along with George Kinder was one of the original "life planners" back in the mid-1990s—struggles, as many planners do, with the best way to get clients to pay a fair price for the many financial planning and career-planning services she provides. Meyers, who sings and acts in local theater and was once an editor of children's books, has the kind of vivacity that engages clients and makes them want to sign on to become a part of her journey.

Cynthia Meyers CFP/Foothill Securities
655 University Avenue
Suite 250
Sacramento, CA 95825
916-927-6487

Sharon Rich founded Womoney, a fee-by-the-hour planning practice in Belmont, Massachusetts, in 1982, making her a pioneer in a business model that is now trendy. Rich, who earned a doctorate in education from Harvard University, worked at first with inheritors, but over the years her clientele has become more mixed. Its emphasis is now on demystifying finances for those who might not be able to afford a traditional planner. Rich charges $160 an hour to do à la carte planning, which she does by functioning as a teacher and coach, giving the client assignments and helping him to achieve independence.

Womoney
76 Townsend Road
Belmont, MA 02478
617-489-3601
www.womoney.com

Evan Roth went to work for Goldman Sachs, specializing in asset management, after he received his M.B.A. from Wharton. In February 2000, he and two other Goldman employees with Wharton credentials—none of whom had yet reached thirty—set up BBR Partners, a multiclient family office in New York. Within three years, the firm had thirty families with $1.1 billion in assets, putting it at the top of *Bloomberg Wealth Manager* magazine's annual ranking of independent wealth management firms. The three partners believe their youth is a plus along with their credentials. Their typical client is a first-generation entrepreneur who doesn't know what to do with his newfound wealth. "We believe that you are your roots," Roth says. "Our roots are high-net-worth families. We take a comprehensive view of all the client's investments and provide totally objective advice."

BBR Partners
420 Lexington Avenue
Suite 2301
New York, NY 10170
212-313-9873
www.bbrpartners.com

Peggy Ruhlin was working as a CPA when she first discovered financial planning and instantly fell in love with the idea of helping people plan their futures, meet goals, and achieve success. The work was certainly more satisfying than crunching numbers for last year's tax returns. Ruhlin's professionalism and accounting background played a big role in shaping the culture at Budros & Ruhlin, a planning practice that's the envy of many firms in the business for its smooth operations and well-planned growth. When Budros & Ruhlin brought in a third and then a fourth principal, all the paperwork was in place for helping these planners buy into the firm. When the firm threatened to grow too large to manage, Ruhlin agreed to take on the role of chief operating officer for two years. "I made them sign an agreement," she said. But she's been running things so well that she was persuaded in October 2003 to extend her contract. Building a firm requires a whole different skill set than financial planning. Luckily for Budros & Ruhlin, Ruhlin's toolbox happened to have both sets.

Budros & Ruhlin
1650 Lake Shore Drive
Suite 150
Columbus, OH 43204-4895
614-481-6900
www.budrosandruhlin.com

Myra Salzer was happy enough working as a chemical engineer, especially since she could do it in the Rocky Mountains, where she lives with her husband and two daughters. After taking some financial planning courses "out of curiosity," she got hooked on it and quit her job to set up a fee-only planning practice in 1983. Things didn't click for Salzer until one day she sat across the desk from a client who twisted her ring to the inside of her finger to conceal a stunning emerald. Salzer had a flash of insight: People who have plenty of money are not exempt from money problems. Theirs are just different. Salzar refocused her business to concentrate on inheritors, adding workshops with experts like Thayer Willis, an inheritor in Portland, Oregon, who became a psychotherapist specializing in people with inherited wealth. Salzer now outsources money management so that she can focus on "wealth coaching" and philanthropy.

The Wealth Conservancy
1919 14th Street
Suite 319
Boulder, CO 80302
303-444-1919
www.thewealthconservancy.com

Judy Shine goes it alone. She runs Shine Investment Advisory Services as a sole practitioner. Shine, who has been a financial planner for twenty years, employs a staff of seven and is willing to outsource some of her work. But she's not willing to take on a partner. "All you have to do is get a few drinks in people and they'll tell you how much they hate their partners," she says. Critical to managing $350 million for 175 clients is being very selective about whom she accepts as a client. Shine wants the client who really needs her firm, someone who knows nothing about money and is looking for a safe haven. She's not worried about competition from Wall Street. "Corporate America is so diseased that it could never take away our business," she says.

Shine Investment Advisory Services
6143 South Willow Drive
Suite 100

Englewood, CO 80111
303-740-8600
shine@shineinvestments.com

Mark Spangler was a fairly traditional financial planner. He was president of NAPFA and an advocate of fee-only planning until 1998, when he cut his practice from two hundred clients to just twenty. Spangler's primary interest had always been in investing, and he decided to set up what he calls a "family office" of wealthy individuals whom the Securities and Exchange Commission considers "qualified investors," so that he could get creative with investments. The participants turned out to be mostly middle-aged tech millionaires who had retired early, so what Spangler ended up with was not merely an investment pool but also a high-tech think tank and an incubator for start-ups.

Spangler Financial Group
2802 10th Avenue, East
Seattle, WA 98102
206-720-6114
www.spanglergroup.com

Mark Tibergien, partner at the accounting and consulting firm of Moss Adams in Seattle, is one of the leading consultants on practice-management issues for financial planners, including business valuations, strategic plans, and succession plans. He has consulted with hundreds of financial planners during the past several years. He also writes a column for *Investment Advisor* magazine.

Moss Adams
1001 Fourth Avenue
Suite 2700
Seattle, WA 98154
800-243-4936
www.mossadams.com

Ben Utley is part of what Dave Drucker calls a "new breed of advisors"—young people in their twenties and thirties who feel so comfortable with technology that they can start out as sole practitioners using their computers as their staff. Utley was studying chemistry in graduate school at the University of Oregon in 1992 when he became interested in investing. He worked in a pharmaceutical lab and thought he might have a leg up on researching drug stocks like Merck and Cyanamid. The research fascinated him. "I found myself hopelessly drawn to finances," he says. Like many planners, he started by selling mutual funds and, like many planners, he didn't have the appetite for sales. He got his CFP and set up shop as a fee-only planner. Most of his clients are doctors, which he attributes to his chemistry background, his fluency with numbers, his training in Latin, and his understanding of science and the human body. His office is completely paperless. He works with a virtual study group online and looks for economical ways to outsource parts of the job.

Utley & Associates Inc.
1859 Heitzman Way
Eugene, OR 97402-7516
541-463-0899
www.utleyassociates.com

Robert Veres, publisher of *Inside Information,* an industry newsletter, is a familiar face at planning conferences, where he often speaks or moderates a panel. Former editor of *Financial Planning* magazine, Veres has been observing the planning industry for more than twenty years. His speaking bureau says Veres is "recognized nationally as the editorial guru of the investment-advisory business." He was named one of the industry's Movers, Shakers, and Decision Makers by *Financial Planning* magazine in January 2001.

Inside Information
491 Country Drive
Mars Hill, NC 28754
828-689-3930
www.bobveres.com

Robert Willard has been called a "financial bodyguard," mainly because of the risks he's willing to take on for the handful of clients he serves. Although he has eighteen clients, he thinks the magic number might be three or four. But what he does for these clients! They're all professionals whom Willard has selected, mostly doctors, who've used him in nearly every aspect of their businesses. He helps them decide whether to buy or lease equipment, how to structure their businesses, and what kind of direct investments to make. One of his coups is the private mortgage fund he set up, which clients use to loan money to homeowners that Willard has vetted. The fund gives clients a way to earn decent income at a time when markets are offering extremely low returns. Willard has made some mistakes, but when he does, he takes over the investment and manages it himself. Case in point: He had lent money to a project to convert a big piece of land in Colorado Springs, but the deal fell apart when the developer discovered the environmental restrictions on development. So Willard took out a second mortgage and worked out a deal to develop the land himself.

Willard & Co.
1040 South 8th Street
Suite 101
Colorado Springs, CO 80906
719-444-0330
REWillard@earthlink.net

David Yeske admits that he once had trouble with boundaries. Every time a new client decided to hire him, Yeske got depressed because he knew he wasn't going to be able to handle the work. He tried hiring an associate and when she was hired away from him, he felt relieved. Supervising her had become yet another thing he couldn't get to. Finally, Yeske realized he had to focus on deciding what type of business would suit him and what kind of clients he could best serve. He pared down his client list to ninety-five, and he now does much of his work online. His public website and private client pages, which include a "to-do list" for each client, are the focal point of his business. Yeske uses hot links to show clients how to reach an estate attorney if they need to update documents. If they need to reallocate their 401(k) plan funds, Yeske provides specific instructions. This business model allows Yeske to have time for a diversified portfolio of activities in his life. He finished an M.A. in economics and is working on a doctoral program in finance. He also teaches classes, takes on leadership roles in the financial planning industry, and writes magazine columns. Yeske believes all these activities enrich his relationship with clients. Yeske could have made time for these pursuits by taking the obvious approach of hiring a staff to do his client work. But he enjoys working with clients too much to do that.

Yeske & Co. Inc.
220 Montgomery Street
Suite 424
San Francisco, CA 94104
415-956-9686
www.yeske.com

In Search of the Perfect Model

Introduction
Inside Stories

IN THE MID-1980s, the slug tracks of unscrupulous salespeople eager to collect commissions for selling risky limited partnerships, bad life insurance policies, and expensive, poor-performing mutual funds crisscrossed the financial planning industry. It was a consumer's nightmare. But it was also an investigative reporter's dream, and I was writing a column for *Financial Planning* magazine. Bob Veres, publisher of *Inside Information,* a newsletter for financial planners, was editor of the magazine at the time and called the mid-1980s "the golden era of financial planning," because "any planner who didn't rob the client blind was a hero." To outsiders, financial advisers were indistinguishable from insurance agents and stockbrokers; all ranked near the bottom of the list of desirable occupations, right along with used-car salesmen.

What a pleasure, then, during the past fifteen years, to watch financial planning evolve into a respected profession, thanks to the dedication and hard work of a group of advisers who revised the examination for certified financial planners and pumped some prestige into the certified financial planner designation, built networks to share each other's knowledge, and imported the technology and tools—such as passive investing and Monte Carlo simulations—from the institutional market for use with their clients.

A sophisticated toolbox is now part of a top adviser's image, but it's not all that distinguishes this new breed of planner from others in the industry. What an easy task prospective clients would have in finding good planners if that were all there was to it. Unfortunately, the skills these advisers can pull out of the box aren't signified in the letters after their names. Still, you know them when you meet them. So permit me to introduce you to some of the most remarkable of the bunch.

The top planners you'll read about in these pages are problem solvers: they help clients work through sticky family-money issues;

they listen to one client talk about the pain of divorce and hear another one blame himself for a child's drug problems or a sister's suicide. Some advisers "do it all" for clients, planning their vacations, buying travel tickets, shopping for family gifts. Most are willing to take risks to get a client on track. Barbara Pope, of Barbara J. Pope in Chicago, had the guts to tell a client that he would always regret it if he cut his daughter out of his will. Janet Briaud, owner of Briaud Financial Planning in Bryan, Texas, told one of her clients that his innocence about money had led to his undercharging clients and cheating his family. James Budros, partner at Budros & Ruhlin in Columbus, Ohio—a gourmet who has cooked with the late Craig Claiborne, former food editor of the *New York Times*—dropped by to prepare a meal for a newly widowed client during the holidays. Cynthia Meyers, owner of Cynthia Meyers CFP/Foothill Securities in Sacramento, California, attended an audition with a client in her seventies, helping the retiree to begin a second career as a singer. These advisers—and dozens of others—have set themselves apart from their competition in the brokerage and banking and other financial service businesses by customizing their planning to suit each client's needs; by continually educating themselves on charitable trusts, alternative investments, and IRA distribution rules; by sitting on the client's side of the table; and by charging fees rather than commissions.

Despite all these changes inside the profession, planners don't look all that different to consumers. Even some outsiders with considerable financial savvy claim to be in the dark. Consider this headline in the *Wall Street Journal*: "If You Think Picking Stocks Is Hard, Just Try Choosing a Financial Advisor." It marqueed one of Jonathan Clements's weekly "Getting Going" columns in May 2002. Clements opened the piece with a joke to make his point: "Heard the one about the broker, the financial planner, and the insurance agent? A customer walks in and says: 'I've got this terrible problem.' The financial planner responds, 'What you need is a comprehensive financial plan.' The insurance agent says, 'What you need is cash-value life insurance.' And the broker says, 'What you need just changed, so let's make another trade.' " Clements concluded, "that pretty much sums up the business of buying financial advice." An accompanying graph called "Hired Hands" told readers that 1.8 million insurance agents, 677,000 brokers, and 300,000 planners populate the industry. That amounts to nearly 3 million purveyors of financial advice, and even experienced shoppers might have trouble sorting them out.

Good planners aren't any easier to recognize in the U.K. "There are more than enough people to go around who are happy to call themselves 'financial advisers' or 'financial planners,' but their quality varies widely," says Andy Jervis, a planner from Loughborough, Leicestershire, England. Most advisers have an axe to grind. "In this country, transaction-led advice is still the norm, and the major institutions are much more interested in using staff as salespeople to maximize product sales than in creating real relationships based on solid advice," he says. "I have often asked myself, If I were not doing this kind of work and needed good advice, where would I go? I struggle to come up with an answer."

Many industry professionals concede that the problem is real. They say the profession is going through an identity crisis. Judy Lau, principal at LauOlmstead in Wilmington, Delaware, wants to know how she can differentiate herself and become the "Prada of financial planning." David Greene, of Greene Consulting Associates in Atlanta, says the wealth management market "remains highly fragmented, with no clear leader either nationally or even in a local market of any significance," and although "many firms are saying they deliver the best solution, the general buying public has yet to see a clearly differentiated leader." And we hear the inevitable from Mark Hurley, CEO of Undiscovered Managers, a mutual fund company in Dallas: Planning as we know it is in its death throes, waiting to be gobbled up by the big banks and by brokers and insurers.

So even as advisers come into their own, many are worried about the future, about people like Jessica Bibliowicz—the daughter of Wall Street veteran Sanford Weill—who's rolling up dozens of individual planning and insurance firms into one big advisory firm called National Financial Partners. Some advisers wonder whether they should sell out to someone like Bibliowicz and pocket the money or try to remain independent instead. They worry, too, that technology is squeezing them on one side and the big players like Merrill Lynch, a New York financial services company, and Prudential Financial in Newark, New Jersey, are bearing down on the other, leaving less room in the middle. Some prominent firms, like Kochis Fitz Tracy Fitzhugh & Gott in San Francisco, are approached regularly by companies that want to buy them out, to invest in them, or to make them part of a national network of planning firms that combines marketing power and offers the advantage of size. Tim Kochis, CEO of Kochis Fitz, likes the idea of keeping his options open. Other firms, like Evensky, Brown & Katz in Coral Gables, Florida, are planning to raise capital to build a network of affiliates and become one of the largest planning firms.

No one has found the perfect answer. But like Judy Lau, independent advisers all over the country are wondering how to distinguish themselves, how to become the Pradas of planning. David Greene says the standouts will be those who provide truly objective consultations to identify a client's wealth management issues followed by an unbiased discussion of alternative solutions. I agree. But what exactly does that mean? How would you describe your way of getting to the heart of that job in a thirty-second elevator speech, which is what Mark Tibergien, a consultant at Moss Adams in Seattle, asks his financial adviser clients to do.

So we're back to square one. The more we hear about what the best financial advisers do, the more vague it sounds. I know dozens of financial planners who put their clients first and provide excellent advice and service. And their methods often have little in common. Ross Levin, president of Accredited Investors in Minneapolis, has his wealth management index to measure a client's progress whereas Richie Lee, president of Lee Financial in Dallas, emphasizes human capital as the most important asset his clients possess.

I can see the trouble a consumer might have in telling the difference between Levin's wealth management index and a stockbroker's rainbow of solutions. The big firms employ huge marketing departments to come up with clever, catchy slogans meant to convince consumers that they'll do it all. Unfortunately, in many cases, presentation is everything.

How can a planner build a practice that a consumer can recognize as offering something of real value? I've talked with dozens of advisers who've thought long and hard about strategies for the future, about their firm's structure and marketing niche, about how to specialize, how to build a big firm or how to survive as a sole practitioner, what to bring in-house and what to outsource. They see that their next big challenge will be to come up with a clear-eyed business strategy, something they can work into an elevator speech: "I specialize in financial planning for gays and lesbians," or "I charge an hourly fee to do à la carte financial planning," or "I operate as a private family office for fifteen families," or "I've never met any of my clients. We do everything online."

The flip side of a strength is always its weakness. The fact that planning can't be pigeonholed means that advisers are offering unique, individualized services. It also means that each planner needs to do some soul searching while choosing a strategy. Many of the most successful practices evolved from the adviser's passion and creativity rather than any expertly articulated design. Kermit Johns and Jennifer Hatch bought Christopher Street Financial in New York because, as gays themselves, they recognized that gays have to deal with special issues in retirement and estate planning, real estate purchases, and insurance. Elissa Buie in Falls Church, Virginia, realized, after she hired a business consultant, that her best clients were the ones she knew the most about. So the consultant helped her design a screening process to identify clients with whom she could develop that kind of close relationship.

Almost invariably, the most successful practices spring from issues connected to the adviser's life. Take Roger Gibson, president of Gibson Capital Management in Pittsburgh and author of *Asset Allocation* (McGraw-Hill), the bible of that discipline. In 2001 he gave a speech that many advisers said changed their lives. Gibson talked about how he had diversified his personal portfolio, sorted through his strengths and his weaknesses, trusted his instincts, and faced decision points head-on to become a better money manager, a better father, and a better person. He had started the process by trying to make lists of key events in his life: the biggest challenges, biggest mistakes, and biggest rewards. What he quickly discovered was that he couldn't untangle the many things that had happened to him. They were all rolled up together. Indeed, he said, his life hadn't really started until it seemed to be over.

Gibson veered off at this point in the speech to describe how in 1986 he had bought his wife a large diamond as a tenth-anniversary gift. She responded by asking for a divorce. Shortly after that, his business assistant quit. The divorce ate up his $300,000 nest egg. He was forced to sell his business partnership and set up shop in his home. At the time, Gibson hardly saw this period as a high point in his life. Now he believes it was his salvation. Had it not been for these crises, "I would have spent my life as a dead man," Gibson says. "I would have been walking around. But spiritually I would have been dead."

What Gibson, a highly technical and analytical guy, did was to go with his gut. He sued for joint custody of his two children and became Mr. Mom. He wrote a book that established his reputation in the field. He remembered being told that the definition of a marvelous person was "someone who relentlessly pursues his interests." He picked up his clarinet again. He began to study depth psychology and Buddhism. He earned a black belt in Tae Kwon Do. He diversified. He became a whole person.

One lesson stands out for financial advisers trying to define a practice: The main job of a life isn't planning for college for the kids or for retirement. It's to become an individual, "a single one," as the Danish philosopher Søren Kierkegaard says. Although financial advisers disagree about how involved a planner should be in a client's transformation, they should know that the intangible difference we're trying to define has something to do with this notion, with achieving coherency in a life, with becoming a whole person. Ultimately, it's about looking within to find the inside story.

Part One

The Quest

Chapter One

A Profession Comes of Age

FINANCIAL PLANNERS HAVE proved to be a tough lot. In a sense, they've created themselves from scratch and grown up in a hostile environment where the competition has fought to squelch them at every turn. As their trade has become a profession and more of a threat to traditional financial experts like lawyers, certified public accountants, insurance agents, and stockbrokers, efforts to do them in, buy them out, or mimic their work have accelerated.

Some advisers, like Richie Lee in Dallas, think we've reached only chapter two or three in the story of financial planning. Thirty years ago, Lee says, when he started as a financial adviser, about fifty people were in the business. Today, more than 100,000 practitioners are "out there trying to figure out how to best do this thing," Lee says, and the "quality of the work is light-years ahead of what it was thirty years ago." Still, Lee cautions against trying to wrap up the story just yet, when planners are still experimenting and trying to find the best models. "Certain things that work well will grow," he says. Lee's fear about any effort to freeze frame the industry and assign catchy names to a half-dozen models is that it will end up pigeonholing everyone involved. "The experimentation is just starting to happen," he says. "Advisers need to go through the experience itself and see where they end up. I hope we don't group ourselves into these little pens and stop experimenting."

Lee makes a good point. But the pioneer work done by the first-generation planners, many of them baby boomers now thinking about retirement, offers younger advisers many lessons that can serve as shortcuts in building their practices. Many of these veteran planners began practicing in the early 1980s, when a financial adviser was little more than a name for someone who sold financial products. She might have worked for Smith Barney or New York Life or American Express Advisors, or he might have worked out of his spare bedroom. Then when the Tax Reform Act of 1986 wiped out the tax advantages of limited partnerships and the Dow Jones Industrial Average nosedived the next year, thousands of planners who had been in the business to make an easy buck dropped out; membership in the International Association for Financial Planning (IAFP), the industry trade group, plunged from around 24,000 to 12,000, according to Bob Veres. At the 1992 IAFP convention in Anaheim, California, the September issue of *Investment Advisor* magazine arrived with a cover story titled "IAFP: Rest in Peace."

The old financial planning sales model associated with the IAFP was to live on in brokerages and insurance agencies. But dedicated independent advisers began to look for ways to serve clients, to solve their problems rather than just sell them products, and they looked for a way other than commissions to charge for those solutions. By then, a small group of fee-only advisers had already organized as the National Association of Personal Financial Advisors (NAPFA), based in Buffalo Grove, Illinois, and they were beginning to sing the praises of fee-only planning, a refrain quickly picked up by the press. And in the spring of 1991, I attended the first meeting of the Alpha Group, a national network of about fifteen experienced advisers, who meet regularly to share knowledge and ideas on asset management and financial planning. A couple of years later, the Alpha Group appeared in caricature on the cover of *Barron's* with a story about the new breed of planner: independent and high minded, someone who put the client first. Little pockets of this new breed began to gather all over the country, focusing on the opportunities to network and develop their practices and offer top-drawer services. They were no longer salespeople but financial experts who drew up plans for all their clients' financial needs, from mortgages to insurance to estate planning and retirement-plan distributions.

Still, the group was crippled in many ways and they knew it. Financial advisers had no single regulatory body, and the diligent couldn't distinguish themselves from the flim-flam men. Any effort to create a regulatory body would be resisted by accountants, lawyers, insurance agents, and stockbrokers, who didn't want to give up any turf. No uniform standards were in place; these determined planners were on their own, hammering out their practice-management issues and due diligence methods and investment standards, networking and seeking new ideas.

When Bloomberg L.P. asked me in 1997 to write a compliance guide for financial advisers, the topic seemed at first blush a solid idea. I would learn more about the rules myself and be better able to distinguish good planners from bad. Along with most consumers, I believed that the purpose of hiring an adviser was to goose up portfolio returns, and I wanted to know how to identify someone who could do that.

But the more I looked at the regulations, the less worthwhile they seemed. Indeed, they looked like busywork. And the long and short of it was that virtually anyone could declare himself a financial planner. I couldn't find much of anything that could distinguish a quality adviser in this morass of regulations. I saw clearly the difficulty of what planners were trying to do in creating a profession in an industry with no real guideposts to help. So rather than writing a compliance guide, I looked into what the best planners were doing in the mid-1990s and how those who survived the tsunami of 1986–87 had managed it. The result was *Best Practices for Financial Advisors* (Bloomberg Press), which focused on due diligence, fiduciary responsibilities, marketing, and avoiding conflicts of interest.

It turned out that what the best planners were doing was building relationships with clients. When I interviewed advisers for the book, the task they said they loved most was working with clients. Over the second half of the 1990s, top planners attracted more new clients than they could handle, helped by a dazzling stock market and baby boomers who had created significant wealth. Marketing wasn't a critical issue anymore. Still, planners did have some concerns about their businesses, mostly having to do with what services they wanted to provide and what kind of clients they wanted to work with. When they were first building their practices, they would take on "anyone who could fog a mirror," says Deena Katz, of Evensky, Brown & Katz. But a point came when they could afford to be selective, turning away clients they didn't consider a good match, pruning their client lists to get rid of those who were troublesome.

The luxury of being selective about clients has helped make planning a more rewarding profession. I spend a good deal of time with financial advisers and I rarely hear them complain about clients the way some of them did five years ago. They simply don't take the ones they don't like. Many of them size up prospective customers and decide in fairly short order whether someone is a good fit. Mary Merrill, a financial planner in Madison, Wisconsin, for example, says she refuses to work with people who have substance-abuse problems or those who are negative or whiners; she takes only clients who are upbeat and want to accomplish something with their lives. Another planner told me that a couple with several million dollars came in for a get-acquainted meeting. Both chain-smoked and treated each other rudely. They had no hobbies or interests and no goals other than to prevent their children from getting their money. "There's nothing I can do for you," this planner told them, knowing he couldn't help them make good use of their money if they had no personal values.

This new breed of planner who traveled the high road and could afford to be selective became a guru of sorts by the turn of the century and was quoted in the *Wall Street Journal, Business Week,* and *Fortune* magazine much more frequently than were CPAs and insurance agents and bankers and stockbrokers. Not surprisingly, other would-be wizards in the industry began to call themselves financial advisers. Some wire houses have paid bonuses of $100,000 to brokers who get their certified financial planner designations. Imitation is the sincerest form of flattery. But as many of these would-be financial caretakers got their CFPs so that they, too, could join the ranks of the elite, earn a good income, and have a fulfilling job, the title of financial planner began to lose its distinction once again.

And where do things stand now for our veteran financial advisers, the survivors of the 1986–87 meltdown? They've gotten more sophisticated and improved their tools and their Monte Carlo simulations; they've reviewed their businesses and defined where they're headed. The top planners are always getting better at what they do. The ones who like working with clients are continually looking for better ways to do that. As Richie Lee says, people are finding their groove. "Some guy like Dave Drucker [president of Sunset Financial Management in Albuquerque, New Mexico] decides what he's best at—running a solo practice—and is teaching everyone how to outsource," Lee says. Eleanor Blayney, partner at Sullivan, Bruyette, Speros & Blayney, says her McLean, Virginia, firm hired a bright college graduate who wanted to learn about planning, but it quickly became clear that his forte was finding technical solutions for planners rather than for clients. So that's what she had him do.

As in any growing industry, there are specialties and subspecialties, and we're only beginning to uncover some of them. The story of how planners evolved from salespeople to a sought-after group of prized advisers who can afford to be selective about their clients is instructive and still unfolding. The planners profiled in this book are some of the industry's most fascinating works in progress.

— 🌺 🌺 🌺 —

Chapter Two

Identity Crisis

OWARD THE END OF 1999, Richie Lee and David Diesslin, president of Diesslin & Associates in Fort Worth, Texas, invited a dozen of the top planners from across the country to come to Dallas for a two-day meeting with a futurist—one of those professional brainstormers who helps you define what you want and how to make it happen—to work on developing possible scenarios for the future of the profession. A few nonplanners like Mark Hurley, of Undiscovered Managers; Bob Veres; Robert Clark, a columnist for *Financial Planning* magazine; and myself—all long-time industry observers—were invited along as well.

We talked about the looming threats from outside the profession, ranging from companies like Financial Engines that dispense investment advice on the Internet to the droves of stockbrokers from Merrill Lynch and Smith Barney and the legions of insurance agents from New York Life Insurance Co. and Equitable, now a product line of AXA Advisors, who had announced that they would be joining the ranks of advisers. We talked, too, about demographics and baby boomer trends, the fact that people will live beyond age 100, that the boomers had begun to search for meaning in life, that many of them will be looking for third, fourth, and even fifth careers, and that many boomer kids seem to be at sea both ethically and financially. Planners had their work cut out for them.

These are thorny issues, but the group had been well chosen. The handful of advisers meeting in that little room in Dallas had distinguished themselves in the profession without any kind of formula for success. They had developed as planners in a dozen different ways, partly by instinct and intuition, partly by pragmatism and strategizing. Now they wanted to share their success stories and figure out how to stake out a claim, how to define the methods for what had been achieved almost by happenstance. It was time to build a model that would help them identify the kind of clients they could best serve in the future, to ward off competition, and to separate themselves from the masses who would soon begin calling themselves financial advisers.

These planners were proud of their accomplishments but uncertain of how they would manage to stay on top. Judy Shine, founder of Shine Investment Advisory Services in Englewood, Colorado, like many in the group, knew that the success of her firm depended on her strengths—her competence, her personality, her problem-solving skills—and that without her there would not be a firm. Others in the group were more like Peggy Ruhlin, partner at Budros & Ruhlin in Columbus, Ohio, who had already spent a good deal of time evaluating her practice, planning for succession, making certain that the business did not depend on her. But all of them realized that the heat was on in the planning industry. What was once the domain of a cozy, elite group of professionals who greeted one another at conferences and shared problem-solving ideas had become a cockfight. And the folks in this accomplished group were being watched by thousands of people who wanted to mimic them and uncover their secrets.

Even one-time allies were suspect. These independent planners would never have been able to build businesses if not for the mutual fund information published since the mid-1980s by Morningstar, the investment research company in Chicago, and the asset management services offered by Charles Schwab & Co., a discount broker, which many advisers used as a back office to track investments and prepare reports for clients. Now that planners had achieved such surprising success, Schwab was sending letters to some of its advisers' clients, trying to recruit them directly. Many planners were beginning to see the relationship with Schwab as an uneasy one, and they didn't know whom to trust. Morningstar, too, was moving into the advisory business with model 401(k) portfolios and stock and mutual fund recommendations. Even the Vanguard Group, in Valley Forge, Pennsylvania, the low-cost provider of funds used by many financial advisers, was offering its own brand of low-cost investment advice.

Indeed, not all of the advisers meeting in Dallas were happy to have Mark Hurley there, so soon after he'd caused such a fuss in the industry that fall with his doom-and-gloom report on the future of planning—"The Future of the Financial Advisory Business and the Delivery of Advice to the Semi-Affluent Investor." Hurley had predicted intense competition and consolidation in the financial advisory business in the decade to follow as well as the emergence of forty or fifty huge firms with a minimum of $20 billion apiece in assets. His report warned that the financial planning business had been isolated from traditional market forces, that the supply of clients exceeded the capacity of advisers, who had no real competition, and that a tidal wave of change would completely reshape the business. The net result would be to create a hostile, competitive environment in which advisers would no longer be willing to share their professional secrets as they had for a decade. According to Hurley, advisers had few choices: They could do nothing and watch their profit margins shrink; they could sell out to one of the emerging companies that was building a regional or national presence; they could build a giant firm themselves; or they could find a niche, as did Tom Connelly and Bob Keats of Keats, Connelly and Associates in Phoenix, Arizona, who focus on Canadian retirees in the United States and the investment, estate-planning, and other financial issues unique to dual citizens.

Big firms, Hurley insisted, would become problem solvers for their clients, too, offering financial planning, asset management, insurance, tax planning, tax preparation, estate planning, and advice on charitable giving, all for less than 1 percent of assets. "Your real value added is the diagnostic function as opposed to the advice function," he told planners. "People don't want investment management; they want lifestyle management." Niche firms would be able to charge more because of the specialized advice they would offer and the barriers to entry they were able to create.

But some of the planners in the room, like Shine and Judy Lau, were sole practitioners and liked it that way. They didn't want to become giant firms. "I want to work with clients," Shine says. "I don't want to supervise people who work with clients." Shine thinks of her practice model as closer to a psychotherapist's than to, say, Bessemer Trust's and says she continues to find she has to defend herself for not wanting to grow her business—even though her firm once again landed in 2003 on *Bloomberg Wealth Manager* magazine's annual ranking of independent financial advisory firms. Hardly small potatoes. But Hurley was convinced that sole practitioners like Shine would continue to function only if they didn't mind existing at a subsistence level once profit margins collapsed.

Powerful companies like Merrill Lynch would stop at nothing to get clients away from individual planners, Hurley said. Shelling out $150,000 to acquire a new client is peanuts to such a large outfit, whereas such spending is unthinkable for a small advisory firm. Independent advisers countered that the big companies could never capture their clients because firms that size simply don't understand the nature of the wealth management process, which, for the independent, goes far beyond a simple retirement projection and considers every aspect of a client's life. They felt confident that the big firms couldn't duplicate the kind of relationship they had with clients. "Nobody pays us but our clients," is the motto of Keats, Connelly. But insurance agents and stockbrokers, even if they converted to fees, would still be attached to a huge firm whose goal is to push its products.

A cursory look at results from the "Financial-Performance Study of Financial Advisory Practices" conducted by the Financial Planning Association (FPA) in 2002 seems to support such fearlessness. From 1999 to 2001 the typical independent firm gained 16.7 percent in assets from new clients at the same time the stock market lost 11.9 percent as measured by the S&P 500 Stock Index. And independents did a great job of managing their clients' assets. Client portfolios fell only 5.3 percent in 2001, thanks to the cautious, diversified investment approach these firms took.

But rosy pictures aside, it appears that Hurley's predictions are coming true. Hurley, a smart businessman who cut his teeth at Goldman Sachs and Merrill Lynch, has made some valid points about the business, which many chose to dismiss. Yet the 2002 FPA study provided startling validation for his forecasts. Hurley wrote his report in 1999, the same year the FPA did its first study. By 2001, just two years later, the margin compressions he had anticipated happened in spades. At the average small advisory firm, revenue was up 6.9 percent for the two-year period, overhead expenses were up 32 percent, and professional staff compensation was up 12.7 percent, while owner compensation was down 3.9 percent. Operating profit slipped 28 percent and net profit fell by exactly one-third. Indeed, even planners like Tom Connelly, who've created a comfortable niche with barriers to entry, expect to see a decrease in fees of perhaps 25 percent and realize that they've got to become more efficient and more profitable.

Hurley was right, too, in suggesting that institutions like Merrill Lynch would begin offering advisory services rather than just transaction-based services and that technology would become a bigger factor in providing them. Already, TurboTax, the Web-based software for tax filing, can produce a superior tax return—and with more accuracy than many accountants.

Hurley's ideas clearly have merit, but when the dust settles, it may turn out that he has oversimplified the advisory world. Lawyers and accountants have no barriers to entry in their profession, other than getting a law degree or a CPA designation. Yet their practices don't divide neatly into merely two strategies, big or niche. Perhaps it's a question of how one defines strategy. Webster says it's "the art or skill of careful planning toward an advantage or a desired end." Maybe that end doesn't necessarily have to lead to becoming either big or a niche. Certainly, many small, marginal planning firms are going to disappear. But there may be room for more variations than Hurley suggests. A firm may not be serving a niche, but it may nevertheless be known for certain strengths that set it apart.

Connelly doesn't buy the idea that survival depends on being big or having a niche. "If you just run a good business and do what you say you're going to do when you say you're going to do it," he says, "you're already ahead of most businesses." Like Lee, Connelly believes there's still plenty of room for experimentation, for different approaches and individual answers to the question of how to advise clients to use their resources to create a fulfilling life. To make his point, Connelly, with whom I share an interest in books about the musings of the desert monks, reminded me of an inscription he saw over the door of a Buddhist monastery: 1,000 monks, 1,000 religions. Tim Kochis, in San Francisco, also believes that the practice will move in the course of this decade toward quality, specialized firms or boutiques.

Whichever winds prevail, it's the independence of their firms that advisers are most afraid of losing in the margin compression Hurley describes. That may be why becoming a large firm is not an attractive alternative for most of these independents. Harold Evensky in Florida, who is arguably the best-known name in financial planning, tried, with some coaching and financing from Hurley, to create a national network of the best and most successful firms. Many of the advisers I talked to, like Connelly, say they gave the idea some thought. But in the end, the negatives outweighed the many positives, such as providing an answer to succession planning, economies of scale, and a feeder system for new clients. "We looked at the possibility of joining," Connelly says. "We didn't think we could fit in." As Connelly sees it, each individual firm has a different vision and a different way of doing things. "Most of us are dysfunctional," he says, "and we can't thrive in a bureaucracy. That's why we went to work for ourselves in the first place." One thousand monks, 1,000 religions.

My sense is that independence in advisers is something clients prize. I've been an entrepreneur for nearly twenty years and I invariably prefer to do business with people of my own tribe. Connelly says his firm has had the same experience. One big client was debating between hiring Keats, Connelly and Northern Trust Co., a national trust company in Chicago that competes with financial planners to offer personalized services to the wealthy. Choosing Connelly's firm, the client said, "You're an entrepreneur just like me."

There's a lot to like about having an entrepreneur working for you: the enthusiasm, the high-touch service. Consider this: The two most talked about and most-feared competitors in financial planning in the past couple of years were Financial Engines, Nobel laureate William Sharpe's online financial adviser, and myCFO, a Web-based provider of customized investment and advisory services to wealthy families. Financial Engines has had problems with its software and has not grown as expected. And in the fall of 2002, myCFO all but disappeared, having been absorbed into the Harris wealth management group in Chicago, a division of the Bank of Montreal. Evan Roth, cofounder of BBR Partners, a large advisory firm in New York, had told me just two months earlier that myCFO was one of the biggest competitors in BBR's market. What happened? Too much tech and not enough touch, was the epitaph insiders wrote.

Advisers must develop a relationship with clients, and they must have a claim to fame—something special to offer, such as family-office services or rarified estate planning or charitable-giving expertise. They might cater to executives who need help sorting through their executive-compensation packages, as Tim Kochis does. Whatever the strength, advisers like Kochis—who has earned an M.B.A. and a law degree and has worked as national director of personal financial planning for Deloitte & Touche and also for the Bank of America Executive Financial Counseling Group—are not about to be swept under the rug as brokers and insurance companies move into financial planning.

Still, expertise must go hand in hand with business savvy. Mark Tibergien, a principal at Moss Adams, an accounting and consulting firm in Seattle, who has consulted with four hundred financial advisers over the past couple of years, "trying to get them to think like businesspeople," says he's seeing some real progress. Interestingly, his guidelines for a workable strategy are a bit looser than Hurley's. To turn a practice into a business, Tibergien says, a planner must take a long-term view. You need a vision. Think: Five years from now my business will look like this. Or: In 2009 my firm will be recognized as the leader in executive compensation issues. Once you've identified a vision, you can create the mission for your business, which, Tibergien says, must be reduced to a thirty-second elevator speech that describes which clients you're serving and why, what you're providing, and what makes you unique.

The third step is to expose the gaps, strengths, weaknesses, opportunities, and threats to your vision: what stands between you and where you want to be. By exposing the gaps, you can come up with tactics. Tibergien says it isn't sufficient to simply identify a market. "You must think about how it will affect your culture, compensation structure, who you hire, and what kind of tools you buy." Financial advisers—at least, those who are doing it right—are seeing a true evolution from practice to business, he says.

Firms need to look too at their capabilities, at what they can do in-house and what they would have to outsource in order to build that particular business. They must know what kind of people they need to recruit and how to train them. It's unlikely that a sole practitioner can set his sights on developing a practice as demanding as a multiclient family office, although Robert Willard of Willard & Co. in Colorado Springs, Colorado, has been able to do something just as comprehensive because he's willing to take on a good deal of risk for his small group of clients. Willard travels all over the country, analyzing businesses his clients might buy. Later, if an investment falls apart, he's likely to take the business over and run it himself.

Hurley, Tibergien, and others in the industry stress the need to face reality, insisting that advisers look at their practices with a cold eye and a calculator in hand. Clearly, a transformation is under way in the financial planning industry, although perhaps not quite the one Hurley envisioned. It's no time to be an ostrich. But the most fruitful side of the question to explore may be the subjective one. To uncover clients' goals, many planners ask them to define success. Maybe you should do the same before deciding on the strategy for your firm. If your goal is to have more time with your family, you won't want to start building a trust company or a multiclient family office. If it's to make $1 million a year, you won't want a fee-by-the-hour practice. "If you want to sustain a strategy, you have to have a passion for it," Tibergien says, "and if it collides with your personal vision of success, it won't work out."

The keys to success in financial planning in the future may not all be clear yet, but on one point, agreement seems universal: You'll have to decide—if you haven't already—how to structure your firm so that it can deliver services efficiently and attract the right clients. The tricky part, of course, is to find a business model that fits not just your clients' needs but your own.

— 🌣 🌣 🌣 —

Chapter Three

Known Quantities

S O NOBODY IN THE STATE can plan for the needs of new business owners with your kind of foresight. Or maybe there isn't an adviser in the county who can sort through sticky divorce issues the way you do. But if nobody knows about it, what good does it do your business?

Before we talk about the ideal specialty or the perfect model for your firm, let's consider the essential little step of letting people know you exist. No matter what your firm's niche or size, you'll need to separate yourself from the crowd. To do that, consultant Mark Tibergien likes the "famous person" strategy of raising the planner's profile in the industry, which he considers a necessary growth stage for many advisory businesses, at least in the short term. He cites as examples planners like Harold Evensky and Deena Katz, and Meg Green, founder of Meg Green & Associates in North Miami Beach, Florida. Green, he points out, gets noticed in restaurants because people recognize her from her television appearances.

Famous is relative, of course, and you may not wind up getting picked up by the networks, like Ginger Applegarth, president of Applegarth Advisors Group in Boston, an adviser who turned her planning practice into a platform for speaking about personal finance and became a well-known television and radio personality. Instead, you might be a household name only to doctors in your area—a profile Bill Howard in Memphis, Tennessee, worked hard to achieve and turn into a very lucrative business. Or you might be a celebrity only within the profession, like planners Peggy Ruhlin in Columbus, Ohio; Tim Kochis in San Francisco; and Judy Lau in Wilmington, Delaware— names that would appear on most everyone's list of the top dozen planners in the country. Being well-known in the profession can be valuable in many ways. You're invited to the most exclusive network- ing and workshop programs in the industry. You learn from other plan- ners, and you top the referral lists of other financial professionals.

Of course, even quasi-celebrity status won't make you a competent adviser. Still, many successful planners believe it's been well worth their time to court the press and to get involved in professional orga- nizations. These associations provide stepping-stones to the next level of success. In my thirty-year career as a journalist, I've run into plenty of people who wanted to get their names in the paper and only a few who had any idea how to do it. I don't recommend calling report- ers or sending letters with story ideas. That's putting the cart before the horse. Most reporters want to talk with knowledgeable planners whose expertise is recognized in the field. More often than not, jour- nalists will call a planner they see quoted in the *Wall Street Journal* or the *New York Times* or someone who's an established name in the planning world. I've heard advisers complain that many of the best planners never get quoted; instead, the same names appear again and again. That's probably true. But a reporter on a deadline does not see it as his job to uncover a new face in the planning business. He wants to get the story done and will call the people who've been reliable in the past. And the first step for advisers who hope to rate a place on a reporter's short list is visibility within the profession.

Making the grade takes a little determination, like the kind dem- onstrated by Nancy Langdon Jones, president of NL Jones Financial Planning in Upland, California, who won a spot in *Financial Planning* magazine's annual survey of the financial planning industry's movers, shakers, and decision makers of 2002 for the way she turned herself from a nobody into a somebody. Of course, nobody is a nobody, but back in 1994, when Jones was president of the San Gabriel Valley chapter of the International Association for Financial Planning (IAFP), she learned the hard way that she was barely a step above anonymous. Jones was being considered for nomination for a spot on the national board. As part of the screening, Ross Levin, president of Accredited Investors in Minneapolis, Minnesota, called to interview Jones. She thought the conversation had gone well. But when she saw Levin later at the IAFP conference, he told her she hadn't gotten the nomination. "I fought for you," he said, "but there wasn't a single person on the board who had ever heard of you."

Jones was disappointed—and determined to do something about it. When she got back home, the job of getting better known went to the top of her priority list. She volunteered to help the Certified Financial Planner Board of Standards and was assigned to the committee to rewrite the CFP exam. At conferences, she introduced herself to leaders in the profession. She got on the media list for the CFP board and on the IAFP list and joined the front line of planners who got referred to reporters. Advisers on this list are categorized according to areas of expertise. Jones chose the specialties that listed the fewest advisers. One of the most frequently asked questions she's addressed on behalf of the CFP board has been, Who are financial planners and why would anyone want to be one? "I can't count the calls I've gotten on that one," she says.

Jones has also written a book—*So You Want to Be a Financial Planner: Your Guide to a New Career*—which is available online at Amazon.com. She is particularly excited about this online book because she can continually update it and keep it current. The book has led to active online networking: answering questions, meeting new advisers, getting involved in new projects. Jones came to the profession by happenstance; she wrote her book to help others rely less on chance and avoid her mistakes.

And Jones has made her share of them. Like many advisers, she didn't start out intending to become a financial planner. After getting degrees in psychology, theater, and English, she worked as a realtor and then as office manager for a CPA, circling around the services she would eventually provide as an adviser. In 1983, while Jones was working as a realtor, the College of Financial Planning sent a representative to talk to her group of realtors about pursuing careers in planning.

Interest rates were hovering around 16 percent at the time, and Jones didn't feel comfortable with the creative financing deals her peers were setting up so that clients could manage to buy a house. She'd never heard of financial planning as a career, but she was excited about the idea of helping people decide whether they could afford to buy a house. It was certainly a step up from trying to collect a commission by selling them one that was out of their price range.

Many of the top advisers I've known transitioned to financial planning in similar ways. They started in insurance or stocks or in some type of sales job because they had the notion that they wanted to help people with financial issues. When they discovered that they were actually pushing products rather than giving advice, they became frustrated with the whole business. Many of these people were later the groundbreakers in creating a new profession that was truly about planning for the needs of the client rather than peddling products for a broker or insurer.

Jones got herself ready to serve clients by taking the series of courses required for financial planning certification—and then some. When she took the insurance course, she got her insurance license. When she studied investments, she took the Series 7 test. And after the tax course, she went to H&R Block to get certified as a tax preparer. Jones loved the coursework and she loved the idea of helping people use their resources to achieve their goals. "From the beginning," she says, "what appealed to me was the planning process."

When the coursework was completed, Jones went to work first for Waddell & Reed, a national financial services company in Overland Park, Kansas, and later for a broker/dealer as a registered rep. But she discovered that to be paid for planning work, she had to sell mutual funds and limited partnerships at an 8 percent commission. She had finally acquired a broad range of financial knowledge, but she found being a rep was worse than being a realtor. At least when she was in real estate, the clients knew exactly what her goal was. As a rep she felt she was posing as a financial adviser but was in truth an undercover salesperson. "I had a really hard time turning my hat around and selling something," she says.

By the early 1990s, it became clear to her that she had to get out from under selling products and do financial planning. But clients didn't want to pay for planning, and "I almost lost my shirt." Her fallback was her tax-preparation training, and she built up a tax practice with one hundred clients. Realtors in the area referred clients to her for tax preparation and financial planning. "I was making about five cents an hour, but that's what I wanted to do," says Jones. "The tax preparation kept me alive."

Once Jones prepared a financial plan for a client, she sent him out to buy the investment products. "But the next year they would come back and I'd find they'd been sold the wrong thing." So Jones was forced to make sure her clients got the right investments, and that meant supervising the purchases herself. In 1992, she talked with Schwab and discovered she could buy funds for her clients without using a commission. But picking investments still gave her sleepless nights, so in 1994 she formed a partnership with a colleague who had an affinity for making investments. Jones did the rest of the planning. Unfortunately, the two didn't click as a team, and in 1995 Jones was the cover girl on *Investment Advisor* magazine under the headline: "Can This Partnership Be Saved?"

It was the investment management that kept tripping Jones up, so she decided to outsource it. She first tried a turnkey operation for the job; later she met Michael Ling on a financial planning interactive Internet board. Ling, an economist who has his own planning practice called Berkely Inc. in Boise, Idaho, loves doing research and assembling portfolios and Jones hired him to do hers. "We've been working together for seven years, and in the last couple of years [2001 and 2002], we've been returning minus 3 percent or so," she says. "I used to second guess Mike all the time; I don't anymore."

The Jones-Ling relationship is a good example of the kind of outsourcing between planners that allows each to do his best work. Jones works with seventy families and describes herself as "touchy-feely," while Ling is much more analytical. Jones, who is in her early sixties, has worked out a buy-sell agreement with Ling, in his early forties, who will buy her practice in two or three years.

And thanks to her hard work in raising her profile, Jones's retirement, when it comes, won't go unnoticed.

— ❀ ❀ ❀ —

Part Two

The Seekers

Chapter Four

The Hourly Planner

B Y THE SECOND HALF of the 1990s, many financial advisers had moved from the sales side of the planning table to the client's side. The key challenge they faced in doing so was how to make sure clients understood what that meant for them, how best to show consumers that planners could truly be their advocates. The National Association of Personal Financial Advisors (NAPFA), with its fee-only anthem, made some headway in getting the message across, insisting that advisers who charge fees eliminate most conflicts of interest. The press bought into the fee-only refrain, applauding the objectivity of such planners. But wannabes soon muddied the waters by calling themselves fee-based—or even fee-only—planners when they weren't. Some of these planners had two phone numbers, one for their fee-only services and the other for their brokerage services. Others used the same number for both. When the mud hardened, a large group of elite planners acknowledged that the fee-only approach was not as sanctified as it appeared; it was possible to charge fees and still be incompetent or even dishonest.

Gradually, top advisers sought other avenues to distinction and began to call themselves wealth managers, a name that carried both the heft and nuance they sought, coming as it did from Harold Evensky, who was arguably the best-known name in financial planning and certainly among the most highly respected. In 1997, the publication of Evensky's heady book, *Wealth Management: The Financial Advisor's Guide to Investing and Managing Your Client's Assets* (Irwin Professional Publishing), marked a watershed in the financial advisory business, outlining a curriculum for planners who wanted to consult with the wealthy and anointing them with a name that stuck. Not long after Evensky's book came out, Ross Levin, in Minneapolis, published *The Wealth Management Index* (Irwin Professional Publishing), a book detailing his firm's way of measuring its clients' wealth and their progress toward goals. Then in 1999 came the launch of *Bloomberg Wealth Manager* magazine, the first publication in the trade to focus exclusively on the problems facing independent planners advising clients of high net worth.

The books by Evensky and Levin and the achievements of the top-tier advisers, along with their new and exclusive moniker, gave those who'd earned it a degree of credibility and respect that had eluded them when they were thrown into the same pen with stockbrokers and insurance agents. This hierarchy is all to the good, but it has intensified a problem in the industry: too many financial planning practitioners racing to make it over the same fence. They all want to manage the wealth of high-end customers. That market has been sliced and diced in any number of ways, with planners offering soup-to-nuts services to wealthy families, sometimes handling mundane chores like vacation planning and home repair, arranging loans for family businesses, and even hiring security firms to protect clients against kidnapping.

All of these services are worthwhile, but the rush to care and feed the opulent has meant that when one of my hoi-polloi friends asks me to recommend an adviser, I can't come up with a single name that's suitable. Most planners I know accept only new clients with a minimum of $1 million in assets. The crowd that remains—cut off from such objective financial advice—could feed a swarm of product pushers. Clearly, most investors don't have enough assets to qualify for the services of a wealth manager. So most of these less-than-wealthy customers end up in high-load mutual funds, with no attention whatsoever paid to insurance, estate planning, and other key financial issues.

Enter the hourly planner, the problem solver who will accept the client who wants advice one piece at a time: Can he afford to buy a home? How much money will she need to retire? Must he sell his business to settle a divorce? The hourly-fee planner can help clients come up with answers they can trust, because these planners do not sell products or manage money, so they receive no commissions.

Many of my planner friends get a bit riled up about this model, arguing that you can't tell someone whether he can afford to buy a home unless you put together all the pieces of the puzzle. I don't buy that. Most Americans are clueless about money issues. Even a little advice can help a lot. One friend of mine at the gym, a forty-year-old mother of three who's still paying off credit card bills for the Chinese food she ate in college, would likely be well served by help applied even with the broadest brush. She never got her degree and is eager to go back to school, but her finances are in a mess. Another friend I referred to an hourly planner knew so little about finances that she had to ask me what he meant when he told her to liquidate every-thing. Neither of these clients can afford a $5,000 financial plan. But they certainly need help.

Hourly planners are the perfect fit for these people. The client can do a little bit at a time, accomplish something, and feel he's in better financial health right away. For example, I sent one friend to an hourly planner after she'd lost more than half of her retirement money investing in the aggressive tech stock funds a broker had sold her. A hard-working, small-business owner, she was panicking, fearing she'd lost any chance at retirement. The hourly planner told her to sell all her funds. "I was crying like mad," my friend told me. "I thought I could wait for these stocks to come back." But the planner showed her that if she pumps $20,000 a year into her new portfolio of index funds, there's an excellent chance that she can retire as planned. This adviser earned nothing for recommending these funds, which went a long way toward persuading my friend that it was the right thing to do. And a taste of success increases a client's appetite for more.

The market for this kind of planning seems to me to be large. The baby boomers and Gen Xers whom I chat with online, for example, want to manage their own money, but few of them care to learn about insurance issues and estate planning. So they need financial advice from time to time. And they're content to seek the answers as the questions arise.

—— 🌺 🌺 🌺 ——

Sharon Rich: An Hour's Worth

When I wrote an article several years ago about Sharon Rich, founder of Womoney, a financial-planning practice in Belmont, Massachusetts, that charges $160 per hour for à la carte planning, I got some cantankerous mail from advisers. That's no way for a serious planner to make a living, they scoffed. It didn't help that Rich, the daughter of a wealthy Houston family, was motivated as much by her wish to make a contribution to society as by her desire do planning per se. Rich's loose affiliation with clients didn't sit well with advisers either, but I find that to be one of the more appealing aspects of her approach.

Today, thanks to Sheryl Garrett, the hourly model has been franchised and made readily available to planning practitioners across the country. Still, Rich deserves credit for being the first, as far as I know, to offer client services in this way. This pioneer has been doing piecemeal planning out of her home office for twenty years, and there's more than a little to be learned from her. Indeed, Garrett, a groundbreaker in her own right, says she learned much from Rich.

When Rich says she is a fee-only planner, she means it literally. She does not sell products. She does not manage assets. She does not keep extensive files for clients. She helps them solve financial problems; much of the actual work is done by the client. Rich sees her job primarily as teaching money awareness. Her background is in teaching. She taught high school English before going to Harvard University for a doctorate in the psychology of education. It was chiefly her politics that got her involved in planning. Browsing in a Boston bookstore in the early 1980s, she saw a book titled *Robin Hood Was Right: A Guide to Giving Your Money for Social Change* (Vanguard Public Foundation). The book was about how to create social change, and it led her to the Haymarket People's Fund. Founded in 1974 by George Pillsbury, part of the Pillsbury baking family, the fund was the first of several set up by the Haymarket Group, a foundation that grants money to grassroots groups for the purpose of promoting social change. In working with the Haymarket Group and with other women who had inherited wealth, Rich learned how important financial planning really was. "I saw that people needed to find a place to talk about money and to ask questions and feel safe to be stupid."

Rich's approach to planning strays considerably from the gospel according to traditional planners. She doesn't schedule regular meetings with clients. She waits until they call her. "I have one client I see once a month," she says. "Some I see once every three years, and I have someone I haven't seen for eight years. My idea is to have people call me when they need me." That might be when they're struggling with the question of whether they can afford to buy a house or take a severance package or when they want to set up a retirement portfolio. Most client meetings are scheduled to run one and a half to two hours.

Rich starts things off by asking the client to bring in all his files, tax returns, company benefit booklets, insurance policies, loan agreements, wills and trust documents, stock option agreements, and statements from investment accounts and checkbooks. She sits down with the client in front of the computer and enters all the data, asking the client to look up the necessary figures from the documents he's brought. When the client leaves, he has all the critical numbers including cash flow information, net worth, retirement and college projections, and financial goals. Rich sends the client home with as many as twenty homework assignments. For example, one client came in with an annuity in a retirement plan. She sent him home to find out the penalty for getting out of the annuity contract. Another woman was using a stockbroker for her investment portfolio and her returns were dismal. Rich helped the woman develop a list of ten questions to ask the stockbroker. "If I find out the answers for her, it doesn't teach her anything," Rich says. Another client was assigned to make two changes to her automobile insurance, increasing the deductible and the liability coverage, after Rich explained why it was necessary. Yet another client was instructed to read a book about socially responsible mutual funds. "I send them to do the homework," she says. "They're not paying me to do it." In a sense, Rich does what many financial journalists try to do: assist do-it-yourselfers. The difference is that Rich holds them by the hand and is available to catch them if they fall.

Although she does not manage money, Rich is not ideologically opposed to it. "Assets under management is a full-time business," she says. "Planners have to grow their office to be competent at both planning and asset management." She prefers not to manage assets for a number of reasons. "First, I'd lose sleep." And second, she has a number of clients who like to do it themselves; all they need is a coach. She subscribes to Morningstar's services so she has the resources to review funds and offer advice. "My forte is problem solving," she says. When clients want investing advice, she shows them how to look up the information online, how to compare different funds, and how to screen them. Third, and most important, Rich doesn't want to change her lifestyle or grow her business; she wants to continue working at home while her two daughters are in school.

Rich believes that a planner must match her vision of the world to her practice, and she admits that her own practice started out with the purpose of making a political statement. She worked at first with inheritors like herself, believing that if people felt more comfortable about their money, they would feel better about giving it away. But over the years, her clientele has become more mixed, with an emphasis on those who can't afford a traditional planner. Her own experience of making peace with money taught her that conflict with money is a universal problem that has little to do with poverty or wealth. Although planning is no longer a political statement for Rich, she enjoys meeting new people, listening to their problems, and helping solve them. "What I love most about my business are the stories," she says. "I'm combining my background in psychology with financial skills."

Rich says at least once a month she meets with someone who wonders how to set up a practice like hers. "I just met with four women who are new to the field," she says, "and I know of at least a half-dozen people in Boston who would like to set up practices like mine." Rich figures she clears about $100,000 a year, which is modest compared with the $1 million many wealth managers take home. But her responsibilities and lifestyle are nothing like theirs, either.

Rich spends no money on marketing because she's not accepting new clients. She estimates that a new planner could set up an hourly-fee business for about $10,000 if he worked from his home. She has a separate home office with a separate entrance. Her children's play-room doubles as the waiting room. She has space for a meeting room, and she's invested in a computer and a fax machine. And, of course, a planner needs Lotus software, errors-and-omissions insurance, and some files and bookcases.

But Rich warns that until the clients start coming in, you need seed money. One way to give yourself a financial safety net would be to start the practice part-time on weekends before quitting your day job. Rich has found there's a great need for what she's offering. "My business has been full since 1996," she says. "This past week alone, I talked to seven people who would use me if I were available."

Build it, and they will certainly come—at least for an hour or two.

Diana Kahn: The Doctor Is In

WHEN DIANA KAHN decided in 1994 that she wanted to become a financial adviser, she hooked up with one of the industry's most prestigious firms—Evensky, Brown & Katz. Evensky targets the high-net-worth market, and Kahn was drawn to the complexity and sophistication of the planning required to serve such clients. "Lots of stockbrokers and insurance brokers claimed to be planners," Kahn says, "but they didn't take a look at each individual situation before making recommendations." Evensky, Brown & Katz certainly provided tailored advice, but the firm's hallmark of working only with clients who meet a certain minimum asset requirement became a problem for Kahn. She found that she didn't click with the high-net-worth market.

Kahn credits Katz with helping her to recognize that she wanted to be a family practitioner for clients' money, someone who would help those who had means as well as those who couldn't make ends meet or were saddled with debt. "Plenty of investment managers wanted to manage money for high-net-worth individuals," Kahn says. "Nowhere did I see unbiased general planners who would provide affordable advice, no matter what the asset level was." And she wanted to charge all clients the same price, whether they were wealthy or on the verge of bankruptcy. She also hoped to help clients find other financial professionals who provide affordable advice.

In December 1997, Kahn set up the Financial Pharmacist in her home in Aventura, Florida. She charges by the project, a $400 flat fee that includes two hours of meeting time as well as analysis. If two hours are not sufficient, Kahn charges $50 for each additional hour. At the end of the year, each client is invited to return for a financial checkup, which costs $200. If the client waits more than a year to come back, the cost is $400.

Kahn hasn't had trouble getting referrals, because planners like Katz, who know her work, are happy to pass along clients who don't meet their asset minimum. And Kahn is happy to offer a cure.

Sheryl Garrett: When Less Is More

THE MODEL SHARON RICH developed for providing financial advice based on hourly fees had two major problems that kept it from being widely applicable: It was unavailable to most consumers because so few planners had set up this kind of shop, and it was considered an unrealistic model for planners because it was unlikely to provide the level of income "wealth managers" sought. But by 2002, when I met Sheryl Garrett, who in 1998 had set up a similar practice in Shawnee, Kansas, she had already franchised her business, making the hourly-fee model seem a more viable option for planners, especially those just getting started. It worked for planners, and it worked for consumers. Indeed, Garrett got great publicity that year for the Garrett Planning Network. *Newsweek* columnist Linda Stern recommended Garrett's low-cost services to her baby boomer clients who'd been burned by the market. And the *Wall Street Journal*'s Jonathan Clements made the case that hourly-fee planners were the only ones with the client's interests at heart.

To be fair, Clements had a point. The difficulty consumers have in identifying good planners has been one of the thorniest issues in the business. There is no simple answer. But both the press and consumers like easy solutions, and that's why today hourly-fee planners are moving toward the holy ground that NAPFA members held five years ago. The press can point to hourly planners and say: Here's a group that doesn't sell products and has no conflict of interest; it offers you straight advice for an hourly fee.

Indeed, when friends ask me to recommend an adviser, I nearly always suggest someone who charges by the hour, because I consider the advice affordable as well as objective. Garrett's network—at www.garrettplanning.com—has grown so large that hourly planners are now available to consumers in most parts of the country. I've followed up with all the people I referred to such planners, and they have not been disappointed. When I write about hourly-fee planners in *Bloomberg Wealth Manager* magazine, I get many enthusiastic letters and e-mails from advisers who've taken this route.

Garrett, of course, may be the most enthusiastic of all. Like Rich, she sees herself as a teacher. Unlike Rich, she is not wealthy. In fact, the Internal Revenue Service audited her 1988 tax return, presumably because her taxable income of $1,100 seemed too low for a financial adviser. "When we got through with the audit," she says, "they gave me a refund of $83." Garrett's doing quite a lot better than that now. But like so many advisers, she went through several incarnations before discovering the kind of planning that suited her best and would bring her success.

Garrett was drawn to financial planning as a teenager because of her interest in investing. She picked it up quickly and spent free time with a financial calculator, checking mutual fund returns and working out portfolio possibilities. When friends and relatives came to her for help, she enjoyed solving their money problems. And she got an early start on solving her own. "When I was nineteen, I decided I would never be dependent on anyone," Garrett says. She went to college, got some business experience, earned her certified financial planner designation, and went through the training program at Investors Diversified Services (IDS)—the former planning arm of American Express. She considered these steps "a good plan for someone with no financial experience." But the cold calls made her sick to her stomach every morning. Each IDS planner was expected to make one hundred cold calls a day. Garrett would dial six digits of the seven-digit number and then pretend to talk—hardly an effective way to make money, which is why her 1988 income was her all-time low.

After IDS, Garrett went to work for a planner in a family office, then for a pension consultant, and finally for an adviser who did fee-offset work. (In a fee-offset compensation structure, the planner charges a fee but may also use products with commissions, which are then subtracted from the fee.) By that time, Garrett figured she'd earned her stripes and she left to become a partner in a fee-only wealth management firm. Her partner handled the personal finance, and Garrett was responsible for investments.

Garrett knew she'd reached the goal most planners aimed for. But she saw very soon that the work didn't suit her. She didn't feel comfortable with the wealthy clients who were coming to her for help.

She felt like a pencil-pusher and a personal secretary. "I was doing a lot of paperwork, and I didn't feel as if I was making a difference in people's lives," she says. What's more, she hated telling someone with $200,000 that they were just small potatoes and her firm couldn't take them on.

Garrett was also aware that scores of planners spend years trying to convert their business from commissions to fees, believing fees to be the only compensation structure that can give them income certainty, objectivity, and independence. Still, she hated being on retainer. She felt hemmed in by the 24/7 obligation, and she wasn't happy exchanging personal freedom for a good income. Garrett likes to backwoods camp, for example, and she found that she wasn't at liberty to go off somewhere, out of the range of a phone. "Part of it was pure selfishness," she says. "I didn't like the way I felt pushing paper around for people who didn't appreciate it." Nor was the pace right for her. "I felt as if I was bogged down in projects that would never get done."

In 1998, Garrett left her wealth management practice when she saw an opportunity to set up the kind of business that would suit her better. She believes that most Americans need financial help but that few of them require a comprehensive financial plan or a full-time financial planner. They need a nip here and a tuck there. They need to be taught how to take care of their own finances with an occasional stitch or two. And Garrett made up her mind to offer that. She set up Garrett Planning Network, a planning practice similar to Rich's that would charge by the hour and welcome clients of all income ranges as well as those who couldn't afford a complete financial plan but needed help with one or two aspects of planning. Working by the hour, Garrett reasoned, would better satisfy her need to make a difference with the people she most wanted to help. It would also free up her time so that she could go on wilderness backpacking trips without carrying along a cell phone to soothe clients coming down with the jitters over market volatility.

Garrett's former partner soon referred clients whose total assets were too small for her firm, and other local fee-only planners began to do the same. In fact, Garrett, a member of NAPFA, got a call one day from a couple complaining that no one from NAPFA would take them because they had only $400,000 in their retirement account.

"That made me feel sad for them," she says. And that's her kind of client.

But Garrett helps many different kinds. Nearly every prospect who interviews with her becomes a client. Some are millionaires who want to do their own investing but require a little advice. Others are working-class people who can't afford the cost of a complete financial plan, so she provides a modular plan, a little bit at a time. "I pretend that I'm talking to my sister. Maybe she needs a lot of advice but she can't afford it all right away," says Garrett. "So I start with things we can do first." Occasionally, a client comes in for a check up and is doing everything right: no debt, good insurance coverage, estate plan in place, good investment mix, and good savings habits. "That's when it's just a joy."

Garrett's workday is incredibly varied. She may meet with the fifteen-year-old son of a client, who wants to open an e-trade account, or with clients who want to know if it's time to refinance their home or whether they should buy or lease a car. One couple came to her because they couldn't see eye to eye on money. The wife thought her husband spent too much; he thought she was a killjoy. Once the wife saw that they were in good financial shape, she loosened the purse strings. Another couple came in because they were miserable in a home they didn't like, paying a 10.5 percent mortgage. Garrett persuaded them to sell the greatly appreciated home and build their dream house. Garrett's help cost them about $700. Garrett also has a relationship with Consumer Credit Counseling, a group that helps people get out of debt. The debt counselors like to send their graduates to her because once they're out of debt, the graduates may have $300 or $400 a month to invest and the planning helps them make a fresh start.

Like Rich, Garrett doesn't need to keep fat files on her clients because she works through the problem with each client in person. In most cases, clients are given homework to do, and Garrett hopes they'll learn enough to become self-sufficient. Nor does Garrett necessarily have a long-term relationship with a client. They don't have standing appointments; they come in only when they need help. "Now I'm the trusted adviser that everyone longs to be instead of an indentured servant to people who don't appreciate me," she says.

Garrett charges $180 an hour for financial advice. Her fees are

Richard Chambers: A Menu of Services

RICHARD CHAMBERS, founder of Investor's Capital Management in Menlo Park, California, and a member of Garrett's network and of NAPFA, lets the clients decide how he can best address their investment needs. At the initial, free, half-hour consultation, Chambers first determines whether the client needs investment advice; if so, he follows up by developing an investment recommendation that spells out the client's goals and needs and incorporates the results of a risk-tolerance assessment. The cost of the recommendation, including a written report and a one-hour meeting to explain it, is $300.

At the meeting, Chambers presents several options. The first is a self-directed index-fund portfolio with a meeting once a year to rebalance. The second is a self-directed portfolio of actively managed funds. This option includes monthly e-mail updates and ninety-minute meetings twice a year to compute performance, consider tax issues, and review other financial planning matters. The cost is $600 per year. The third option is to have Chambers do the implementation for $1,200 a year or 12 basis points after the first $1,000,000. The last option is for Chambers to manage the portfolio of funds he recommends, as well as any other assets in the existing portfolio, for a fee that starts at 80 basis points. Most clients choose the second option.

structured much like a lawyer's, applied in five-minute increments for telephone calls and short visits. Averaging fifteen to twenty new clients a month, she puts in about eight to ten hours for a first-time client, with a total fee that ranges from $500 to $2,000. But she does have bigger plans. She intends to structure her practice like a law firm into which she'll bring younger certified financial planners (CFPs), who will earn one-third of the billable rate, with the other two-thirds going to Garrett and to overhead. In 2002, she hired two CFPs along with a paraplanner, whose salary is $24,000, with billable time of $60 an hour. She owns the building she works in and has additional space, "so adding people is adding profit," she says.

But bigger has come sooner than expected for Garrett—not to her practice but to her idea. Consumers all over the country called her, wanting to become clients. And novice advisers offered to intern with her for free. Many of them told her they wanted to be fee-only planners but didn't want to be asset gatherers. The next step became clear. She decided to license her business model for a fee of $6,500 plus a retainer of $1,200 a year. Sixty people joined her network in 2002, the first year of operation. The fee includes a three-day training program as well as Garrett's software and reports, including a sample of every form Garrett uses, her risk-tolerance questionnaire, and the press kits she distributes to the media. To qualify for her network, planners must meet the stiff requirements for NAPFA membership, although they need not join. Members are encouraged to use her Internet community and attend an annual retreat as well as sit in on three or four monthly teleconferences. Garrett figures a new planner would need an additional $8,000 to $15,000 for computers, phones, furniture, compliance, marketing, some software, and business-registration fees.

I've gotten letters from planners—all of them pleased—who have joined Garrett's network. Gregory Neal, managing principal at Neal Financial Planning in Towson, Maryland, wrote, "Not only do hourly and flat fees work well for clients; they work for planners too. It's getting very crowded in the wealth management business and one of the least competitive markets is the one that's the largest: hourly and flat-rate services for the middle market." Others write to talk about how they manage money for clients. David Ressner, former journalist and now president of Ressner Financial Planning in St. Louis, Missouri, and part of Garrett's network, says he recommends only index funds and passive-asset-class funds like Vanguard and Dimensional Fund Advisors (DFA). "Passive management removes another variable from the advice process and gets us one step closer to the ultimate goal: complete objectivity," says Ressner.

Some advisers who've been in the industry for a long time make light of Rich and Garrett and their fee-only model. I don't see why.

The hourly model is a real breakthrough, making objective financial planning available for the first time to the middle class and to people who in the past had to rely on tripe like "The Best 10 Funds to Buy Now" in *Money* magazine. I believe this segment of the market will be a fast-growing one. I can see, too, how it would have tremendous appeal to planners who want to create a business that matches their own lifestyle, the way Garrett has.

— ⚘ ⚘ ⚘ —

Chapter 5 *Five*

The Niche Planner

WHEN MARK HURLEY's 1999 research report, "The Future of the Financial Advisory Business and the Delivery of Advice to the Semi-Affluent Investor," predicted that survivors in the financial planning industry would fall into two groups—megafirms and niche firms—many planners decided right away that building a $20 billion business was an unattainable goal. If Hurley is right—and not everyone agrees that he is—a niche, by default, is the only way to go.

Hurley's predictions have been the subject of much debate. In a similarly controversial report in 1995, assessing the future of the investment management industry, he made many similar predictions including the notion of an imminent industry consolidation that would leave in its wake a small group of large institutions and many small niche companies. His take on the investment management industry turned out to be accurate. But there are reasons to believe that the money management business is not a precise model for the financial advisory industry. Money management, for example, lends itself to using leverage and economies of scale. If Bill Gross, manager of PIMCO Total Return fund, manages $1 trillion, he probably won't need to change his strategy much as more money rolls in. But financial advisers provide a personal service, so it's not clear that a planning firm can gain the same advantage from economies of scale.

The niche model, however, has some real appeal. What adviser wouldn't want to insulate his business against competition by providing a service to a specialized group of customers, especially if the practice has significant barriers to entry for other planners? The clients' needs define the niche, Hurley says. "Ideally, clients in a niche will share some very complex problems for which solutions are essential to their financial success. The more complicated and specialized the problems, the greater the [viability] of the niche." But even those who have defined and penetrated a niche are not home free, he says. They must operate efficiently, continue to fend off competition from similar niche practices, and anticipate clients' changing needs.

A successful niche business is considered a plum, and Hurley devoted a second report on the financial planning industry, called "The Future of the Financial Advisory Business Part II: Strategies for Small Businesses" issued in September 2000, to defining niche planning firms. The report acknowledged that most planners would not gravitate to the megafirms. "The vast majority of firms are committed to remaining small so they can continue to provide the best possible service to clients and keep company cultures intact," Hurley wrote. "The purpose of this second paper is to provide a road map that smaller advisory businesses can use to position themselves to become niche competitors." The good news, according to Hurley, is that niche companies can sell their products at premium prices. The bad news is that clients will pay that premium only for "products they perceive as essential to meeting their needs and that include necessary features not available in generic products."

Perhaps because of his first paper's ominous warnings, Hurley tried to soothe planners a bit in the second one, telling them that although some firms sensed danger in his predications, a smaller group saw opportunity. "We believe the next five years offer advisory-industry participants a once-in-a-lifetime opportunity to build great businesses," Hurley wrote. "Only a handful of niche businesses currently exist. Literally hundreds of niche segments lie waiting for the taking. And the current benevolent operating environment in the industry provides a window for advisers to reposition their businesses." So in the niches lie the opportunities. "But the window is very small," the report warned. Those who "hope to prosper in the future need to take steps now to prepare for the coming changes to the industry."

Mark Tibergien, at Moss Adams in Seattle, has consulted on strategy and valuation with hundreds of financial planning firms taking such steps. Tibergien believes that the niche strategy will emerge as the most dominant, but he finds the term niche is often used incorrectly. People say, My niche is the high net worth market. Unfortunately, that puts you in a crowded field, Tibergien explains. A niche, in fact, is a market segment that's limited and definable, such as doctors or college professors. It might also be a demographic segment, such as retirees or gays and lesbians. "When you take a niche approach, it means you're somewhat of a generalist, but you identify a market and come up with products and services to serve it," Tibergien says. "Every practice is limited in terms of time, money, energy, and people. Deciding where you want to go is always a resource question."

Key to the niche strategy in financial planning, Hurley tells me, is to define the client you're after. Using the dermatologist—his wife's occupation—as an example, Hurley explains that such a client's net worth is tied directly to his ability to make money. "Helping them make more money is the most important thing an adviser can do for them," he says. To make this niche strategy work, you must first understand how a dermatology office works and be able to offer suggestions on how to make it more efficient, Hurley says. Second, you must corner the market. In Dallas/Fort Worth, there are 200 dermatologists; a planner who wants that niche should aim to serve 150 of them.

But defining the client first strikes me as putting the cart before the horse. The wiser path, surely, would be for the adviser to first define himself. Planners solve people's problems, so they need to determine what kind of problems they can best solve. Take William Howard Jr., founder of William Howard & Co. in Memphis, Tennessee, for example, who specializes in advising doctors. Howard decided early on that he liked working with doctors. Having done a lot of disability insurance work, he was familiar with doctors' needs and believed he could leverage that knowledge. In 1989, he went to the Shelby County Medical Society in Memphis and offered to provide financial planning for the group's doctors. The medical society didn't bite right away so Howard hung in there, offering to write a financial planning article for each issue of the membership publication. His patience paid off, and he has built a strong practice that serves mostly doctors.

Howard's practice remains solid despite the low barrier to entry for his target market. Another enterprising planner could set up a similar practice tomorrow to serve doctors, and Howard would be forced to either rely on the loyalty of his clients or cut his prices. My bet is Howard can count on loyalty. Clients will hold strong allegiance to the person or firm whose work has made meaningful and positive changes in their lives. When it comes to personal services—people who do work around my house, for example, or who give me a Thai massage or plant our gardens—I don't think I'm alone in my immunity to any temptation to switch solely to save a dollar. These people's services are important to me, and I hope they're better paid than others in their field because they're worth more. Consider, then, how highly valued a good financial adviser must be.

My dictionary defines a niche as "a place or position suited to or intended for a person's capabilities, occupation, or status." And despite the tendency to define niche firms in terms of the client—like the dermatologist—the most successful niche firms seem to be those in which the niche fits the planner as well as it fits the client. One of the best examples of a financial adviser who took the time to know his own strengths is George Kinder. When he graduated from Harvard, Kinder didn't really want to work at all. Instead, he took two years off to study the world's major religions and try his hand at writing and painting. Finally, forced to find employment, Kinder took the CPA exam, planning to work only during tax season and allow plenty of time for meditating and pondering the human experience. The energy Kinder gave to looking within surely helped him find his niche as a planning guru who could help clients do the same. As the adviser many would call the founder of the "life planning" movement, Kinder created his own market niche: Helping people discover what they want to do with their lives and showing them how to use their resources to accomplish it. Kinder now relishes his work, probably because he's found the only thing he enjoys doing as much as studying religion, writing, and meditating.

Other examples of planners who looked first to their own strengths to define their markets are people like Jennifer Hatch and Kermit Johns at Christopher Street Financial in New York, who believe that being gay gives them a better awareness of the needs of their gay clients. Johns says he understands perfectly well how it feels when—after a couple has been together for twenty years—one partner dies and his family descends en masse, trying to claim the inheritance of the surviving partner. Although four big brokerage firms target the gay market in New York, Christopher Street Financial has a unique advantage because of the special knowledge of the owners and employees.

Market niches that evolve from a planner's professional or personal experiences might just as easily aim to serve divorced women, college professors, or entrepreneurs. Bob Keats, for example, a Canadian who has acquired dual citizenship, has spent more than a decade with his partner Tom Connelly, a Minnesotan, studying the tax structures, tax treaties, and all the special financial circumstances faced by their niche of Canadian snowbird clients. Likewise, Cicily Carson Maton, in Chicago, who struggled through her own difficult divorce with no financial knowledge, went on to acquire the skills to set up a niche practice for the finances of divorce.

Planners fortunate enough to identify personally with individuals of high net worth must select a slice of that widely courted market. Myra Salzer did that when she founded the Wealth Conservancy in Boulder, Colorado, a firm that serves inheritors—people who inherit enough money so they need never work again. Salzer spends a good deal of time on the psychological issues that inheritors struggle with—lack of self-esteem, suspicion, guilt—and runs workshops with a psychologist who is an inheritor herself.

But sometimes the niche emerges from the values planners hold. I'm reminded here of Lowell, Blake & Associates in Boston, whose founder, James H. Lowell II, a member of one of Boston's most prestigious families, believes that the wealthy should give something back. He also thinks most charities are worthless because they're not run like businesses and they waste the contributions they receive. So Lowell sets up his own charitable endeavors for clients, giving them the opportunity to invest in timberland preservation or the rehabilitation of a working-class neighborhood or films that promote the preservation of endangered wildlife.

It's difficult to think of a successful planner who hasn't found his niche. The best planners have worked through difficult issues for themselves and found their own answers. That's what makes them so good at counseling others. In the following profiles we'll look at some specific niches and how they were developed.

— 🌺 🌺 🌺 —

Myra Salzer: The Rich Niche

WHAT DOES AN INDEPENDENT wealth management firm have that its big institutional competitors lack? Creativity and agility, for starters. Creativity is nourished by allowing space for the ideas that tumble around in your subconscious and by having the liberty to go with your instincts and intuition. Translating those instincts into action is where agility comes in.

That's the kind of readiness that was part of the picture when Myra Salzer was working in the early 1980s as a chemical engineer in Boulder, Colorado, and decided out of curiosity to take some courses offered by the College of Financial Planning in Denver. She quickly got hooked on financial planning and began to put plans together for friends and acquaintances. Soon she was looking for ways she might get involved in the planning business without taking commissions and without leaving the Rocky Mountains, where she lived with her husband and two young daughters. "I couldn't have lived with myself if I were trying to sell a product," says Salzer. So she saved up two years' worth of salary to support a start-up, fee-only practice and left her engineering job in 1983 to set one up.

Unfortunately, the market for fee-only planning in Boulder at that time was virtually nonexistent. "I had planned for zero dollars and zero cents to come in for two years," Salzer says. "But I hadn't figured it was possible to go below zero." She couldn't even make enough to cover overhead. Still, she wasn't about to give up.

The turning point for Salzer came the day she found herself sitting across the desk from a couple who had acquired a great deal of wealth in a very short time. The wife wore a large emerald ring, which she kept nervously turning to the inside of her hand. Salzer later asked the woman privately if there was anything wrong. There was. The husband, it turned out, had just given her the ring, and although she was embarrassed to wear it—especially in front of her family—she was reluctant to take it off and risk offending him. "How can you show your father a $60,000 emerald," the woman told Salzer, "when he can't even make his mortgage payments?" Salzer saw what was wrong: The rich had their own unique money problems, particularly those who had not earned the wealth themselves or who didn't have money when they were growing up. "There are challenges to inheriting or marrying into wealth that most people haven't considered," Salzer says. Not the least of these challenges are guilt and a sense of worthlessness—the sense that everyone wants something from you, and you can't figure out who you are and what you should do with your money.

The experience of the lottery winner is the most dramatic example of the unhappy changes sudden wealth can bring. Many dream of such windfalls, but the story for the real winners rarely turns out to be a happy one. Indeed, the most frustrating experience Linda Lubitz ever had as a financial planner was with a postal worker who had just won $24 million in the Florida lottery. The client was referred to Lubitz's firm—the Lubitz Financial Group in Miami—by another client. The couple had by then been ripped off by a furniture dealer and set upon by friends, relatives, and passersby. As a result, they had become paralyzed and couldn't make any money decisions.

Circumstances aren't so different for people who inherit great wealth, Salzer found. They're convinced that people care only for their wealth and not for them. When I wrote about Salzer's work in a column for the *New York Times*, I got plenty of mail from folks who had trouble mustering sympathy for the plight of the rich. "Oh, cry me a river," one man wrote. Several more suggested the unhappily well off find charity work to do or simply give their money away and free themselves of the burden. But as most financial planners know, the problems of the wealthy don't always lend themselves to such simple solutions. I saw a classic example of this with a psychotherapist who had become one of my regular sources. She specialized in the problems people have in dealing with money. Ironically, when her father died, none of the work she'd done with clients helped her through her own money problems. She resented her father because although he left her a fortune, he'd never spent money on her as a child. Receiving the money at his death was an unworthy substitute for affection while he was living, and the money became a terrible burden. She couldn't invest it because she felt he was looking over her shoulder. She felt paralyzed. Her father and their troubled relationship loomed over the entire inheritance, and she felt no freedom in gaining this money.

Salzer intuitively saw the same conflicts in her client's discomfort with owning the emerald ring, and she turned that insight into a powerful niche practice for inheritors—called the Wealth Conservancy—aimed both at managing their money and providing the psychological and emotional support to help them deal with the side effects of sudden wealth. There is a good deal of inherited wealth in Boulder, so Salzer soon came up with the idea of doing workshops designed for that group. "Naive as I was," says Salzer, "I didn't think of the workshop as a marketing opportunity as much as an opportunity to let inheritors know that they're not alone and that it's safe to talk about their money." She called attorneys, accountants, and clinical psychologists and set up the first three-day workshop in September 1989 with twenty participants. When an attorney gave a short presentation on prenuptial agreements, the participants turned it into a lengthy discussion on how to protect assets without draining the romance out of a relationship.

Salzer now plans further ahead for workshops, sending out questionnaires to identify key issues and interviewing each participant in advance for a couple of hours. On the workshop's first day, everyone introduces himself and talks a bit about his relationship with money. "The purpose of the workshop," Salzer says, "is to explore the effects of inherited wealth and to see how that has stopped you in life, how to get beyond those blocks and how to let money empower you rather than imprison you."

Joining Salzer in her workshops is Thayer Willis, author of *Navigating the Dark Side of Wealth: A Life Guide for Inheritors* (Equine Graphics Publishing) and heiress to the Georgia-Pacific fortune built by her father and uncle, the Cheatham brothers. After spending years resolving her own conflicts with money, Willis became a psychotherapist and worked with other inheritors. Willis says that inheritors are removed from the life experiences that bring maturity to us more fortunate poor folk. In Salzer's workshops, Willis explores issues like self-esteem and feelings of isolation and worthlessness.

Salzer's research on inheritors has helped her build the firm into a national practice serving about twenty-five inheritors, with net worths ranging into the hundreds of millions of dollars. Although Salzer has had clients with net worth as high as $600 million, she feels she makes the most difference with people whose net worth is between $5 million and $20 million, because they have financial options and challenges "but not so much money that they can't still screw up and blow it."

Salzer outsources money management to SEI and uses index funds at State Street or Parametric so that she can focus on what she calls "wealth coaching," as well as philanthropy. She also looks into new issues that affect inheritors. "Inheritors tend not to get things handed to them," she says. "There are always strings attached." They may have a limited partnership with a brother or stock in a family company. So she is developing a new workshop on how they can gain autonomy and a measure of control over their lives. "I had one creative idea in my life," Salzer says, "and everything else came from that."

Minimum fees at the Wealth Conservancy are $5,000 a quarter. New clients tend to pay from $100,000 to $200,000 for the first year, with a reduction in fees the second year. Salzer employs five people at the firm, but she doesn't have a succession plan. "I have no intention of retiring," Salzer says. "I'm just beginning." She says she is not building equity in her firm but having a good time and supporting herself comfortably.

Salzer emphasizes that she doesn't have the rich niche sewn up. When she started in the 1980s, the market was practically virgin territory. Now other planners are using the issues of sudden wealth as the focus of their practice. Finding ways to differentiate her services from those of the competition requires constant vigilance. For Salzer, that's half the fun.

James Lowell: Giving Back

JUST HOW ESOTERIC do the issues that define a niche practice have to be? Not very. If we believe that the main threat to independent planners is competition from the brokerage behemoths, with their low costs and high technology, the key to creating a niche can be as fundamental as truly getting to know clients, sharing their values, and satisfying them individually by meeting an important need. As the most successful of these niche practices show, that formula works best when planner and client are cut from the same cloth.

Such is the case with Lowell, Blake & Associates, a Boston financial advisory firm, whose founder, James H. Lowell II, believes people with money have an obligation to do something for the world. Lowell isn't content or even inclined to urge that clients give money to charities. Quite the opposite. He believes most charities don't know the first thing about operating like a business and that they merely squander the money they're given. "If you don't have anything better to do with your life than work as the development officer of a charity, you're a totally useless pimp," says Lowell. "You'd provide more service working at McDonald's." Lowell's solution is to design his own philanthropic projects for his clients, projects that fulfill passions. Of course, the firm also invests clients' money in traditional financial markets, charging clients a flat retainer fee that amounts to a maximum of one-half percent of assets to cover all aspects of financial planning. But it's the firm's unique approach to charitable giving that is its cornerstone.

I've met many financial planners who say they won't work with wealthy clients who choose to give little or nothing to charity. But I've yet to find anyone as outspoken as Lowell about the need to put wealth to good use, a distinction clearly connected to his roots in one of Boston's distinguished Brahmin families. The Massachusetts physician John Collins Bossidy once said of Boston's two leading families: "The Lowells talk to the Cabots, and the Cabots talk only to God." But the view from those heights doesn't particularly impress Lowell. In fact, he believes families like his are part of the problem rather than part of the solution because they contribute to the hidebound elitism that governs most charities.

Lowell is the youngest of six children. His father was the sole trustee of the Lowell Institute—the family foundation—until Lowell's oldest brother, John, took over the job, which he in turn will pass on to his oldest son. Lowell has been unimpressed with both his father's and his brother's stewardship. "The last original idea my brother had was when he was two years old," Lowell says. And therein lies the problem, he says. The old-money families who can afford philanthropy are hung up with political correctness and lack vision, whereas the people with vision and passion don't have the financial resources.

Lowell doesn't give a damn about political correctness. And he doesn't mind telling clients they should be giving more money away or telling them where it will do the most good. When a client says an alma mater is asking for a contribution, Lowell warns that if she gives it, the school will hit her up for twice that amount the following year and then four times as much the year after that. What's worse, the money will not be spent on anything useful.

Lowell believes that the giver should be involved in the gift and that he should decide for himself what cause he wants to help. The fact that philanthropy is a big concern of baby boomers doesn't hurt Lowell's practice, but he certainly didn't set it up with that in mind. The key to effective charitable giving, as Lowell, Blake sees it, is to identify worthwhile charitable endeavors, put together limited partnerships to finance them, and then sign up clients as investors.

A secondary goal is to help charities learn how to help themselves, so Lowell is always on the lookout for people with passion and a project. That's how he happened upon Charlton Reynders III, fresh out of Princeton University and eager to make a film to educate people about whales and the threats to their survival. Lowell thought Reynders had both vision and passion and agreed to do the project provided they could create a model that would help charities learn something about operating like a business. Lowell, Blake investors put up $350,000 for the $3.5 million film, which was made by the National Wildlife Federation. More than seven million people saw the film, and the National Wildlife Federation got more than $2.7 million back on its

$1.65 million investment. The National Wildlife Federation later pumped some of the return from *Whales* into a film about dolphins. To support that effort, this time Lowell, Blake set up a limited-liability company rather than a partnership: One-third of the pot went into the film *Dolphins* and the other two-thirds into two venture-capital partnerships. Lowell, Blake got top billing in the credits for *Dolphins* at its screening at the Museum of Science in Boston.

Lowell, Blake also deserves credit for raising money from clients to buy 17,000 acres of timberland in Maine—a project that fits well with Lowell's longstanding passion for forests. Part of the land purchased, which includes mountains and a lake, was set aside for campers and hikers, and parts of the shorefront were donated to the state of Maine. The working forest was sold as timberland with restrictions on how it may be cut. Clients got a 50 to 75 percent total (not annualized) return over nine years. That certainly isn't a get-rich scheme, but clients who participate are more interested in the good their investments are doing.

Considerable good resulted from the firm's investment in the rehabilitation of a working-class neighborhood in nearby Lynn, Massachusetts, which had been devastated by the 1990 recession. Lowell, Blake bought a dilapidated crack house and some other run-down buildings, renovated them, and turned the neighborhood around. Investors received 10 percent income a year as well as 10 percent capital appreciation and helped revitalize the community.

Just as important to Lowell is revitalizing individuals. One of his favorite causes is mental health. "I've seen so many clients struggle with depression and anxiety," he says, "and I'm proud to say I've struggled with it myself." He doesn't put much stock in doctors and institutions for breakthroughs in mental-health care. So for clients who share his concern, he looks for places where their contributions will do the most good.

Because returns on the philanthropic projects are limited, Lowell, Blake permits clients to put only 1 to 2 percent of investable funds into such charitable projects. Still, the firm wants to show both investors and the community that with a lot of hard work and some investors who are willing to recognize reasonable profits, a lot can be done. And Lowell doesn't hesitate to tell a client, "You've been so successful, you really must put something back into the system." He says 75 to 80 percent of his new clients are eager to do it; those who aren't are asked to move on to another firm.

Indeed, client participation is the watchword at Lowell, Blake. In the fall of 2000, the firm introduced the Mentor Charitable Fund, which permits clients and others to donate money to charity and to get involved in how the money is spent. The letters in "Mentor" stand for medicine, education, nature, tolerance, opportunity, and responsibility, the key areas in which donors may contribute. The minimum contribution is $5,000, and Lowell, Blake subsidizes the fund, charging less than 1 percent for management and administration, which includes consulting on finding the right spot for the donation. You can be sure that spot will not be a big organization like the American Cancer Society, because Lowell, Blake is about individualism, vision, passion, and the belief that each of us has some power to make changes.

Like most strong financial planning firms, Lowell, Blake does a good job picking stocks and taking care of estate planning and other financial issues. But its approach to charitable giving—the idea that you can invest in, say, a wildlife film, go to the screening, and become a part of something beautiful and worthwhile and, not so incidentally, make a little money on it—is very appealing to a certain type of client. It's another example of how a founder's personal vision became a vision for a firm.

— 🐾 🐾 🐾 —

Cicily Carson Maton: Port in a Storm

YOU DON'T HAVE TO look far to see that the most successful niche planners are the ones who trust their instincts and build a business from their strengths. But there's at least one successful niche that was inspired not by the founder's expertise but by her sorry lack of it: Cicily Carson Maton's firm Aequus Wealth Management Resources in Chicago helps solve the financial problems of people going through divorce—and that's not something Maton was always able to do.

When Cicily Maton was divorced in 1982, she had no career and knew next to nothing about her finances. She had good reason to be terrified. But she'd always been active in politics, and she was able to line up a job quickly as Illinois State Finance Director for the John Connelly for President Committee. Once she started working, she began meeting financial planners and knew very soon that what she wanted to do was help people with their money problems.

When Maton got her certified financial planner designation in 1986, she got job offers from the big insurance companies and brokerages. But she wasn't interested. Selling products didn't fit her definition of helping people. Newly remarried, she told her husband that she believed she had two choices: She could work for a big company or she could build her own firm and go to work for herself. She wanted to do the latter. But she warned him that if he agreed, he would have to support her until she got rolling. In exchange, she'd support him later on. He agreed enthusiastically.

As fate would have it, one of Maton's first clients was a woman going through a divorce. "She was emotionally distraught, and I sympathized with her," says Maton. "And that's when it dawned on me that here was a whole unserved group of people." Maton decided on the spot to specialize in financial planning for people going through divorce. After researching the field and talking with divorce lawyers, she took out full-page ads in local newspapers in affluent areas to advertise her divorce seminar: "The Financial Realities of Divorce."

She charged $50 for the seminar, and twenty or thirty people would show up. Later she developed workshops on divorce and provided organizational guidelines, with instructions on how to hire a lawyer and put together a team of people—the divorce lawyer, a mediator, therapist, financial planner, and, in some cases, a career counselor or coach, a forensic accountant, and a business appraiser. She talked about her own divorce and how frightening it was to know so little about the financial details of her marriage. From each seminar, she got planning clients, many of whom are still with her. In fact, she now handles the finances for four generations of one family.

When Aequus takes on a divorce client, Maton has the person sign a letter of agreement covering the divorce-planning work. The firm provides no investment advice during this period. If the client wants to continue with the firm after the divorce, a new contract is drawn up. Maton uses the divorce-planning period as a screening process. Some divorce clients don't require ongoing planning advice; others turn out to be people she doesn't want to continue working with, so she doesn't offer them a second contract.

Maton's divorce-planning services are provided strictly by the hour. "The minute they sit down, I start charging an hourly fee of $200," she says. By 1988, about half of Maton's work was divorce planning. Today, she takes about a dozen divorce cases a year, all of them through referrals. Although she says she wouldn't turn away anyone who wants a one- or two-hour consultation, she tells couples who don't have a good deal of wealth that they would be better off looking for a less-expensive alternative. "They get the most value working with me when the situation is complicated, with many assets," she says.

Clearly, complications don't scare Maton. She's also a divorce mediator. "I do a fair amount of face-to-face mediation, and we work out a financial settlement together," she says. "I think that's where I'm at my best, but mediation doesn't work unless there's some degree of trust left." Typically, one spouse approaches Maton about the possibility of mediation and then brings the partner in. "I've got to win that person's trust in ten minutes," she says. "Usually, I can do it." Couples are rarely listening to each other anymore at this point because the emotional baggage has obscured the logic behind the decisions they must make. "I act like an interpreter," Maton says. By and large, the couples who get the most from mediation are those who have children that they plan to raise together and who want to come out of the divorce with a working relationship.

Maton can now speak from experience about children and working relationships. In 1990, Maton's daughter, Michelle, joined the firm, after graduating from Stanford University with honors, and the two began to broaden the firm's practice beyond divorce work. Maton saw that most clients come to a planner when they're in crisis—when they've lost a spouse, lost a job, lost a child, or become disabled. "Seventy-five to 90 percent of new clients are in crisis of some kind," she says. However different the crisis, the strategy for addressing it is similar. For example, Maton tries to limit the number of decisions the client must make during a difficult period. This prevents the client from doing anything that might be harmful in the long run. Instead, she attempts to provide a safe place and a clear path for working things through, and the advice presented goes well beyond the financial. Maton—who started race walking in her mid-sixties and competes in two marathons a year—tries to get clients to practice fitness in all areas of life. And she doesn't hesitate to impose some of her own values while she's drawing up the budget for a financial plan. For smokers, she takes cigarettes off the expense list, for example, tells them they'll have to quit smoking, and shows them how they can better use the money. For others, she adds the cost of weight training to the budget, which, she explains, is cheaper than medical bills.

Given the firm's concern for the "whole" client, it's not surprising that Maton and her daughter have moved in the direction of dealing with the psychology of money and how it fits into a client's life. When former financial planner Susan Bradley's book *Sudden Money: Managing a Financial Windfall* (John Wiley & Sons) came out in 2000, the author also introduced the Sudden Money Institute through which she gives seminars on the topic. Aequus signed on for the membership fee of $4,000 a year. "Not all of our clients are sudden-money recipients, of course, but the process for dealing with all clients in crisis is very similar," Maton says. Bradley's seminars have helped Maton develop a turnkey operation that provides clients with something she calls a "stewardship policy." Maton talks to each one about the role money plays in his life, what values he has concerning money, and how money will influence his future plans. She then puts together a statement that summarizes what the client considers most important and what his goals are.

To learn more about helping clients define their goals, Maton and her entire staff attended a workshop based on *The Seven Stages of Money Maturity: Understanding the Spirit and Value of Money in Your Life* (Dell Books) by George Kinder of Kinder and Co. in Littleton, Massachusetts, and Maui, Hawaii. There they met Ed Jacobsen, a psychologist with a Ph.D. and a Wharton M.B.A., who was writing and working as a consultant. Maton hired Jacobsen as a consultant for her firm. She told him she wanted him to build on the Kinder seminar to help her staff discover what they wanted individually out of life, what goals they had for themselves, and how those goals might dovetail with the goals of the firm. "Right from the beginning, Michelle and I thought we could have a work environment that enriched everyone and where everyone had a good time," Maton says.

When the staff met with Jacobsen the first time, he asked them each to recall and describe a time when they set a goal and accomplished it and to focus on what characteristics helped them make it happen. "He pulled from each of us our personal characteristics and made a flip chart of everyone's strengths," Maton says. "We learned things about each other in a very positive way." In fact, Maton says she learned more about her daughter's passion for conservation in the meetings with Jacobsen than she'd learned in all the years before.

Maton's effort to look within applies not only to the client but to the firm and reflects the care with which Aequus's staff was put together. Michelle is also her business partner; Maton's husband, Sheldon Lee, who retired as owner of a manufacturing plant, is now the company's controller. And several of Maton's employees were once her clients. While helping Lois Carlson work through her divorce, Maton told her it would be a good idea for her to get a job. Carlson said she had no skills. When Maton asked her what she liked to do, Carlson said she liked to shop. So Maton hired her one day a week to do the shopping for all the supplies and everything else the office needed. The arrangement worked out so well and freed up so much time for the mother/daughter partners that Maton asked Carlson what else she enjoyed doing. Carlson told her she liked to talk on the phone. So

Maton brought her in for two more days a week to call clients and chat with them: How was your trip to Alaska? How is your daughter doing in her first year of college? Have you recovered from your surgery? Is there anything else we can do for you?

Not long after that, Carlson's daughter, Fran, graduated from college with a degree in fine arts. Maton hired Fran, too, as a general assistant: Fran is now working on her certified financial planner designation and Maton intends to use her as a planner. Client Nancy Caldie's divorce consultation also led to employment at Aequus. She was hired as a receptionist and also books appointments.

The firm's goal is to stay small so that each client gets plenty of face time and each staff member can make time for personal goals. For her part, Maton plans to continue race walking. In fact, she has a race-walking coach, walks four days a week—including one walk of up to twenty miles—and works out with weights two days a week. Maton's husband would like to be in a warmer climate for two months of the year, and they've put that goal on the agenda. Michelle would like to be able to spend two months a year on a volunteer conservation project in Africa. Maton sees all this as doable. More and more, the firm's clients are dispersing across the country—to California, New York, Florida, Montana, Tennessee—so that working from a different location in the winter will not be a problem. "I can be having a telephone conversation with a client, and we can be looking at the same thing on the screen," she says. Clients who plan to move express relief when Maton tells them the move won't affect the planning relationship.

All the while, of course, Maton keeps her goals for Aequus in mind. Like other planners, Maton realizes she needs to do something to distinguish the firm's strengths from those of the big corporate firms. "I know what I want to do," she says. "But I realize that Merrill Lynch says the same thing I do: 'We want to help you achieve your dreams.' I don't think a corporation can deliver on that like an independent, but a person searching for planning advice doesn't see that." So Aequus continues to meet regularly with Jacobsen to talk about how the firm might set itself apart. "He's still a consultant but practically on our permanent payroll," Maton says. They talk about clients they may be having problems with and about how to approach problems in different ways and find new solutions.

The firm's solutions to date, however, have served it quite well.

Maton says Aequus gets a number of referrals from trust officers, estate-planning lawyers, and elder-care firms. But she'd also like to forge an identity as being a positive force in the community. Susan Bradley's Sudden Money Institute has developed Money Camps held at fancy resorts where affluent children can learn about money in the morning and swim and play tennis in the afternoon. Bradley plans to license the camps to institute members. A license permits a member to conduct three camps as long as one of them is for charity. Fran Carlson of Maton's staff sits on the board of Child Serve, an organization for inner-city children, and Maton is planning a money camp for them. "Our marketing is going to go in that direction," she says. Aequus also belongs to The National Association of Personal Financial Advisors (NAPFA) and gets referrals from that group.

Aequus still charges fees based on assets under management, but Maton plans to change to retainer fees. The up-front financial planning fee for nondivorce clients is now $3,000 to $7,000, depending on how complicated the financial situation is. If the client signs on to continue working with the firm, the fee is 1 percent of up to $1 million in assets and a sliding scale for amounts exceeding $1 million. The fee includes asset management, which Maton does with index funds. Aequus has one hundred long-term clients as well as thirty clients at any one time going through the financial planning process and another ten going through the divorce process. Some of those in the two latter groups leave when they reach their immediate goal; others sign on to stay—often through thick and thin. Over the three years of the bear market, Aequus didn't lose any clients. In fact, says Maton, "clients would call to say, 'How are you doing in this terrible environment?'"

Quite well, apparently.

— 🐝 🐝 🐝 —

Tom Connelly: Birds of a Feather

I CAUGHT UP WITH Tom Connelly as he was heading for Singapore to make a presentation to planners there on what constitutes a niche practice and why a planner should consider developing one. His firm, Keats, Connelly and Associates in Phoenix, Arizona, is often singled out as one of the most successful niche practices in the country, so I was eager to hear what he planned to say.

Keats, Connelly serves the special needs of Canadian snow-birds, many of whom retire in the Phoenix area with dual U.S.-Canadian citizenship. These clients' investment-, tax-, and estate-planning problems are unique, and Connelly believes the firm has developed a niche that is nearly impregnable because of the time and money it would take for another firm to break itself in. "Some barrier to entry is important," Connelly says. "For us that barrier is knowledge of the two separate tax codes and the tax treaty that sits on top of them and the two countries' very different investment regimes."

"A niche practitioner routinely solves second- or third-order problems within a tightly defined group," Connelly explained in his Singapore presentation. One niche might be estate planning for residents of Singapore who have interests in Hong Kong, he told the group. Or it might be the employees of one specific institution, members of one particular profession, or inheritors of great wealth. Connelly also sees Muslims, who must abide by usury restrictions, as a group needing special attention. People who feel strongly about socially responsible investing and clients who wish to be active in philanthropy are likewise candidates for niche markets. Providers of niche services, he says, can charge premium prices because they will gain a strong, loyal client base. But they should always be looking for new value-added services for their customers.

Connelly didn't start out looking for anything of the kind. He was a geologist, which, I think, says a lot about his approach to life—fairly technical and scientific. Yet there was nothing scientific about the way he found his niche business. "Most niche practitioners stumble into their opportunity," he says. "You bloom where you're planted." Connelly was originally planted in Minnesota, where he got a degree in geology before doing graduate work at Arizona State University and then taking a position as an exploration geologist. He liked the work even though he didn't care much for its transient nature. Hoping to gain a strategic advantage, he got a master's degree in business administration and was hired as a geologist right out of school, with the promise of a permanent job. The company closed two weeks later. So much for something less transient.

In 1986, Connelly switched to financial services and went to work for a Canadian company in Phoenix, selling contractual plans, which is just about as far as you can get from fee-only planning. A contractual plan is a legal contract between the investor and a mutual-fund company. A client might decide, for example, that he wants to invest $10,000 over fifteen years, and the fund company draws up a contract and tells him how much he must invest each month to reach that goal. Contractual plans typically carry a load of about 9 percent. As with an insurance policy, most of that load is paid in the first year of the plan. It's not a particularly consumer-friendly way to invest. But many a reluctant investor probably feels pleased once the fifteen years have passed and he's acquired a nest egg with money that might otherwise have been squandered on restaurant meals and ski equipment. (Sounds familiar, right? It's the forced-savings argument we hear from cash-value insurance salespeople.) The stability of the money in these plans makes the manager's job easier, and some funds like Fidelity Destiny I and Destiny II have performed very well as a result. But let's not try to make a silk purse out of a sow's ear. Connelly was a geologist looking for a new career, and financial services—even if the service wasn't exactly insightful—held some appeal for him. The subtleties of fees and commissions were not yet a concern or even clear to him.

Things soon changed after he met Bob Keats, a Canadian who'd come to Arizona as branch manager for the company Connelly was working for. Keats got dual citizenship. Connelly got his certified financial planner designation. And the two began to do seminars for Canadian winter visitors to the Southwest, with Keats covering financial planning and Connelly the investments. In late 1987, they both left the Canadian company—each to work on his own—and Keats wrote a book called *The Border Guide* (Ontario Motorist Publishing Co.), which came out in 1992 and gave him higher visibility within their targeted market.

By now both men were eager to work for fees rather than commissions. Keats had been an engineer and a member of the Canadian armed forces; so each had a work history with a professional code of conduct and neither liked the commission business. "We wondered why we couldn't just give people a straight deal and still make money," Connelly says. But it was slow going. "Bob was doing seminars in trailer parks."

Change was in the air, however. In *Barron's*, Connelly and Keats read about people who manage money using no-load mutual funds. They read about Judith and Keith Maurer, who in 1984 founded Fee for Service, a discount insurance brokerage in Tampa, Florida, and sold low-load insurance. (The company is now called the Fee Insurance Alliance and owned by General Electric.) So in 1990, they teamed up to form Keats, Connelly and Associates, a financial planning and investment management firm that charged fees based on assets under management. Canadian snowbirds made up 50 to 70 percent of the clientele, but the firm emphasized integrity as much as its specialty. "Nobody pays us but our clients," Connelly says. "We don't even take trips or rewards of points or any kind of soft-dollar arrangements."

By the late 1990s, the firm had moved from asset-based fees to retainers, eyeballing the size of an estate and setting a base fee. For cross-border clients, the fee bumps up by 30 percent. Sometimes the firm adds a multiplier for complexity or for a "PIA factor," which designates clients who show telltale signs of turning out to be a pain in the ass. All the time spent on each account is tracked and the fee is adjusted if necessary at the end of the year.

Connelly believes it's money well spent. He says the firm takes the place of an employee who would do all a family's financial work, including bookkeeping and estate planning. Keats, Connelly has a staff of eighteen, including ten professionals, three of whom are partners. The third partner, Dale Walters, is a certified public accountant and a personal financial specialist (PFS), a designation given by the American Institute of Certified Public Accountants. He has a good deal of expertise in 529 plans and stock options. The team includes five certified public accountants, one chartered financial analyst, five certified financial planners, and nine staff members who have earned master's degrees.

Although the dual-citizenship expertise is Keats, Connelly's strength, the firm provides a complete range of services for each client—meeting with families, handling bookkeeping, and coordinating all the legal or insurance work that's farmed out. "If we're working with an attorney to do the estate planning, we'll get all the legwork done. All the client has to do is sign the paper," Connelly says. "If we're recommending insurance in an estate plan, we'll go out and get the insurance."

In 1997 and 1998, when the equity market was outdoing itself each day, Keats, Connelly, like a lot of independent planning firms, lost a rash of clients "because of its investment philosophy," Connelly says. "Diversification didn't look so hot." The firm lost about 5 to 8 percent of the assets it had been managing. That upheaval, among other things, prompted the firm to add a family-office model to its snowbird niche. All of the firm's family-office clients are on retainer, although Keats, Connelly will take referral clients from Charles Schwab & Co. for asset-based fees. Today, the firm has 175 clients including the family-office clients, for which it provides complete financial planning services. But the family-office group is not yet earning its keep. "Our margins there are not much above zero," Connelly says. "We're trying to develop the technology and figure out how to get more economies of scale." He says the firm hopes to become more efficient and to get more and bigger clients and that it's already "seeing activity from deca-millionaires."

But Connelly does not take the future for granted. He agrees with Mark Hurley and Mark Tibergien that a planning practice must be run like a business and that margins in the industry will be compressed for the near term. "We're planning on a 25 percent decrease in fees over the next several years," he says. But he doesn't believe that survival requires becoming a giant firm or having a watertight niche. The brokers and insurance firms are not going to lure away his clients, Connelly says. "There's plenty of room for small, independent businessmen with good technical background and good investment theory who know how to run a business like a business."

Although he's worked hard to make his niche succeed, Connelly believes the key to success in any business model is client service. "If you just run a good business," he told the practitioners in Singapore, "and do what you say you're going to do when you say you're going to do it, you're ahead of most everybody in your field."

— ❋ ❋ ❋ —

Janet Briaud: Higher Learning

ABOUT TEN YEARS AGO, I was asked to write an article about the career self-help books that were so popular at the time. The thinking reflected in these books, which included *What Color Is Your Parachute?* (Ten Speed Press) by Richard Nelson Bolles and *Do What You Love, the Money Will Follow* (Dell Publishing) by Marsha Sinetar, seemed a bit too New Age for me and I declined. But as I've talked with planners about their business strategies, I've seen much evidence that they share a similar career sense, the notion that once they found their own personal niche, they'd discover the niche for their business.

So it was with Janet Briaud, who was pictured on the cover of the July 2002 issue of *Financial Advisor* magazine above the cover line "Niche Practices" and has become known for her work with professors at Texas A&M in Bryan, Texas. Indeed, whenever advisers talk about a successful niche practice, the name Briaud Financial Planning invariably comes up. Yet when I called Briaud to find out how she selected and developed her niche, she balked. "I'm not convinced that I even have a niche," she says, "and if I do, I don't know if you can equate that to success."

Starting out, Briaud's goal was simply to find something she loved to do. Once she found it, she claims she would have been willing to do it for fifteen cents an hour. The exaggeration makes her point, but there's more than a little truth in it. Briaud says that what consultants like Mark Hurley don't understand about financial advisers is that they're less interested in maximizing every dollar than in creating the quality of life they want. "Mark looks at it from a business point of view," she says. "I look at it as something I love to do. I want to help people and what I make is enough."

Briaud's firm makes her more than enough. She manages $150 million for 210 clients with the help of ten employees, three of them planners. Briaud admits that having so many clients with the same employer saves her time because they all have the same employee benefit plans and the same 403(b) retirement plans, but she argues that doing a good job—rather than merely serving a niche—is the key to a successful practice. "How many people who work for you do a really good job?" Briaud asks. "Think about your lawyer, the people who clean your house, or mow your lawn. How many of them do a really good job?" Good point. When people who work for me do a good job, I don't question what they charge. I usually give them a raise because I don't want to lose them. I'll bet anyone who's ever had an unreliable baby-sitter or an accountant who took shortcuts feels the same way.

Doing a good job has been Briaud's calling card all along, but she says it's only since Hurley's industry reports started trumpeting the advantages of a niche practice that hers got so much attention. "For years, everyone felt sorry for me," she says. "They assumed I was struggling, with a middle-market clientele." At one advanced-planning meeting, an adviser who works with doctors spent an hour talking to her about why and how she should switch from professors to physicians.

But Briaud wasn't thinking about money when she got involved with planning for college professors, and she doesn't think about it much now. Like most niche planners, she came to hers from her own life experience. Briaud says she never thought about investing or managing money growing up in New Brunswick, one of six kids in a poor family. "I thought some people had it figured out and some didn't, but I wasn't too interested in how they'd done it."

Briaud, who's Canadian, met her husband, Jean Louis, who's French, at the University of New Brunswick, where he was getting a master's degree in engineering and she was an undergraduate. Jean Louis didn't speak much English, but Briaud spoke French. Briaud got a degree in education, taught for three years, and the two got married and went to the University of Ottawa for graduate work—Jean Louis for a Ph.D. in engineering and Janet for a master's degree in physical education administration.

Jean Louis began teaching engineering at Texas A&M and Briaud taught physical education there for a year before she took time off to have two children, Natalie and Patrick. While the children were young, her husband did consulting work on the side and Briaud took care of the books and invested some money they'd saved. She put $4,500 in a fund with an 8.5 percent load, and her investment sunk to $2,800. That made her angry. "I'm going to figure out how this works," she told herself. And she did. At the library she studied the old *Weisenberger Guide to Mutual Funds*, now out of print, and decided to put their money into the Pennsylvania Mutual Fund. Later, when the fund made it to the Forbes Honor Roll, she felt pleased with her research. Almost overnight, financial reading became an addiction. She read *A Random Walk Down Wall Street* (W.W. Norton & Company) by Burton Malkiel, professor of economics at Princeton University and father of index investing, and began a steady diet of all the financial publications she could get her hands on, enjoying them so much that she referred to them as "dessert reading."

An even greater influence on her view of money and how to make it, though, was her husband and his approach to his work. Before she married, Briaud says, she figured work was work and you tried to get away with doing as little of it as possible. But her husband loved to work. "He loves his students. He loves his research. He's a good writer and he loves that, too. He spends enormous amounts of time on it because he enjoys doing it so much," she says. She wanted to find the same passion in work of her own. From the beginning, Briaud has seen that search as a personal journey. "You have to look into your own heart first and see what you want to do and what you might love doing," she says.

All the better, of course, if someone else is also on the lookout for you. For Briaud, that person was her running partner, who came across an article about the certified financial planner course and suggested that Briaud enroll. She did, starting in 1984. "I studied religiously two hours a day," she says. She took the exams in Houston and started her own business in 1986, when she finished the coursework. Briaud wanted to invest with no-load funds, much the way she did with her own family savings. But personal finance, not investing, was the most compelling part of the package for her. A friend of her husband's gave her office space, and soon she was writing articles for local newspapers and making presentations about financial planning at the university. As for clients? "Any warm body that came in the door, I'd take on," she says. "It didn't matter."

Sometimes, even getting paid didn't matter all that much. Briaud started out charging hourly fees but hated the time-consuming billing.

"I did some work for one client who never paid me," she says. "I never billed him." Another client told her she didn't charge enough and paid her extra. So Briaud went to a flat fee of about $500 a year per client. She charged her biggest client $1,000 a year and considered it a fortune. All the other planners in her area were selling product, which made Briaud think that the idea of planning for a fee was something she'd come up with on her own. In the mid-1990s, she began basing her fees on assets under management but kept some early clients on at the old fees. Newer clients pay 1 percent of assets up to $400,000, 75 basis points to $2 million, and 50 basis points above that. "I've never gotten rid of a client because they paid me too little," she says. "They were there when I needed them. I'll keep them until they're down to their last nickel."

Such loyalty may make Briaud seem like a soft touch, but if she is, it doesn't appear to be hurting her business. In Schwab's 2002 "Report on the Best-Managed Firms in the Advisory Business," prepared by Mark Tibergien, Briaud Financial Planning is listed among the twenty best-managed firms in the country based on business practices in advertising, communicating with and crediting referral sources, using a disciplined process to screen clients, training professional staff, recruiting, and several other measures. In 2003, Briaud Financial Planning once again made the list in *Bloomberg Wealth Manager* magazine's annual ranking of independent financial advisory firms. And whenever I'm invited to attend a meeting of some small group of elite planners, Briaud is there.

Her firm no longer relies on the warm-body approach to building a client base. About 60 percent of her clients are college professors. Given her location, Briaud's concentration on academics was more a matter of good sense than inspiration. "I'm in a college town, and that's all we have," she says. Yet she insists that the professors are a perfect match for her. "They fit my personality very well," she says. "I think that's what makes it all work—when you find a group of people that fits your way of working."

In Briaud's way of working, money has never been the primary motivator, a characteristic shared by her professor clients, who typically value education and learning more than riches. "The professors are not greedy," she says. "They may be greedy intellectually but not financially." And yet she says they are the true millionaires next door.

In a college town, "it's cool not to have the best and newest thing. The older the car, the better. They pride themselves on being frugal. They save and they have a notion of what is enough."

That notion often makes them more willing to listen to reason when it comes to investments. In 1999, for example, Briaud was concerned about Y2K and the astronomical valuations in the market. She talked to her clients about it, telling them, "You have enough. Let's take something out now." Her clients were willing to listen and take some money out of tech stocks, she says, but for clients in, say, Austin, Texas, with its high-tech business, this argument would probably have been a tougher sell.

Briaud keeps client money at Schwab and Fidelity and at TIAA-CREF, the company that manages educators' pension plans. But the bulk of her clients' investments, about $100 million, is with Vanguard. Although Briaud is moderate to conservative on investments, she's willing to encourage big risks when it comes to decisions on personal money matters. One of her clients, a consultant, was having trouble charging the fees she was worth, because of the influence of her father, who had been a minister and taught her that money was dirty, that it got in the way of spirituality. Briaud called the client in for a talk and went through the seven stages of money maturity based on George Kinder's book of that name. "I talked about innocence and innocent thinking," Briaud says, "and helped her see that she was stuck there, that giving to the church was her way of filling up her spiritual bank account so that God would take care of her." She was giving to the church and expecting a spiritual return. Briaud explained the difference between "innocent" giving—which is almost manipulative, done with the hope that you will get something in return—and the kind of giving Kinder calls "aloha"—which is giving out of a spirit of pure generosity. Briaud asked the client if she knew any spiritual people who had a great deal of wealth. She did. Undercharging for services, Briaud explained, was unfair to her family. She wasn't taking care of herself or them. "She really got it," Briaud says. "After our conversation, she went out and doubled and tripled her fees. I was exhilarated after that conversation."

That's because Briaud draws tremendous satisfaction from helping clients see when they're getting in their own way—which is what she did for another client's new wife who came to talk with her. Both husband and wife had been through nasty divorces, and the woman had recently received radiation treatment for cancer. The couple had planned to build a house together, but now the wife was considering using the $100,000 settlement from her first marriage to buy a condo that would belong only to her. "My husband has a lot of confidence in you," the wife told Briaud. "I want to know what you think."

Briaud's response was direct. She took the client's hands in her own and trusted herself to say the right thing. "This is not about money," Briaud said. "You're both caught in your past bad experiences, and now that you're sick, you're afraid and you're moving away from each other. You can't afford this condo and you don't need it. What you need is to start moving together." Briaud feared the couple would lose their relationship unless they could work this out. "They both had to learn to trust again and to commit," she says. "Fear had taken over the love they once had."

Briaud's financial advice for yet another couple took her again into territory where planners don't often go. This young couple had inherited a great deal of money, but they'd blown a lot of it and were adrift. Briaud advised them to raise their human capital. "You've been given this money for a reason," she told them. "There's something you're supposed to accomplish." She asked them to complete some exercises including writing a family autobiography, describing ten people they really admire, and listing the personality traits they admire. "The good we see in other people is really about who we are," she told them.

Such terrain is the logical next step in financial planning, Briaud believes. Planners start out mastering the technical competence to do what they need to do. That done, they inevitably move on to the counseling side. "I do it with every client," she says. "It's part of a very long goal-setting process, and the more I do it the better I get at it. To make a difference in someone's life is the highest level of planning. It's about changing people's thought processes." If that means she's crossing the line into therapy, Briaud's not concerned about it. "A psychologist tries to change something about a person," she says. "I'm not trying to do that. If they need help, they must go to a psychologist. I'm trying to help them see what's there."

Briaud didn't start out with such confidence. As she's grown in her practice and as a person, she feels more comfortable relying on her instincts in dealing with clients. She has become fascinated by the theories of where instincts originate. In fact, among her chief reading interests now are books on spirituality and psychology. She's dabbled in *A Course in Miracles* (Foundation for Inner Peace), an allegedly inspired text offering a way to universal love and peace, channeled during the 1970s by Helen Schucman, professor of medical psychology at Columbia University. Briaud also listens to tapes and goes to conferences to learn more about Taoism, Buddhism, and inner knowing. "I'm always thinking of how to use intuition with clients," she says. "The more you go into yourself, the more you can do that with clients. You keep peeling off one layer after another. Start wherever you feel comfortable or—better yet—slightly uncomfortable."

Given the success of Briaud's practice, the answers, either way, are sure to be helpful.

— 🌼 🌼 🌼 —

Chapter and Verse

"LEARNING IS VERY IMPORTANT to me," Janet Briaud says, which is one of the reasons she's so effective with her clients. She regularly attends conferences to improve her technical competence, but she is just as interested in learning about the places where psychology, spirituality, passions, and dreams interconnect. In fact, if she were going back to school, Briaud says, she'd probably study spiritual change and psychology and how they relate to our feelings about money. Although she has been on her own spiritual quest for many years, she believes she still has a long way to go. In her reading, she relies a good deal on synchronicity, looking into books mentioned by friends and clients.

The following books, which Briaud often recommends to clients, are among her favorites:

> ➤ *The Artist's Way: A Spiritual Path to Greater Creativity* (J.P. Tarcher), a book by Julia Cameron that provides a twelve-week self-discovery course to unlock creativity. One of Cameron's suggestions for seekers is to freewrite three pages in longhand every morning when they first get out of bed—a kind of random thought walk in which you slap down whatever comes to mind. Cameron calls them morning pages and argues that they often help her to see what's amiss in her life and recognize what she really wants. So many of these dreams remain under the surface of everyday busyness, Cameron says, and the morning pages tap into them before our rational minds can filter them out or toss them aside as unrealistic. Briaud has discovered much from her own pages and looks for ways to apply new insights to clients. "I look for clients' dreams and find out what would really excite them," Briaud says.

> ➤ The books of Carolyn Myss such as *Why People Don't Heal and How They Can* (Wellspring Media) and *Sacred Contracts: Awakening Your Divine Potential* (Harmony Books), which is about archetypes and how to determine who you are and what you're meant to do. Myss, who once spent time in a convent,

can "read" people, Briaud says. That sounded farther out than I normally like to go, but I read *Sacred Contracts* nonetheless and found it interesting. What's more, I later recommended the book to a woman who introduced herself to me at the gym and told me about her work as a psychotherapist and writer. Three weeks later, when I saw her again, she said the book had changed her life.

➢ Mary Anne Williamson's books, such as *Return to Love: Reflections on the Principles of "A Course in Miracles"* (HarperCollins). Briaud recommends them to clients when she thinks Myss's books might be too complicated.

➢ Neale Donald Walsch's *Conversations with God: An Uncommon Dialogue* (Putnam Publishing Group).

➢ *The Celestine Prophecy: An Adventure* (Warner Books) by James Redfield, a book about people who give us energy and those who drain energy from us.

➢ The Toltec books, such as *The Four Agreements: A Practical Guide to Personal Freedom* (Amber-Allen Publishing) by Don Miguel Ruiz and *The Mastery of Love: A Practical Guide to the Art of Relationship* (Amber-Allen Publishing), also by Ruiz.

➢ The books of Thich Nhat Hanh, a Vietnamese monk who wrote *The Miracle of Mindfulness* (Beacon Press) and *Peace Is Every Step: The Path of Mindfulness in Everyday Life* (Bantam Books).

➢ *Tuesdays with Morrie: An Old Man, a Young Man, and Life's Greatest Lesson* (Broadway Books) by Mitch Albom.

➢ Joseph Campbell's books, such as *Myths to Live By* (Arkana).

And each night before she goes to bed, Briaud reads—make that rereads—a bit of *The Seat of the Soul* (Fireside) by Gary Zukav.

Christopher Street Financial: The Trust Factor

THE BASIS OF any good relationship is trust. And that goes double when the relationship involves money. Most niche practices succeed because the client sees something in the planner that allows him to open up and give such trust a chance to develop. Sometimes, as with Keats, Connelly and Associates and their Canadian snowbirds, the key is expertise. The clients know they need help that they won't find in the average stockbroker's office. In other cases, the planner and the client are simpatico.

Both of these strengths are part of the mix at Christopher Street Financial, an advisory firm in New York, which, from its office on Fifth Avenue, serves the special planning needs of gays and lesbians. "We maintain our offices on Fifth Avenue because that address will play in Peoria," says Kermit Johns, president, hinting at plans to expand the business across the country. Johns is co-owner of the firm with Jennifer Hatch, managing director.

Peoria notwithstanding, the name Christopher Street certainly plays well among gays and lesbians in New York, calling to mind as it does the rebellion in 1969 that began at the Stonewall Bar on Christopher Street in Greenwich Village and became the turning point in homosexuals' struggle for civil rights. If you ask New Yorkers to name a place they associate with gays and lesbians, chances are good that they'll say Christopher Street. Johns and Hatch didn't come up with the name, though, or with the original idea for the firm. When the two met, Johns was in the financial department at Time-Warner Communications. Hatch had sold bonds at J.P. Morgan Chase & Co. and stocks at Bear Stearns. Christopher Street Financial was founded in 1981 by Bob Cassaletto, who, according to Johns, was one of the first openly gay brokers on Wall Street. Cassaletto did only the investment management piece of financial planning and only for male clients. "He was a bit of a misogynist and had no women in the firm," Johns says. Still, Cassaletto was good at what he did and the name has served the firm well.

And the firm has served its clients well. Of course, investing needs are no different for men than they are for women, singles or couples, straights or gays. But unmarried couples—whatever their sexual preferences—have other thorny financial problems, many of which they don't learn about until it's too late. Unless a couple is legally married, for example, they cannot make unlimited gifts to each other. They must abide by the $10,000 per year annual gift exclusion. So if one partner adds the other's name to the title of a house, it can lead to disaster because the Internal Revenue Service views that move as a gift of half the price of the house and begins to calculate gift taxes. Nor may unmarried couples take advantage of the unlimited marital deduction in their estate planning. Although little can be done about some of these inequities, gay and lesbian couples need to know about them and plan accordingly.

The death of a partner can raise especially difficult problems for same-sex couples. Often the family of one partner—or of both—disapproves of the relationship. When one partner dies, his family may claim all the assets of both partners if the surviving partner has no records to show what belonged to whom. And—unless proper records are kept—if one partner dies, the entire value of the couple's home may be deemed to be part of the deceased's estate, with estate taxes due on it. What's more, a surviving unmarried partner is not permitted to roll over the deceased's IRA or claim any of the retirement benefits owed from a company pension plan after a partner's death.

Few people in these predicaments are aware of the pitfalls until it's too late. What's worse, gays and lesbians may be reluctant to discuss these issues with a straight financial planner. But that's the beauty of how Christopher Street Financial serves its niche. Hardly anyone there is straight. Both Johns and Hatch are homosexual, as are all their employees and most of their clients. Mixed in are a few people who were referred from other clients and who happen to like having a planner they feel they can trust. When a prospective client is drawn to their firm, "there is always this affinity that comes into play," Johns says. "Someone has been disenfranchised in some way, and we understand it because we've been through the very same thing." Johns, who is in his early fifties and is in a long-term relationship, says he remembers going to planners for financial advice and when he told them about his gay partner, they sort of crawled into the corner on the other side of the room, hoping he'd go away.

By 1997, when Johns and Hatch bought Christopher Street Financial, there was far less stigma attached to being gay. A strong affinity remained among the group as a whole, of course, which had been devastated by the AIDS crisis. "I remember when my friends were dropping like flies," Johns says. Although some sections of New York had become a haven for gays—at least compared with other parts of the country—Wall Street was not one of them.

"It was difficult to be gay on Wall Street," says Hatch, who worked at some of the most prestigious firms on the Street. Johns and Hatch saw the opportunity inherent in identifying themselves as resources for all the life planning and wealth management needs of gays and lesbians and gay and lesbian couples. Johns had both experience and interest in technology and saw, too, that the firm could use the Web to identify itself as an intermediary for all the general financial needs of gay clients, including obtaining estate attorneys, mortgage brokers, insurance agents, accountants.

To seize that opportunity, the two took a firm with five brokers earning commissions and converted it—within five years—into a fee-based practice with sixteen employees serving all the financial needs of more than two thousand clients. Not all the work is done in-house. The firm uses SEI Investments for investments; Manhattan Mortgage Company, a mortgage broker, for mortgage shopping; and an estate attorney. But all the work is coordinated through Christopher Street Financial. All new clients pay fees rather than commissions, although the firm is still in the process of converting some of the existing clients to fees. Johns sets a $1 million asset minimum for clients he works with himself, but the firm will take on clients with as little as $100,000 in assets.

Whatever the client's net worth, the first conversation a Christopher Street planner has with a client is about his life goals and lifestyle. "Sometimes a couple is together for forty years, yet when one partner dies, his family comes out of nowhere and takes all the assets," Johns says. So Christopher Street focuses first on estate planning, writing a will, naming an executor, and signing medical directives and powers of attorney. Unmarried couples are also advised to create ownership agreements for large assets such as real estate and to keep extensive records of each partner's contributions to assets.

Johns says he and Hatch made plenty of mistakes at the beginning. But he believes they've worked out the bugs now, so much so that they're toying with franchising the model, opening branch offices, or affiliating with gay or lesbian planners in other metropolitan areas, perhaps giving them the Christopher Street stamp of approval. The firm already has clients all over the country, but Johns, along with Mark Tibergien at Moss Adams, is looking at other ways to take full advantage of the niche.

Not that the gay niche has gone unnoticed. Johns says several other firms—including Merrill Lynch and American Express—are aggressively marketing to gays and lesbians in New York. Christopher Street works hard to keep a close relationship with clients. The firm planned an evening with the Paul Taylor Dance Company at its rehearsal studio and invited top clients along. It also held a wealth management conference for individuals of high net worth. Of the fifty people who attended, 90 percent later became clients. A conference the firm sponsored at the W Hotel, one of New York's trendy night spots, and a booth it sponsored at a classic car show also landed some big clients.

So which came first for Christopher Street Financial—or for that matter, any other niche firm—the chicken or the egg? Was it a case of a firm tailoring itself to a recognized market or a matter of two people exploring the issues most meaningful to them and responding to the same needs in clients who shared their values, goals, and problems? However it came to be, Hatch says making the switch from white-shoe Wall Street to Christopher Street Financial was a welcome change, like going from a suit-and-tie job to a week full of casual Fridays. You feel so much more comfortable. That's what happens when the planner and the client have more in common than a business transaction.

—— 🌸 🌸 🌸 ——

The Multiclient Family Office

W HEN I WROTE a personal finance column for the *New York Times* during the early 1990s, many of my best sources were partners in charge of personal financial planning at the accounting firms once called the Big Eight. I came to them with questions when the Internal Revenue Service issued a private letter ruling or when distribution rules changed on pension withdrawals. At times when most practitioners were scrambling for answers they could trust, these were people I could count on to get it right. Many of them have since migrated to family-office practices, perhaps for the joy of independence but most definitely for the challenge and the variety of the planning issues such firms address for a single wealthy family. The services typically start with investment management, tax and estate planning, wealth-transfer planning, charitable giving, and record keeping and reporting, and often go on to include lifestyle management and goal-setting services, not to mention making sure the house on St. Bart's has its fence painted. Barbara Pope, for example, one of my most trusted sources on tax issues when she was partner in charge of personal financial planning in Chicago at Price Waterhouse, left the firm some years ago to operate a single-family office in Chicago. Pope owns the business and has just one client, the family whose office she runs. Another Price Waterhouse alumna,

Carol Caruthers, who was national partner and headed the company's personal financial planning practice from her office in St. Louis, Missouri, is now president and CEO of Fiduciary Counseling, in St. Paul, Minnesota, a large family office that oversees trusts, estates, and foundations and provides financial services to clients of privately held corporations and partnerships.

These moves are not a coincidence. Family offices are one of the hottest topics in financial planning today. Wallace Head—another transplant, who was once a partner at Arthur Andersen in Chicago and later went to work for Sanford C. Bernstein and then for the Strong Funds—landed at the Family Office Exchange in Chicago, as president and chief operating officer. The exchange, founded in 1989 by CEO Sarah Hamilton to help families deal with issues of wealth, provides services for family offices nationwide. Hamilton had worked in the personal trust department of Harris Bank.

I asked Head what drew him to the Family Office Exchange. "The handling of families with significant wealth—$25 million or more—is going through a dramatic change; in fact, the growth of family offices and multiclient family offices is the most exciting thing happening in our area," he says. The fun part, at least for Head, has to do with what he calls "the complexities on the technical side as well as on the emotional side," not to mention the international implications. "You rarely find a family with more than two generations living in one country," he says. Add to that second-generation divorces; rivalries; the purchase and maintenance of boats and homes around the world; and layers and layers of bill paying, insurance, and bookkeeping chores. "It's a mess," says Head, "which is great for a planner." And getting messier all the time. At least 30,000 families in the United States have a net worth of $30 million or more, Head says.

The Family Office Exchange is a professional association that serves as a clearinghouse for best practices and concepts in wealth management. Its members are families of exceptional wealth, the executives who work in family offices, and professional advisers. The exchange offers three types of membership: The first, of course, is for a family office; in this category are 310 members that describe themselves as servicing multiple generations of one family. The exchange provides opportunities for family-office members to exchange information and discuss confidential issues. The second category is for the multifamily office—an organization that provides family-office services to more than one family—which has about forty members and is the fastest-growing group. The third membership category is for advisers, consultants, and others who provide advice and services to family offices. There are 140 members in this group. By separating the categories, the exchange can more easily prevent solicitors from attending the same conferences its family-office executives will attend.

One member of the exchange might be someone like Pope, who must make a succession plan for her firm. Pope could decide to grow her office by serving more than one family. Or she could sell out to a larger firm like Frye-Lewis Capital Management, a wealth management firm in Chicago. One woman who came to the exchange for help ran a small family office built by her father and managed $200 to $300 million in wealth. She felt she had to decide whether to accept other families or to turn the reins over to someone else. Another client might be a family that has recently liquidated substantial assets and needs help in deciding whether it wants to establish its own office. Setting up a single-family office requires at least $50 million in liquidity, Head says. It becomes a separate business to be managed, and the costs are steep. If the family decides to go it alone, the exchange helps them design the office, tells them what staff it will need, and helps the family find them. If the family prefers not to have its own office, Head and Hamilton talk to them about multi-family offices and how they work.

Multifamily offices are becoming very popular for a number of reasons, Head says. The first is cost. "To get the talent you need to run a single-family office costs a lot of money," he says. "If you have a couple million dollars, the effort, oversight, and risk management might be too much." Sometimes a family doesn't want to take on that responsibility, or the family members may not have any experience at it.

It should be no surprise, then, that many advisory firms are morphing into multiclient family offices (MFOs)—firms modeled after a family office, but serving multiple families and/or unrelated clients. "In America, emulation goes well beyond flattery," Head says, "and so if someone sees a new business model, everyone claims they do it." But not every adviser is suited to this model, he says, particularly if they lack the flexibility to deal with a range of personalities or if they're overly focused on the numbers and insist on going by the book. The issues that come up in a family office are large, especially those having to do with transferring value within the family, risk management, and conserving the family wealth.

The planning often encompasses the work of identifying family values and helping to teach youngsters how to deal with wealth, and it will more than likely include building a family foundation and certainly dealing with philanthropy in some way. "There is tremendous complexity in most wealthy family situations: layer upon layer of trusts, partnerships, charitable lead trusts, and remainder trusts as well as issues that affect people who don't reside in the United States," Head says. "Once you get beyond six or eight people in the family, it gets very complex. And when you get beyond two generations, issues surface that can have an impact in many different directions."

"What do you do, for example, with kids who never need to work?" Head says. "That's an important issue." So are intergenerational conflicts and the control money can exert over family members. Any adviser who works with wealthy families must be adept at understanding the family's culture, heritage, and values. As planner Charlie Haines of Charles D. Haines, LLC, in Birmingham, Alabama, discovered, that can mean getting a psychologist on staff and going well beyond typical financial issues.

Like all of the other models that planners are adopting, the multiclient family office has to be right not only for the client but for the planner. "You have to ask yourself, 'What are your personal goals? Where are you trying to go?'" Haines says. In terms of fit, Haines, who is building a multiclient family office, is hardly the fellow I would have picked ten years ago as the one most likely to listen and sympathize when it comes to the highly charged emotional issues that come up in a family office. In fact, Haines, an M.B.A. from the University of Virginia, is more the quantitative type, who goes by the book, as Head would say. Haines is nothing if not a businessman, however. He wants to grow, and he realized early on that a family-office practice would require a wide range of skill sets, some of which he didn't have. Still, he set to work putting together the kind of firm that could serve all the needs of a family. Haines loves solving problems, and I suspect that building the firm has been a delight to him for that reason.

Many smart planners would likely find a multiclient family office a satisfying model. But whenever something is hot or trendy, many plunge in too fast. Today, many firms want to call themselves a multiclient family office, because it sounds so prestigious, so much more like a white-shoe trust department than the local office of a brokerage firm. Indeed, some advisory groups have firmly targeted this market and are going gangbusters. Of all the models, though, this one seems to require the biggest commitment in terms of effort, revenue, and personal time. As Haines told me a couple of years ago, "My wife says she never sees me anymore."

Planners aspiring to this model be warned: You could face tough family issues in more ways than one.

— 🌸 🌸 🌸 —

Mark Spangler: Birthing a Clan

MARK SPANGLER CALLS the practice he's created a family office whose members happen to be unrelated. I call it ingenious. In 1998, Spangler cut his client list from two hundred people of varied net worth to twenty qualified and accredited investors and formed a network called the Spangler Financial Group. Spangler and his clients pooled their money so they could diversify their portfolio of stocks and bonds with real assets like oil and gas, timberland, and real estate.

Spangler's firm is in Seattle, and most of his clients are high-tech folks who retired very early on stock options, so his network has become a family of sorts. Members often research wealth-related topics like the best ways to teach money matters to kids whose parents don't need to work for a living. Together they also serve as something of a high-tech think tank and incubator for new businesses. Although Spangler couldn't have envisioned what the network would become, the evolution was logical: from the start, he has been fascinated by—and incredibly adept at—computer technology and the businesses it spawns.

The oldest of ten children, Spangler was expected to take over his father's insurance brokerage, Spangler Insurance, when he finished college. He got the necessary licenses, and by the late 1970s he was on course to run the agency. But it didn't quite fit. What Spangler was more interested in doing was offering total financial advice to a handful of clients—specifically, business owners—whose financial planning and investment management needs are typically more complicated. His father's agency had half a dozen clients who were business owners, and in 1982, Spangler took them on as clients. "Here I was in my late twenties, making $40,000 or $50,000 a year," says Spangler, "and I thought, 'This is as good as it gets.'"

Hardly. Within a decade, the business owners were retiring and Spangler was collecting new clients, most of them people who worked at high-tech firms like Microsoft. "I wasn't smart enough to advertise as a niche or join the right country club," he says, "but they started to gravitate toward me because I understood tech." Most of these clients' portfolios were, of course, heavily weighted in tech stocks. In fact, in the late 1990s, shares of Microsoft made up about 50 percent of their combined portfolios. Tech stocks had served his clients well. They'd grown rich on them. It was clear to Spangler, however, that finding ways to diversify their portfolios had to be the top priority.

But Spangler wasn't finding the answers he needed at the financial planning conferences he attended. So he began branching out and attending meetings of the financial practitioners who managed family offices and endowments. That's when he met the person who led Spangler to change his career path: David Swensen, who runs the Yale Endowment Fund. Swensen was a Yale graduate and an economist with no money management experience when he was hired to manage the fund. "He came at it from a fresh perspective," Spangler says. The asset classes Swensen decided to use were pretty radical for an endowment fund. There were the usual fixed income and equities, but Swensen also bought into hedge funds; private equity; and real assets, such as direct real estate, oil and gas, and direct timber.

Spangler loved it; he'd long been intrigued by investing, especially in alternative asset classes, and he was quickly hooked on Swensen's model. But he couldn't make it work with his practice, which at that time was a typical financial planning firm serving more than two hundred clients with portfolios of various sizes. He had to find a better way.

The problem with planning practices, says Spangler, is that they keep growing, but they don't earn more money as they grow. Two clients can't be served as cheaply as one. Still, many planners keep adding clients and providing more and more services, which increase their workload right along with their costs. To Spangler, the most important number a planner must consider is the profit per client. It doesn't matter how many millions you have in assets under management if you're not making any money. A $100 million practice with ten. clients is preferable to a $100 million practice that has to serve 250 clients. But many planners go from a two hundred-client firm making $1,000 per client to one with three hundred clients, bringing in only $500 per client. "All they've done is mask a real problem," Spangler says.

Spangler had been mulling that very problem when he encountered Swensen and his asset-allocation model. Spangler had "two hundred clients in mutual funds in a typical cookie-cutter practice." Many of them had been with the firm for years and had moved right along with him from hourly fees to assets under management to retainer. "I was working too many hours, and my number of clients kept growing," he says, "but I was not making that much money."

So Spangler identified the firm's twenty-two wealthiest clients and talked with them about developing what he called a family-office model. Within this framework, all the clients—and Spangler too—would pool their money and diversify out of technology and into real assets. The single criterion for selecting which clients would be part of the family office had to be net worth, because each would have to be accredited by the Securities and Exchange Commission before they could invest in the pool. That requirement made it easier for Spangler's other clients to understand why he was dropping them, he says. He was, in fact, changing to a different type of practice. Two of the twenty-two clients he'd selected decided not to join him. The other twenty agreed, and the family investment office wound up with a total of about $100 million in assets.

To address the financial aspects of running the business itself, Spangler called recruiters who worked with family-office managers and learned that a typical salary for the manager of a family office with $100 million in assets might be $400,000 to $500,000. He told the members what the office would cost—including his salary and a staff of one full-timer and one part-timer—and what jobs they would have to outsource. Spangler outsources all the financial planning and tax work and focuses on the investment management. He explained to the group that if they added more members, the cost for each member would, of course, go down, but they would also have less of his time. The group voted to close the office to new members.

The model Spangler built lets him focus on the area of planning that he likes the most and in which he can add the most value. "It's not so much a practice as it is a co-op investment office," he says. "Most planners focus on the area where they bring the least value. They sit in front of a computer analyzing a stock for days, and they still can't make a decision." His advice to all planners: "Put your focus where you add the most value, and get rid of everything else." For Spangler, that area is clearly investment management. The Spangler Group has never lost money.

Spangler set up limited liability companies to pool the funds and adopted nearly all of Swensen's asset classes. Each member's portfolio is customized, but everyone has some of each asset class. He substituted municipal bonds for the corporate bonds Swensen uses, however, because an endowment doesn't pay taxes whereas a family office does.

For the equity portion of their portfolios, Spangler and his clients use separately managed accounts. For example, Spangler had owned Longleaf Partners Fund for years, and Mason Hawkins, the fund's manager, is now one of the separate-account managers for the Spangler Financial Group. Hawkins's minimum for a separate account is $10 million. Spangler writes the investment policy approach for each manager, with one criterion being a very concentrated fund with no more than twenty-five stocks. One managed account has just a dozen issues.

The group uses three to six equity managers and also invests in a hedge fund, bonds, and real assets. Some of the timberland and real estate owned by the group has been purchased by REITs and so the portfolio ends up with stock in REITs. For example, the group owned a piece of timberland that was bought by Georgia-Pacific, which was subsequently bought by yet another company, so the Spangler Group now owns some low-basis stock.

Spangler says his most difficult year was 1999. Most planners say the same thing, of course. But only a year earlier Spangler had launched a brand-new asset-allocation model that de-emphasized technology stocks even as the Nasdaq was soaring. "I had set the whole thing up, and the market kept going up and up and up," Spangler says. "Our overall portfolio made 12 percent; the Nasdaq made 40."

A couple of members—all of whom had made their money by taking flyers on technology and biotech companies—questioned the need to diversify, but no one left, and in 2000, it all came together. The Nasdaq peaked in March of that year, and then started falling. The Spangler Group made 26 percent for the year. In 2001, the return for all accounts was 9.79 percent. In 2002, the composite return was 10.05 percent, and for the three-year period from January 2000 through December 2002, the composite return was 45.24 percent.

All his members are now convinced it was the right choice, of course. Spangler spent a lot of time educating members at the beginning, he says, and that paid off when the markets moved against him. Success like that doesn't go unnoticed. Two of the entrepreneurs who had approached the group for venture capital later asked to join it, and they were taken on, bringing the number to twenty-two. Spangler's gotten a number of other requests from investors wanting to join the group. "But the people who come to me scare me," he says. For example, new prospects who have lost half their money in the tech bust tell Spangler: "You can replace my money. I know you can." This is not the kind of client Spangler wants. Educating the group members took a great deal of work, and he doesn't want to add members with unrealistic expectations.

The group, in fact, has moved beyond the typical challenges of investing. Most of them are people in their forties and not working. "They're grown ups; they can't just go out and play," Spangler says. "It's hard for people not to work even when they don't have to." Spangler gives each of them a regular paycheck. "But after six months, some of them get stir crazy," he says. And that's how the Spangler Group came to get involved in private equity deals. What could be better for a would-be start-up than a group of highly knowledgeable people with some money to invest? "They seek us out because we have both financial capital and human capital," Spangler says. The group may invest $500,000 to $1 million in a start-up, get involved in helping it get on its feet, then sell it for a couple of million dollars. So Spangler is creating wealth as well as preserving it.

Ideas can come from unlikely places. About the same time Spangler started his family investment office, a group called Social Venture Partners started a similar project for charity in Seattle and then moved on to other cities. "It's the very same thing I'm doing, but it's done for charity," Spangler says. "Instead of writing a check to charity, the members decide which charity they want to support and then they invest their money and they roll up their sleeves and get involved." That model is now operating in twenty-five cities, and Spangler says he gets a lot of ideas from watching how it has evolved.

Although Spangler never envisioned his group members becoming deal makers, that aspect of the group's work is now what he enjoys the most. No one is pressured to get involved, of course. "Some don't do anything. They live in Europe. Others decide they want to get involved but pull away later. If something intrigues them, they join right in."

"The venture capital market is just fabulous," Spangler says, with lots of opportunities for knowledgeable people like those in his group. In any case, Spangler enjoys being a contrarian; he likes to go against the crowd. "I love it when I get an idea and everybody wants to throw up, because that's when I know I'm on the right track," he says.

The track for Spangler's practice is clear to him. He wants to create the kind of community that he knew growing up in a family of ten kids. "That's what I try to replace in my world," he says. As a planner, he doesn't take a position on life planning, but when one of the members has a problem, he says, "we find the answers in the community."

The members of the Spangler Group also do a good deal of networking. One member, for example, was going through a difficult divorce. With her permission, Spangler put the word out to the network, and very soon she had a support group. Likewise, members form committees to do research and invite speakers to address money problems they share.

Like other successful advisers, Spangler—who lives just a mile from the home where he grew up—followed his interests and kept his options open. "It's taken a path of its own; I don't close any doors," he says. The problem with practice models is that they're cookie cutter, he says. "The only way you guarantee business success is through innovation and performance." Once president of the National Association of Personal Financial Advisors (NAPFA), Spangler says he never checked with his peers to see whether they thought he was doing the right thing when he launched his family office.

Certainly, his office is a business model that looks very different from most others. Likewise, Spangler doesn't look much like other planners. To spot him at conferences, look for a mop of curly hair and the loudest sweater in the group. I asked him if he still thinks of himself as a financial planner. He does. Nevertheless, he let his certified financial planner designation lapse because he didn't think it was adding anything to his work for the family investment group.

How long he'll continue to run the firm is anyone's guess, but should he leave, succession is not a problem, Spangler says. He will sell the practice to the group when he wants out. "I would probably bring someone on board, and I would stay as chairman of the board and work my way out of the office and then work in a niche that really interests me," says Spangler. "The beauty of this profession is you can do whatever you want."

Agreed, although not many do it quite as well as he does.

Darcy Garner Bhatia: Close Relations

WHEN I MET Darcy Garner Bhatia at a meeting of the New York City chapter of the Financial Planning Association in the fall of 2002, she offered a piece of the puzzle that had eluded me in my efforts to put together this book. I realized that I'd gotten so hung up on profit margins and the thundering institutional competition from the big guys in the business, I'd all but forgotten that the most successful advisory businesses are the ones built on relationships. A client who feels he has a planner he can trust and rely on will stick with him even if he moves to the opposite coast. I suspect that's because all of us have had advisers whom we couldn't connect with in any way—or who burned us so badly that we still have the scorch marks. So when we find someone who understands us—and who happens to be good at his craft—we don't let go.

I met Bhatia at the refreshment table just before the meeting and got the chance to learn a good deal about her. Like many planners, Bhatia had no intention of becoming a financial adviser. She studied psychology and linguistics and behavioral finance before getting her M.B.A. in international business and finance. Her plan was to work for the United Nations or perhaps for a nonprofit or Unicef. She was motivated by altruism rather than by making money and, like many college graduates, had a rude awakening when she saw the types of jobs available to those without experience. She eventually took a job selling mutual funds at First Interstate, even though selling products didn't match her idea of what she wanted to do in the world. "You just need to do this for a little while," her boss told her, "and then you'll be able to help people."

He was right. After a few months selling funds, she moved to the trust department of Pacific Bank in San Francisco, where she managed a half-billion dollars in fixed-income and core equity and was able to help clients with asset allocation and portfolio building and to work with attorneys and estate planners and accountants to pull together the whole picture for a client. She liked the idea that she wasn't selling anything. And she liked knowing that the clients she worked with weren't focused on looking for the highest yield and the lowest fee. They were looking for a relationship; she was too.

When Pacific Bank was purchased by one of the largest banks on the West Coast, Bhatia was offered ten different positions with the larger bank. She didn't want any of them. The bank was consolidating and cutting costs, and she believed the services they were offering weren't necessarily the best for the consumer. Bhatia still believed she could use her business training to help people rather than to skin them. So she moved, along with several other Pacific employees, to another bank in San Francisco called First Republic. Her clients followed. The new spot suited her. She likes solving problems, and she likes working on a team with attorneys and accountants and other specialists. For instance, she had a client who sold two natural gas tankers and she set up and managed an escrow account with the trust department.

Then Bhatia fell in love, got married, and moved to New York, where she went to work for Trainer Wortham & Co., an old money management shop. What caught my attention about her story, though, was that the clients who had followed her from Pacific Bank to First Republic followed her once again to Trainer Wortham. "When relationships are built by working together, often nothing can come between them," she says.

And that, I think, is what Mark Hurley and other business-minded consultants fail to see when they look at the financial advisory business: It's the relationship that matters. Sure, people who earn $50,000 a year are concerned about fees. For them, there are advisers like Sharon Rich and Sheryl Garrett and her network. Thank goodness. Truly wealthy families are not coupon clippers. They want someone who shares their values and sees his mission as helping them solve life's problems, specifically the financial ones.

Bhatia's training in psychology and behavioral finance are noteworthy, I think. She also has a chartered financial analyst designation and is testing to become a certified financial planner. Her combination of talent and experience illustrates one of the reasons it's so difficult to develop a definitive checklist of characteristics that make a good adviser: Caring, empathetic, smart, experienced. Certainly, those qualities would warrant a place on the list. But what leads a client to someone like Darcy Garner Bhatia or Cicily Maton or Judy Shine and keeps them there? It's more than luck. I certainly wouldn't argue that no one at a big brokerage or insurance firm could be a good adviser, but if I had to name one trait that all the top planners I know have in common, it would be their independence.

At Trainer Wortham in New York, Bhatia worked with four other partners and started to do family-office work, which she describes as filling the chief financial officer's job for a family. The five took over responsibility for all the financial decision making for the families they served, including tax- and estate-planning decisions, working with clients on strategic planning, bringing creative solutions to setting up lines of credit, and diversifying portfolios that had concentrated positions in a family-owned company or in stock options.

Then in the spring of 2002, Bhatia; Steven Hoch, former principal and head of client services for Pell Rudman Trust Co. in Boston; Maarten Van Hegel, managing director at Trainer Wortham, where he had established the family wealth management team; and Bert Nowak all left Trainer Wortham to set up their own firm, Highmount Capital in New York. Within six months, Highmount had thirty to forty-five client relationships and $500 million in assets under management, largely from clients who had worked with the partners at earlier jobs.

One of the things that compelled the partners to start their own family-office practice was the desire to create a culture in which they could advise their clients freely and allow them complete investment independence. Big firms like Goldman Sachs want to use their own products, Bhatia says. Trainer Wortham is paid on the basis of assets under management. And Bhatia, who had been a part of several bank trust departments and private firms by the time she joined Trainer, saw that the culture at the firm changed each time there was a merger or a buyout and that the restrictions on which advisers could talk to whom and which investments clients were allowed to choose from changed, too, not on the basis of what was best for the client but because new management was now running things.

Highmount Capital's clients must have a minimum of $10 million in assets. The partners manage the core S&P 500 piece of the portfolio and do some active bond management, but they prefer to look for "best of breed" managers wherever they can find them in international, small cap, and alternative investments. The partners analyze a new client's portfolio when he comes on board. "But we're not given any incentive to keep money in-house," Bhatia says. "We want to do the asset allocation and then farm it out." The partners do due diligence on the managers, and they have a contrarian's approach to asset allocation, moving some client money to the sector that's most beaten up, as was small-cap growth in the fall of 2002. The client pays for the money managers and pays Highmount a consulting fee that amounts to about 1 percent of assets for all family-office work.

Despite the size of the firm as measured by assets under management, the staff is very lean: the four partners, a junior portfolio manager who interned while working on his M.B.A. at Columbia University, one operations person, and a secretary.

Bhatia says the model works because each of the partners is available to talk with any client at any time and will help to resolve any problem. If the client has an accountant he loves, Highmount works with the accountant. If the client needs an accountant, Highmount helps to find one. "It's important to understand what you're good at," Bhatia says. A firm like Highmount can't pay the best estate-planning attorney in New York to join the staff. Instead, the partners must contract for the services of such top people and sit down—along with the client—to work with them.

Bhatia thinks the planning available to high-net-worth individuals has come full circle. First, a client had to make separate visits to the bank and the lawyer and the broker and the insurance agent. Next, they went to big banks as a one-stop shopping place. But the full-service approach didn't work either, she says, because it became too bureaucratic and the client was ill-served by limited product offerings and limited access to advisers. Now, she says, what clients of Highmount want is one person who understands their entire operation, who can make a call to an estate lawyer to iron out a wrinkle; rejigger the portfolio when that's necessary; and keep insurance needs up to date, bills paid, and all the loose ends tied up. "We're not going to walk the dog or make travel arrangements, but we'll send someone to your home to pay your bills," Bhatia says.

Bhatia describes her firm as a boutique multiclient family office shop. The firm's strength, she says, is its unbiased opinions and independent relationships with vendors. "Because we're independent, we're always trying to better ourselves and gain more knowledge."

One of the big challenges for the next year is to decide how fast the firm wants to grow and what kinds of services it wants to add. Bhatia, with her psychology background, is interested in affiliating with a consultant who will work with family dynamics and hold family meetings to discuss the softer side of money issues. Clearly, the firm can't continue to grow at the rate of $500 million assets every six months. Taking the time to pause and consider the best ways to grow is one of the continual challenges of every advisory firm.

— ❀ ❀ ❀ —

Charlie Haines: The Care of Kith and Kin

CHARLIE HAINES IS one of those people who can do anything they put their mind to, including, in his case, picking up a Southern drawl to make the wealthy clients in his practice in Birmingham, Alabama, feel at home. Haines grew up on Long Island and attended elite Northern private schools—Groton and Williams College. Today he heads Charles D. Haines, LLC, a multiclient family office in Birmingham, Alabama, serving about 250 clients, including members of the Forbes 400, with $300 million in assets under management.

Haines differs from many top planners today in that he set his goal of becoming a planner early on rather than happening upon the profession in midcareer. Armed with an M.B.A. from the University of Virginia, Haines went to work for two of the top planners in the country, Lynn Hopewell and Don Rembert, in Falls Church, Virginia. From them, Haines figured he would learn what he needed to know to set up his own practice. And he did. He also developed retirement planning spreadsheets that later became a template for many software programs, exhibiting early on the technical expertise that would mark his strength as a planner.

Although Haines's strengths are many, I suspect that spontaneity does not lead the list. Rather, he's a strategist. He's also incredibly flexible. So when he sees a service that belongs in a planning practice, he's only too happy to offer it, even if that means he has to go outside the firm and bring someone else on board to do it. Perhaps because he grew up rubbing shoulders with great wealth, Haines knew from the start that financial stewardship involves more than just counting pennies. So he has aimed to provide a vast array of services for his clients that keeps them in the fold. He knows what's good for his clients, and he knows what's good for the firm and he keeps his eye on the competition.

From the start, Haines's intention was to develop a business rather than just a practice. Most planners still have a job rather than a business, Haines told me when I first interviewed him back in the mid-1990s. That's the mindset that struck him among members of NAPFA when he joined the group in 1995. Members of NAPFA focus on competence and integrity, he said. But few of them think about the longevity of their businesses. "They're a bunch of counseling-oriented people, who are running boutique firms."

That was not what Haines had in mind. Yet as certain as Haines was starting out about the business he would build, the focus of his practice has changed over the years. As he saw that baby boomer values were wanting in ways that money couldn't counter, Haines, a boomer himself, changed his views on many issues. Haines's father, who had been editor and publisher of *The Long Islander*, a regional newspaper in Huntington, New York, had taught him that money can't buy happiness. In his clients, Haines saw firsthand what his father meant. These people had made some money and achieved financial success, but they didn't feel satisfied. They were searching for meaning in life. So Haines started asking clients questions like: When did you last spend a chunk of time with your best friends? What are your spending patterns teaching your children about who you are and what you value? Haines thought about the questions himself and he wasn't entirely happy with the answers, which led to a decision to spend more time with family and friends.

For many planners, the most enjoyable part of their work is building relationships with clients, but Haines is not in that group. He's the quintessential big-picture person, someone who can point to where the profession is likely to go next. But he readily admits that he can be dim when it comes to social skills: For example, when an excited employee once waved her diamond engagement ring in front of his face to show off her new status, he asked—baffled—if she'd gotten a manicure. Haines admits he is similarly lacking in the instinctive counseling skills many planners possess.

That doesn't mean he doesn't make sure his clients get the range of advice they need. As far as I know, Haines was the first to split the financial planning process into its two very different skill sets: technical and counseling. Nearly ten years ago, Haines hired two employees and set out to train them in both portfolio management and financial planning. One of them eventually told Haines that he didn't feel comfortable with the financial planning tasks. At just about the same time, the other one confessed that he didn't feel comfortable with the number crunching. Haines could relate to how lopsided they felt. His strengths were on the technical side, but he knew that the counseling was important and that his firm needed to provide it. The trick was to figure out which staff member could provide it best.

So Haines hired an industrial psychologist to test all his employees as well as the recruits to determine their strengths and weaknesses. Using the Meyers-Briggs Type Indicator—a personality test that assesses whether a person is introverted or extroverted, a thinker or a feeler, and gives insights into the way people interact and work together—the psychologist found that portfolio managers tend to be "thinkers" whereas financial planners tend to be "feelers." Haines wasn't surprised. "A financial planner needs to be more empathetic, more emotional, to be able to relate to the client," Haines says. "But you don't want an emotional person handling the portfolio." He knew he needed both thinkers and feelers. When he hired new employees, he chose the candidates whose strengths leaned to one side or the other, aiming to strike a balance for the firm.

But even planners who excel at counseling are not equipped to handle a client's emotional problems. So Haines put a clinical social worker on retainer to assist clients facing more sensitive issues. In one case, a couple had trouble balancing the needs of their disabled child with those of the rest of the family. The social worker was a big help, Haines says. He also calls on the social worker if a client's guilt or other money hang-ups block him from implementing planning recommendations.

With the successful business model he's building—a multiclient family office—Haines is making an important contribution to the profession. Even more valuable is the forward thinking that has characterized his success. Thinking, after all, is what Haines likes most to do. Sameness bores him; he prefers to move on to the next challenge. Haines saw before most that clients wanted answers to larger questions than, Can I afford to retire? He decided four or five years ago that the comprehensive financial planning model built on asset allocation, mutual funds, and a retirement plan was nearing the end of its life.

To build the multifamily office model, Haines had to turn away clients who didn't fit the future of the firm. "In the last four years, we have sacrificed growth to put this plan together," he says. "We slowed our growth and hurt our profitability because we were not willing to just ride off into the sunset." Instead, he hopes to be able to offer services to wealthy families across the country. "We think bigger is better for our clients."

Wealthy families, whether they own a business or not, need help with family communication and emotional issues, Haines says. They need a family succession plan that addresses much more than just what happens to the money. Haines's business model includes an on-staff psychologist, who works with all new clients to help them define their life goals, and a philanthropy center headed by a staff member who helps clients set charitable goals and figure out how to accomplish them. The firm also has a family-governance expert and an alternative investments division. Continually on the lookout for additional services he might offer to his wealthy clients, Haines retained a security firm a couple of years ago to screen job applicants for his clients' household staffs and to offer self-defense strategies against kidnapping.

In his search for new ways to serve clients, Haines finds there's no shortage of complex problems to address. Many of his clients are family business owners, and Haines has identified seven different viewpoints within a family business: the owner, the family, the manager/employee, the owners who don't work in the business, the owners who do work in the business, family who are owners but not employees, and employees who are owners but not family. No financial planner is equipped to deal with that kind of complex emotional and psychological interaction. And so Haines has hired a third psychologist, Marty Carter, whom he calls a family wealth counselor, to work with all client families on issues of wealth transfer and multigenerational wealth.

Once Haines finds solutions that work, he attempts to standardize the processes involved. For years, Abe Kaplan, a retired planner whom Haines consults on business issues, told Haines he needed a procedures manual. Haines knew he did, but he kept putting it off. Finally, he decided that his next hire would write the training manual and when that new employee came on board, he was instructed to write down everything the firm did with a client, beginning with the initial meeting. Haines and other senior members of the firm edited it, and now new employees are responsible for providing feedback on how well the procedures work and for keeping the manual current.

Despite the wide range of services Haines's firm provides, it does outsource certain things like bookkeeping, bill paying, legal work and tax compliance, the security training for defensive driving and kidnapping prevention, and family-governance work. Haines says he's still refining the firm's fee structure for all these services. He's moving toward retainer fees, but a fair amount of business is still asset-based. The fees for the psychologists' work are hourly. "The fees are highly customized," Haines says, noting that one family business still has the old model of "yes people" on the board and now wants to move to outside, independent directors, making the service much more complex than a routine review. "We'll have to ramp up the fee," Haines says.

Like so many planners on the leading edge, Haines is convinced the solution he's found is right for his firm, but he realizes it may not work for everyone. "If serving clients this way is your goal, then this is how I would do it," he says. "But that's who I am. Self-awareness is so important." Haines likes change and new situations and working with wealthy clients who can afford to pay for some of the research and development. With clients whose assets are below $1 million or $2 million, "I start to yawn," Haines says. Not because he's a snob but because the ideas he dreams of putting together cost money.

How do you find out who you are as a financial planner? I asked Haines. Start out by making sure your ego is not in the way and by acknowledging your mistakes, he says. But, he admits, few people ever truly find out who they are. "We're trying to help other people do it, but how many of us do it ourselves?" He pays attention to which of his tasks get done quickly and which get postponed. That, he says, tells him a lot.

— 🌺 🌺 🌺 —

All in the Family

SOME FINANCIAL ADVISERS dread the time when a wealthy client needs trust services because that means the bank will compete with them for the client's business. Charlie Haines found a solution: He owns—together with more than one hundred other advisory firms—National Advisors Trust, a trust company with $20 billion in assets. The trust company can be a custodian of client assets and can serve as trustee. And it's a purchasing co-op. In many ways, it accomplishes what some financial planning firms have attempted to do by way of a merger: cut costs and capture economies of scale.

The trust also acts as a co-op to develop services and products to serve the firms that own it, Haines says. National Advisors Trust is getting free research from Goldman Sachs and gets discounts on computer software and hardware. "We cut the fee for products in half," Haines says. Setting up a life insurance trust, for example, costs $500 rather than $1,000. The trustee fee is set at 25 basis points, about half of what advisers would pay to an outside trust company.

If an adviser keeps client money at an independent trust, the relationship with the adviser ends at the client's death because the bank becomes trustee of the assets. "It's the worst time to have our relationship ripped away from the family," Haines says. Setting up a trust company for advisers resolves many of these problems.

Chapter Seven

The Large Firm

I F YOU WANT TO see how varied the opinions of independent advisers can be, ask them about Mark Hurley's forecasts on the future of the financial planning industry. Hurley has proposed that over the next decade Merrill Lynch and the other big brokerages will become the chief competition for independent planners and that a handful of giant planning firms will emerge from the financial advisory fray, squeezing the small and midsize firms to the wall and leaving them no choice but to join a big firm. No two planners I talked to weigh in quite the same way on how much size matters, how much autonomy they're willing to give up, or how much of the personal touch they'd be forced to give up by expanding.

Some planners—like Sullivan, Bruyette, Speros & Blayney in McLean, Virginia—are convinced growth can work for them. They concur with what Hurley says about margins being pinched, and they figure the best way to deal with that is to leverage their talent and standardize as many operations as possible. Sullivan, Bruyette even has someone on staff who spends all of his time looking at ways the firm can do a better job by standardizing procedures. But so far, Sullivan, Bruyette is aiming at becoming a household name only in suburban Washington, D.C.

Even planners who define big in larger terms—like Evensky,

Brown & Katz in Coral Gables, Florida—don't necessarily agree that big and boutique are mutually exclusive. Advisers simply need to decide on a strategy, they say. "They need to make a decision about what they want to do and how to do it and not just let life happen to them," says Deena Katz. "That's what many planners are doing; they're dismissing the changes" in a rapidly changing industry.

"One thing Hurley accurately predicted was that there would be a lot of turmoil in the industry, a lot of organizational ferment," says Tim Kochis at Kochis Fitz Tracy Fitzhugh & Gott in San Francisco. But Kochis doesn't see that turmoil leading to the creation of giant firms. "I've been in this industry for thirty years," says Kochis, "and this one-stop shopping is a wave that builds momentum and then crashes against the shore."

Kochis, a lawyer with an M.B.A., was national director of personal financial planning for Deloitte & Touche as well as for the Bank of America Executive Financial Counseling Group. "I was part of the Bank of America when it was going to take over the world, and I was part of an accounting firm when it was going to take over the world," Kochis says. "The idea is meritorious, but it doesn't happen." That's because big institutions have a short attention span, says Kochis. "They have a bad quarter or two and all bets are off. Although they have large resources, they don't consistently and reliably apply them." So Kochis, who's viewed planning from all sides, believes the boutiques will win the day. "I think five or ten years from now, you'll see mostly small, independent firms." Partly that's because wealthy consumers want the best of breed for the services they need, says Kochis. "A small firm doesn't manufacture or carry proprietary products for those needs and it doesn't have to overcome the institutional barriers." Indeed, these firms are spared any conflict of interest in having to recommend brand products; and unlike wire houses, their research need not support an investment banking business.

Still, arguments citing the leverage and economy of scale of a big firm continue to be compelling to many planners and institutions. News of mergers and acquisitions comes over the Business Wire regularly, like the one in November 2002: "Patriot Bank Corp., a $1 billion financial services company operating seventeen banking and lending offices in southeastern Pennsylvania, announced plans to acquire Bonds & Paulus, a wealth management firm with $65 million in assets, headquartered in Chester County, Pennsylvania. Bonds & Paulus was founded in 1993 to provide investment advisory and financial planning services to high net-worth individuals and families. Bonds & Paulus is to be merged into Patriot Advisors, a division of Patriot Bank that provides wealth and employee benefits, brokerage, and life insurance services. The group hopes to grow through additional acquisitions."

And so do other players in the industry. Every financial planning practice in the country will probably be approached with a similar deal. No one doubts that there will be many more mergers and acquisitions, roll ups, and national networks in the planning business. Many advisers say they've already talked with Jessica Bibliowicz, the daughter of Wall Street veteran Sanford Weill, who's been working to create a big firm by rolling up dozens of small planning firms across the country into her National Financial Partners. Even major planning firms like Evensky, Brown & Katz say they've talked to Bibliowicz. "What she's doing is very interesting," says Harold Evensky, although in the end he and Katz decided not to join her.

Most planners, like Kochis, have explored many different options. "We've been approached by companies that wanted to buy us, or to make an investment for an ownership position, or to invite us to join them to form a nationwide consortium," says Kochis. But he believes his firm already has a good plan for growth. He doesn't think he needs to hook up with any of these strategists to achieve his goals of unparalleled service to clients and enough growth to provide value to the owners of the firm and create value for the next generation of owners.

Still, Kochis is keeping his options open. Others, like Evensky, Brown & Katz, are going further. They're planning to do a roll up of sorts on their own to create a national firm called the Evensky Group.

Not many planners will consider expanding to become a nationwide business. But most planners will be offered a chance to decide if they want to become part of one.

— ✻ ✻ ✻ —

Harold Evensky and Deena Katz: Starting Over

BACK IN THE late 1980s, when *Money* magazine asked me to write a story on how to teach kids about money, Harold Evensky was one of the financial planners I called for advice because I'd seen his name in so many stories on financial planning. Evensky, who knows how to deal with the press, told me he'd get back to me. As it turned out, he called Deena Katz, who was then a financial planner in Chicago, and asked her to give him some quick coaching on the topic. Then he called me back with Katz's ideas. Talk about smart planning.

By the time I interviewed him again—this time for a story for *Business Week* on prenuptial agreements—the two had gotten married and I talked with them both. (And in case you're wondering, they advised clients to have an agreement, although they found it too unromantic to do the same.)

Evensky's name still gets around. He has, more than likely, the highest profile of any financial planner/adviser/wealth manager in the industry. In fact, his book *Wealth Management: The Financial Advisor's Guide to Investing and Managing Your Client's Assets* (McGraw-Hill) helped make the term "wealth management" the standard for the profession. Evensky's popularity with the press has caused more than a few planners to fume. They don't see what makes him or his Coral Gables, Florida, practice so special. From a reporter's point of view, his popularity is easily explained. Evensky always comes up with good material for a story. He's never afraid to give his personal opinion or even to talk about his personal life and the mistakes he's made. And that's exactly what happened when I asked him about his strategy to build a national wealth management firm. He detailed the mistakes he's already made and was eager to talk about how he would fix them going forward.

These days, reporters actually make an effort not to call Evensky for their stories because they're getting skittish at the accusation that he gets too much press. But as often happens, I couldn't find anyone else who approached the problem of business strategy in quite the same way as Evensky's firm. Katz wrote a book in 1999—*Deena Katz on Practice Management* (Bloomberg Press)—in which she discusses what the firm calls concierge service, that is, offering a more comprehensive package of wealth management services than clients can get anywhere else. Evensky and Katz want to take this model—the concierge service/family-office model—and create a template they can offer nationally. With the economies of scale, buying power, and pooled talent of a number of firms pulled together as the Evensky Group, they figure they can offer just about anything including insurance, a medical ombudsman, psychotherapy, as well as traditional financial planning's sacred six: risk management, cash flow, investments, and retirement, tax, and estate planning.

Evensky and Katz say the idea to build a national firm came from their own notion of where wealth management is headed. Evensky chaired the Certified Financial Planner Board in 1998–99, when the issue that came to be known as "CFP lite" surfaced. By that time, the certified financial planner designation had become distinctive, and the press invariably put it on the list of "must-haves" for a competent planner. But for institutional firms like Merrill Lynch, whose salespeople typically do not have the CFP designation, that prerequisite is a problem. So the CFP Board proposed that the CFP designation be offered in two varieties: the regular designation—which requires the applicant to take courses in six different areas (retirement, taxes, estate planning, risk management, investments, and basic planning) and to demonstrate a wide range of knowledge by passing a comprehensive exam, as well as to have three years of experience as a financial planner—and a second one, with less-rigorous demands. The requirements for the secondary designation were still being hammered out when a brouhaha erupted that led to the tabling of the idea and the resignation in October 2000 of the CFP Board's president and CEO Robert P. Goss. Evensky, who had been one of the CFPs long dedicated to making the label distinctive, took a lot of heat for supporting CFP lite.

It was, he says, a growth experience. "All the issues that led to CFP lite also led us to the realization that wealth management was becoming a commodity," Evensky says. He became convinced that Merrill Lynch and similar institutions were committed to getting into full-scale planning and that the field was going to get very crowded.

"We saw that it wouldn't take many steps for Merrill and AXA to emulate what independent planners do," Katz says. Her research on the practice-management book she'd just written had convinced her even more that big changes lay ahead in the industry. Evensky and Katz don't believe the assets under management (AUM) model will remain viable going forward. They think, as does Mark Hurley, that planners will be forced to provide more services for the same fees. "We needed to systematize and formalize our services," says Katz, "so we could deliver them more economically."

The two concluded that the scale of services they offered was not going to be sustainable in the future. "We needed to amortize the costs and spread them over a larger base," Evensky says. They decided to create a support system for independent planners that would allow them to offer top-of-the-line service without reinventing the wheel each time.

"The planets," says Katz, "all suddenly aligned." In 2000, Evensky hired a chief executive officer whose mandate was to take the Evensky Group to a higher level. Exactly how high was still unclear. Katz thought the Evensky Group should start out as a regional firm, buying up other smaller firms in Florida. Evensky believed it should go national, merging with similar firms of similar size. But the new CEO had grander plans than that. "He wanted a national fiefdom," Katz says. "He wanted to create a monster."

The CEO had lined up six national firms and $40 million in financing and was ready to make it happen in April 2001. Evensky liked the scope of the firm, but he didn't feel the CEO was the right person to do the job. Neither did Katz, and at the eleventh hour—with deals waiting to be sealed—they decided that they didn't want to go into business with this CEO. For Katz, the key problem was that the scope of the network was too large. "The cultural differences among the firms were a big issue," she says.

Parting company with the CEO, they scaled down their plans and focused only on roll ups in Florida. The revised plan was to hire someone to manage Evensky, Brown & Katz in Coral Gables while Katz created a corporate office to merge the new organizations, systematize them, and bring in a central, standardized technology. Evensky would chair the policy committee—made up of owners of the different firms—and also the investment policy subcommittee. And, of course, his name would give the new firm immediate recognition and prestige.

But progress has been halting. Katz took six months off in 2001, the chief operating officer they hired did not work out, and in early 2003 Evensky and Katz were still several months away from getting started. Many of their original ideas are still good ones, Katz says, but the new plan is to start more slowly. And with Katz again managing the practice, the two say that once they put the plan back into play, they estimate they'll have six practices on board in eighteen months and twenty-five practices in five years.

The first six practices brought in are likely to be consolidated practices, involving twice as many smaller firms. "We probably won't go after bigger firms," Katz says. "With people our size, there are a lot of ego problems." Owners of smaller planning firms have approached her after reading her books on practice management, eager to join a firm that has all its systems in place. This time, Katz says, rather than looking at $200 million firms, they might look at firms with $50 million to $100 million in assets and put three to four firms together in a single office.

Smaller firms tend to be "much easier to get along with," Evensky says. They also stand to benefit greatly from the technology they gain access to as part of the relationship.

The trouble with many smaller firms, however, is that they have an exaggerated notion of what they're worth, according to Katz. To assist with the appraisal process, Evensky and Katz asked Mark Tibergien at Moss Adams to build a program to help evaluate practices. "Believe me," Katz says. "No one wants to see those numbers. 'What do you mean we're only worth $300,000?'"

But once that hurdle is passed, the purchase price can be worked out, and then the Evensky Group would do a stock swap, so that the smaller firm's owners get a piece of the larger company. Practice value will always be a stumbling block, Katz says. "You have to bring them back to reality." But she says that many small practices are delighted at the idea of this virtual investment in their infrastructure.

The Evensky Group could add value to a small firm in a number of areas, and marketing is certainly one. "It costs a fortune to do any kind of marketing," Katz says. Not only can Evensky and Katz put together a slick brochure, but their names are well-known in planning circles. Both have traveled around the world to give speeches to planner groups in places like Australia, England, Japan, and Hong Kong.

The acquired firm would also receive help with technology, an area in which, Evensky believes, small firms have a particularly difficult time keeping up with institutional competitors and their huge resources. Likewise, recruiting planners could be done on a corporate level. "We used to get quality staff practically [knocking at our doors]," Evensky says. "Now it's much more cost competitive to get good staff." That's where the advantages of having a corporate human resources department would come in. It can standardize the procedures for recruiting and training planners.

Similar savings would apply to the cost of providing life-planning services. Of course, financial planners have always done a certain amount of life planning, Katz says, but most planners don't have the skills to be a therapist or a coach. At the corporate level, the Evensky Group would contract with a national network of therapists and make them available to all the offices. The group would also handle health care issues, such as getting a client to the right doctor. "In our corporate office, we would have medical people and a medical ombudsman. The office will allow the planners to deal with issues that have been too delicate for them to touch as individual planners," Katz says.

One such issue that would no longer be off limits is insurance work, which fee-only planners won't touch because of the commissions. But Evensky planners could provide insurance through the corporation. "No one gets a bonus for using insurance products," Katz says. "There is no commission." The commissions will go into the corporate pot, and the person running the insurance division will be compensated on how well he serves clients.

The question of insurance led to one of Evensky and Katz's toughest decisions regarding fee structure: to relinquish the fee-only status they had worked so hard to achieve. Fee-only firms have blazed the trail to integrity and objectivity in the financial planning profession. But the Evensky Group can't be fee-only and still sell insurance. TIAA-CREF and Vanguard are becoming inexpensive, high-quality players in the insurance market, Evensky says, and planners can serve their clients by offering insurance. If we sell insurance, he says, it means the firm receives commissions, and the definition of fee-only is that you don't get income from anyone but your clients. "So we're not going to hold ourselves out as fee only," he says. They ultimately made the decision by polling their clients, who said that not offering insurance was taking a "holier than thou" approach at the expense of clients.

Planners will be on salary and have some ownership in the corporation, and fees will be set as retainers, spanning different levels of service from low-frills to concierge. The key to cutting costs is to standardize the process in order to leverage the planners' time. "We all do the same thing," Evensky says. "We all have a back office, we all trade, we all do the same functions for our clients that do not require our personal expertise." For example, planners typically help clients renegotiate mortgages or car leases. "It's time-consuming, and it doesn't require our level of expertise," he says. "That's where the Evensky Group could have leverage." The corporate office could go out and shop a mortgage and when a client comes back from vacation, he gets a new mortgage at $350 a month less in payments. Or the office asks: What kind of car do you want? Then all the shopping and negotiating and paperwork are done in the corporate office. Similarly, there are companies that will consolidate all airline miles and give discounts for hotels. The corporate office could negotiate for all the clients of the Evensky Group. Ditto for wireless services or travel agents.

Evensky and Katz have, in fact, polled their clients to see what kinds of services they would like planners to provide. Bill paying was one. So they're also looking at what can be done with key cards, which are similar to smart cards but with much broader use. Essentially, "clients who belong to the Evensky Group of family offices," says Katz, "could present a card and get discounts on a range of products and services."

Economies of scale and a wide range of services are attractive benefits, say Evensky and Katz, but what will differentiate the national Evensky Group from Merrill Lynch is trust, for one thing, and service for another. "They [Merrill Lynch and other institutional firms] can't offer the level of service we're talking about," Evensky says. Continuity is important too. At institutions like Merrill Lynch and U.S. Trust, clients are assured no continuity of service as brokers and bankers come and go.

Katz and Evensky want to be ready to compete as the industry changes and that's what's driving their move, but Katz thinks planners probably have it all wrong in looking for competition only in the logical places. Fifteen years ago, she asked the head of Delta Airlines who his competition was, and he named AT&T, because with improvements in phone conferencing people wouldn't need to fly anymore. "The point is, we're not going to be the only game in town," Katz says. "You've got to think outside the box."

— ✻ ✻ ✻ —

BBR Partners: The Big Boutique

IN THE FIFTEEN YEARS I've been observing the financial advisory business, the top players hadn't changed all that much until recently. Each time someone was elected to the Certified Financial Planner Board of Standards or chosen to head a major trade group, it was a name from the universe of planners I knew. But as we move into the new millennium, not only the players but the pace is changing. The first generation of advisers took years to grow and build their businesses. Today, a handful of new firms are reaching top speeds right out of the starting gate.

One of those pacesetters is BBR Partners in New York, a firm that was set up in February 2000 by three young men—none of whom had yet reached thirty—from Goldman Sachs who thought they could improve on the Wall Street investment banking formula by offering more service to fewer clients. The three—Art Black, from private client services; Brett Barth, from investment banking; and Evan Roth, from asset management—set up a five-year plan to serve as chief financial officer to a group of families, each with a minimum of $10 million in assets. Within three years, the practice had thirty families with $1.1 billion in assets, and it has—for three years running—been at or near the top of *Bloomberg Wealth Manager* magazine's annual ranking of independent financial advisory firms

What accounts for BBR's success? The partners point to an abundance of drive and a minimum of gray hair. "Plenty of people could do this job," Roth says. "You have to want it, to be hungry for it." A certain type of résumé doesn't hurt either. "The credentials help, the fact that we have Wharton degrees and worked at Goldman," he says. One set of clients comes from Wall Street competition; they're the clients who want the same expertise they can get from an investment bank but with more service. "The trusts and estate attorneys will tell their clients, 'You need to get away from a bank or a broker,'" Roth says. So they get away to BBR.

The three partners believe their youth is a plus. "The average age of our clients is fifty-five," Barth says. "Clients want to hire us because we'll be around for them." And the young men have every intention of following through. "Our goal is to run this business for a long time. This is our last job," Barth says.

BBR provides asset allocation, selection of investment managers, advisory services for complex financial needs such as low-basis stock or restricted stock, and access to and analysis of quality alternative investments. Each portfolio is customized. BBR also offers to incorporate and supervise clients' existing advisers, such as attorneys and accountants, and help with philanthropic objectives. Although the firm does not prepare taxes, write wills, or pay bills, the partners oversee the lawyers, attorneys, and bookkeepers who do this work and meet with them semiannually. Like Mark Spangler's firm in Seattle, BBR also creates a forum for clients to interact with one another. In Spangler's case, the clients share an interest in high tech and Spangler acts as an intermediary to help them work together on problem solving. At BBR, the partners might set up a forum for clients who share an interest in a particular wealth-related topic and help them find an expert to teach them more about it.

Roth says the key to the pace of the firm's growth was the decision not to do in-house asset management. "With asset management, you need to grow organically or go out and acquire firms," he says. "We didn't think we had the patience to grow organically." Roth thinks the decision to find and monitor managers rather than manage the money in-house gives BBR a distinctive marketing advantage because the firm has nothing to gain in compensation by picking one manager over another. Roth says other firms could follow the same path. The biggest stumbling block, he says, is the conviction many advisers have that they can't win big business. "Perhaps some advisers don't have the ability to evaluate managers the way we do," Roth says. "But you can outsource that. It's just a question of finding crutches for the places where you have weaknesses."

The partners seem to have adjusted well to independent planning. Roth says the three men felt very conflicted in their old Wall Street jobs because Goldman sold products. BBR decided first off not to do that. The partners also like working with families rather than institutions. "When you work with a pension manager, he wants to keep his job," Roth says. "But with a family, the connection is much more emotional. You won't use a white-paper strategy." If a client has never used bonds and doesn't want to use bonds, Roth says, we can't put bonds in the client portfolio. The strategy must combine technical excellence with emotional insight.

At Goldman, the partners found that the supervision of a client's asset management could become disjointed. A client might sell a business for $30 million and put $10 million with Merrill Lynch, $10 million with Goldman, and $10 million somewhere else. That led to overlapping investments and problems with issues like the alternative minimum tax, which must be addressed by someone who sees the entire portfolio. "What would happen if we had this kind of money and remained a boutique and became very service oriented?" the three wondered. The answer defined their niche: bringing Goldman Sachs expertise to clients on a personal level and without the conflicts of interest. "We believe that you are your roots," Roth says. "Our roots are with high-net-worth families. We take a comprehensive view of all the client's investments in a single place and provide totally objective advice."

The firm's brochure, called "The Evolution of Wealth Management," compares BBR to five other types of advisers, pointing out how BBR solves the shortcomings of each. The local financial planner has no Wall Street experience, BBR says, and his incentives are product sales and commissions. The banks and trust companies have gaps in service and treat clients like numbers. Consultants do most of their work for institutions and do not understand the tax implications for individuals; they do not develop close relationships with clients and are typically highly quantitative. Investment bankers and brokers hide their means of compensation and have an inherent conflict of interest. Family offices find it difficult to attract and motivate top talent, cost a lot to run, and lack buying power and deal flow.

BBR is the superior alternative, the firm says, because the partners combine years of Wall Street experience, incentives aligned with client objectives, confidentiality, a focus on after-tax performance, both qualitative and quantitative approaches, transparent costs, institutional pricing, and a depth and breadth of resources. BBR will evaluate a Walgreen sale-leaseback program or buy a property to turn into a hotel, as well as analyze sophisticated investment products like collar exchange funds.

The partners decided from the start that their model wouldn't work for a client with $2 million or $3 million. "We are not the low-cost provider," Roth says. They set a minimum of $10 million in assets because at that level, the partners believe, a client can get full use of BBR expertise. All but one of BBR's clients have come from referrals; most of the clients are first-generation entrepreneurs who don't know what to do with their sudden wealth, like a Florida woman in her mid-thirties who sold her technology business for $15 million in stock. She wanted both income and capital appreciation as well as freedom from worrying about the investment herself. BBR developed a strategy to sell her single-stock position tax efficiently and also helped her evaluate insurance, mortgage, and legal providers.

The firm has no standard pitch. "The first meeting is different with every client," Roth says. "We do not get questions like, 'When can I afford to retire?' or 'How should I save for college?' We're hired for our investment expertise, then they keep us for the other stuff." The other stuff addresses the needs of wealthy families, having to do with estate planning and family governance. "We spend a lot of time with parents and kids on learning about wealth," Roth says. "But we're not therapists. We don't ask, 'Did the other kids in school make fun of you?'"

If a client needs bill-paying services, BBR is willing to hire a book-keeper for him, but the firm doesn't probe into clients' lives or do what many firms call life planning. The more sensitive questions are typically raised by the clients. "A client will tell us that he spent $2 million last year, and he thinks that's way too much money," Roth says. "So we'll sit down and look at what he spent it on. Was it frivolous? Was it a long-time dream like starting an art studio? We can't impose our standards for what might constitute a lot of money on our clients," Roth says.

Each client is assigned a relationship manager, and the client can ask any question he likes. BBR has a staff of fifteen. All employees are encouraged to get a chartered financial analyst (CFA) designation. Although the BBR partners don't have insurance licenses, broker's licenses, or law degrees, they lead a year-end meeting with the client's accountant, attorney, and other advisers. In mid-2002, BBR hired a chief operating officer, who is a Harvard M.B.A.

The firm customizes each account to that client's needs. For instance, Roth says, a manager might build an S&P 500 position around a stock the client holds. The firm uses ten or eleven strategies—such as high risk, high return; high yield; low risk, stable return—rather than asset classes. BBR charges an incentive-based retainer. "A client should know that we will make more money if they make more money," he says.

Although the business is labor intensive, it's not capital intensive, so the partners did not need to write a business plan for investors in order to raise capital. "We went through the five-year numbers in the first year," Roth says. BBR's goal is to add four to five new families a year and to grow slowly. The best way to get the kind of clients the firm wants is by word of mouth, and, of course, the best way to get word-of-mouth referrals is by treating clients well.

One thing that sets the firm apart is its mailings to customers. Rather than a monthly newsletter that announces things like "Evan's wife just had a baby boy," BBR sends clients articles that the partners consider thought-provoking, along with a little summary. One month it was a study by Dean Baker of the Center for Economic and Policy Research titled, "The Run-up in Home Prices: Is It Real or Is It Another Bubble?" Baker argued for the bubble, noting that there's a strong long-term connection between the rise in the value of homes and inflation and that traditionally they rise in tandem. But home purchase prices rose nearly 30 percent more than the rate of inflation during the past seven years, which means they're likely to drop. Another article, this one by Mark Kramer, chairman of the Center for Effective Philanthropy, titled "Strategic Confusion," argued that the majority of philanthropic foundations in the United States today fail to act strategically in creating the most value for society with the resources they have at their disposal, because they scatter their funding too broadly and pay too little attention to measuring the results of the activities they fund. The article outlines the steps necessary to build a successful, effective foundation.

As Roth says, "You are your roots and that's evident among successful planners. Some of them no doubt visit clients in the hospital and stop in for a cup of coffee when a client is feeling down. That's one practice model. BBR is in a different place. "Clients know we're not roofers or dog walkers," Roth says. "They know what we do." They serve clients who expect Wall Street expertise but are happy to have an extra dollop of service and a trained eye to look over all their investments with tax and estate planning in mind.

— ❧ ❧ ❧ —

Chapter Eight

The Regional Firm

ONCE WORKED ON a project for the American Institute of Certified Public Accountants, where I learned about its various types of member firms. At that time, of course, the Big Eight were among them, but others were members of a relatively new group, the Personal Financial Planning Division of the American Institute of Certified Public Accountants (AICPA). In the midsize range were the Group B firms. They were not as large as the Big Eight, but they were not small financial planning firms either. Most of them were regional accounting firms, and many were probably the best-known accounting firms in their particular area, whether it was Minneapolis, Minnesota; Atlanta; or Portland, Oregon. Many clients preferred a company from Group B to a national firm, simply because it was local.

A decade ago, many of the top financial advisers began to emulate accounting firms and law firms, particularly in terms of their professionalism and standards. For example, the exam for the certified financial planner designation was updated and rewritten to create a greater barrier to entry into the profession, making it more like the respected CPA exam and the state bar exam. Planners have certainly succeeded in raising the bar in all aspects of the financial planning field. And some of them have also chosen to actually build a firm that resembles the model for a law or CPA firm. By that I mean they've standardized their procedures, recruited bright young people out of college, developed a growth track for these professionals, and worked hard to make certain that their financial advisory practices don't rely on any one personality. When Budros & Ruhlin, a financial planning firm in Columbus, Ohio, for example, brought in Dan Roe as a third partner, the firm mandated that clients work with each of the partners in turn for their regularly scheduled meetings. Clients are not permitted to say, "I'll work only with Peggy [Ruhlin]," or "I'll work only with Jim [Budros]." Budros & Ruhlin believes that standardizing procedures and making certain that each partner knows the details of each client's financial plan are good for the client and good for the firm.

Certainly, a book about successful models for financial planning firms would be incomplete without a discussion of this type of firm. Budros & Ruhlin appears on every list of best-managed firms, and I don't want to leave them off mine. Still, it's difficult to assign a name to such an elusive and varied model. Mark Tibergien at Moss Adams calls them regional firms because they're dominant players and sometimes even household names in a certain geographical area. Jim Budros, for instance, reviews restaurants for Ohio Public Radio in his weekly program, *Table Hopping*, and Peggy Ruhlin did a financial-commentary program on National Public Radio. She is also former president of the International Association for Financial Planning (IAFP) and a regular at the most exclusive planning confabs.

Another firm that fits into the regional group is Sullivan, Bruyette, Speros & Blayney, a growing financial advisory firm in McLean, Virginia, which serves the capital beltway and Washington, D.C., area. This firm is committed to growth and has a plan for it.

The characteristics of the regional model apply to many financial planning firms. One firm that I considered including with this group is Lee Financial in Dallas. Like the planners in regional firms, Richie Lee has built his practice into a business and is a major advocate of others' doing so. But Lee is too nontraditional to belong anywhere but with the mavericks.

Still, I recognize that the model under which I place a particular firm is sometimes arbitrary. And perhaps the regional group has more than its share of strange bedfellows. That's because there are a couple of firms I simply couldn't leave out of the book, and the regional model seems as good a place as any to put them. One is Kochis Fitz

Tracy Fitzhugh & Gott in San Francisco. The firm specializes in comprehensive financial planning for executives and in executive-compensation issues. The firm has a high profile in the Bay Area and is often hired by corporations to do planning for its executives. In dealing with stock options and other compensation issues, the firm has few rivals. It's also dedicated to growth and to developing a structure that can facilitate it.

As is the case with most planning firms, the backgrounds of the financial advisers in the regional category greatly influenced the type of firm they built. Perhaps it's no coincidence that the founders of each of these firms had links to the accounting business. Greg Sullivan and Jim Bruyette, for instance, worked as CPAs for one of the big accounting firms before they morphed into planners; Peggy Ruhlin, too, trained as a CPA. Although Kochis is not a CPA, he is a lawyer and an M.B.A., and he headed the personal financial planning practice at both Deloitte & Touche and the Bank of America Executive Financial Consulting Group.

So it doesn't surprise me that when these three firms plotted their growth strategies, they thought in terms of succession planning, recruitment, and staff development. These planners consider succession a major issue. They wanted to build a company—a business that has value and can be sold—one that would outlast them and continue to serve clients. Indeed, they believe that planners who don't plan for succession are shirking their responsibility to clients. Planners with other business models often have the same goal, but for the regional firm, it's a clear priority.

Whatever else the planners in regional firms have in common, they share the desire to build a company that will serve clients and then to develop procedures that can be standardized so that new recruits can learn the ropes. Charles Haines had much the same goal in mind when he assigned the newest employee to write a procedures manual and then had all subsequent new hires add steps to it. A procedures manual, or training manual, for each of these three regional advisory firms would no doubt look quite different. But the fact that advisers are beginning to write them demonstrates a certain maturity—perhaps even a coming of age.

— ❧ ❧ ❧ —

Eleanor Blayney: Getting There From Here

ONE OF MY FAVORITE and most reliable sources of information on financial planning issues is Eleanor Blayney, director of portfolio management at Sullivan, Bruyette, Speros & Blayney in McLean, Virginia. Blayney—who has an M.B.A. from the University of Chicago and is plenty well equipped to chat about alphas and betas, passive management, and suitable benchmarks—is perhaps best known in the business for her thoughtful presentations on investing and measuring risk. But some of my favorite discussions with her have been about personal stuff like her majors in English and French literature at Mount Holyoke and Cambridge University, her trip to visit her daughter in Russia, her tastes in writing and painting and films, her spinning classes at the gym, and the things she may do in the next phase of her life.

In some ways, Blayney is the ideal planner—hard-headed and unyielding about investment goals and proper portfolio diversification but concerned about a diversified life as well. When I called her in early 2003, we talked about the studies on value stocks by Eugene Fama and Kenneth French and Blayney's belief that the term "value" needs to be redefined because it's becoming indistinguishable from growth. Then we talked about her financial planning firm, which I like to use as a good example of a regional model because of the way it began and the deliberate way the partners have planned its growth.

Two of the partners, Greg Sullivan and Jim Bruyette, worked together at one of the big audit firms when they were brand-new CPAs in the early 1980s. Each went out on his own to do financial planning: Sullivan teamed up with Blayney, and Bruyette with Pete Speros. In the late 1980s, Sullivan and Bruyette hooked up again and talked about setting up a fee-based financial planning practice, which was a rare bird at the time but a logical idea for CPAs.

Sullivan, Bruyette, Speros & Blayney was founded in January 1991 as a fee-only planning firm with a very flat organizational structure in which the four partners did most of the work. But the firm had big ambitions from the start. "Greg [Sullivan] has always distinguished himself as a businessman rather than a planner," Blayney says. "We started thinking right from the beginning about how we would create a business."

If Blayney had to give Mark Tibergien's thirty-second elevator speech about the goals for that business, it would sound like this: "We want to become the dominant player in the Washington, D.C. regional market, the name that comes to mind when people think of planning"—or at least when the truly wealthy think of planning. As Tibergien says, a firm's model determines how it will use its resources. Sullivan, Bruyette aims at highly affluent individuals and is building a staff and structure to accommodate growth among those clients. "We've spent a lot of time moving from a fairly flat structure, much like a sole proprietorship, to creating a lot more depth in the firm," Blayney says.

Sullivan, Bruyette has organized its staff of thirty-three into groups of six teams. A team is defined as a partner supported by one or two senior planners. The partner is the relationship manager, responsible for bringing in the business and overseeing the work flow, but the bulk of the work is actually done by a senior planner assisted by an associate planner, a tax specialist, and a portfolio manager. "The team takes ownership of that client," Blayney says.

Each team has a portfolio liaison, which Blayney says has been the most difficult function to organize because most portfolios must be customized. But reporting, at least, can be standardized, and Sullivan, Bruyette uses a service that can provide reports overnight. The firm has also developed a number of planning templates that it stores in a central library. All client data are also stored and maintained on a central database. The firm is working on ways to standardize methods of retrieval, so that, for instance, a planner would be able to pull out every client who might be subject to the alternative minimum tax (AMT) in the current year—something helpful to know because there are certain types of municipal bonds (private-activity bonds, for example) that people subject to the AMT shouldn't own.

Each team should be able to handle one hundred clients, Blayney says. But eventually, as the firm grows larger, it will need to develop new teams, most likely as offshoots of the existing teams. "We've defined what's expected at each level in terms of mastery of different types of planning," Blayney says, so that some staff members are designated as administrators, some as planners-in-training, some as associate planners, and some as senior planners. Developing a planner to the point at which he can consult with a client "so that the buck stops there," says Blayney, takes a long time. But one of the firm's senior planners is already autonomous and directing her own team.

Although the team approach works well in managing the overall client load, "a team can become like a silo of people with no cross-fertilization," Blayney says. So the firm has developed ways to get people talking horizontally and to showcase employees who come up with novel ideas and to share those ideas with members of other teams.

For firms like Sullivan, Bruyette that want to grow, recruiting the kind of financial planners who can generate such ideas has been a major problem. Five years ago, when I wrote *Best Practices for Financial Advisors,* planners were experimenting with methods of identifying good hires. Charlie Haines in Birmingham, Alabama, had set up a scholarship/internship program at the University of Alabama, which he hoped might bring him smart prospects. Some advisers claimed that CPAs made better planners; others said that people skills were critical and that those skills were hard to identify in an interview. Whatever the method preferred, none is foolproof. "And a bad hire costs a lot," Blayney says, "because you leave it far too long." So the firm is trying to "be smarter about screening and testing," to find out how the candidate's work style fits with those of the other members of the practice. "You can narrow the search down to two highly talented people, but you have to decide which one is compatible with your style," she says.

Still, Sullivan, Bruyette tries to think out-of-the-box to find solutions to the problem, and it has been willing to experiment with some unlikely hires. In fact, it has had good luck with smart, curious people with no training whatsoever in financial planning. The firm not long ago was willing to gamble on a college graduate who was a very bright techie who wanted to learn about financial planning. "It quickly became clear that his talent was in helping us grow more efficient with technology rather than in working with clients," Blayney says. "He is the better-faster-cheaper master, and we are his students. He is continually looking to find patterns of inefficiency."

Blayney finds some of the best hires are really smart kids right out of college, with an interest in financial planning. They're typically economics or math or finance majors, but "I'm not likely to turn down an English major," Blayney says, "because that's what I was." Most graduates who choose to work for the firm do it because they like the culture. She says it's not unusual to come in on the weekends and find a bunch of twenty-somethings working on a client project—and having fun doing it.

Another group that has become a resource pool are people who have professional experience but not in financial planning. "There are a couple of stars here who've had other careers and then decided to retool," she says. "They've got mileage, and a little wisdom and street smarts can be so valuable."

I've seen fresh perspectives work well in journalism too. Reporters who write for *Institutional Investor* magazine, which covers Wall Street, have to interview analysts, investment bankers, and pension managers for stories about the most arcane products imaginable. When I was a staff writer for the magazine, the publisher at the time, Gilbert Kaplan, insisted on hiring bright liberal arts majors because he'd found that someone with curiosity who knew how to write turned out a much better story than someone who knew how to create a serial zero-coupon bond but couldn't describe it in lay terms.

In addition to bringing in new talent—wherever the firm may find it—Sullivan, Bruyette plans to grow through acquisition. Margaret Welch, a planner whom Blayney has known for a long time, brought her practice into the firm two years ago and became the fifth managing partner. "We want to grow both organically and by acquisition," Blayney says. "With growth, you either passively accept how it happens to you or you embrace it and channel it."

However the firm's growth is channeled, critical to that growth is achieving a balance between the steps that can be standardized in serving clients and those that must be customized. "We have to continually explore the tension between those two," Blayney says. "We're not making pizzas."

But they do help a client make a life, although Blayney seems to shy away from embracing life planning. "We hear about people's hopes and dreams and phobias," she says. "We're well experienced but not well trained. We have not formalized this or held ourselves out as coaches." Blayney believes a firm needs a psychologist to get into that arena.

Blayney describes the firm as a generalist rather than a specialist. "We're smart on options and retirement planning," she says, "but for many clients it's the breadth of expertise rather than the depth that's appealing."

As for the future, the firm continues to look at mergers and acquisitions, and like other successful firms, it has been approached by many people with different ideas. Blayney is not convinced of the wisdom of a national roll up. "We're the first generation of this profession," she says. "The profession has only come into visibility in the last fifteen years, and it was initially populated by people who came from other disciplines." She thinks there will be more consolidation but that it will come because veterans will want to retire.

Whatever happens, says Blayney, Sullivan, Bruyette will be a survivor. "Whether it's to be a survival of the biggest or the fittest, I think we'll be there." But there is more than one definition of dominance; one is from the consumer's point of view and the other is the industry's view of a firm. "Within the industry, we're seen as one of the most successful, dominant firms," she says. "But dominance to us is when someone asks, 'Where will you go for financial advice?' and the response lists our name in the top three. We're not there yet."

The firm is certainly headed in that direction.

— 茶 茶 茶 —

Tim Kochis: Executive Decisions

TIM KOCHIS LOOKS more like a corporate executive than a financial planner. Dapper is the word that comes to mind. And well-spoken. When Kochis appeared with me on a panel about the future of financial planning a couple of years ago in Lake Tahoe, he was wearing a stunning Armani jacket, a gift from his wife. He's someone who gets noticed. Factor in his experience and expertise and the success of his planning firm, and it's clear that there's even more to him than meets the eye.

Kochis, a Midwesterner who longed to be a Californian, went to high school in Chicago, then went to Marquette University. He has a law degree from the University of Michigan and an M.B.A. from the University of Chicago. I first met Kochis when I was writing a column for the *New York Times* and he was head of personal financial planning at Deloitte, Haskins & Sells. Kochis came to Deloitte from a management position at Bank of America, having taken much of the staff with him when Bank of America decided to get out of the personal-advice business.

Kochis didn't start out with notions of blazing any trails in personal financial planning. With a brand-new law degree and no clear idea of what he wanted to do, he "fell into" the financial advisory business when Continental Bank was hiring law grads in the early 1970s. "We were all about the same age and just making up the job as we went along," he says. Many of his colleagues have stuck with the profession, too, like Wally Head, who is now president and chief operating officer with the Family Office Exchange in Chicago, a group that gives advice to family offices.

From Continental Bank, Kochis went to Hewitt Associates, a leading employee-benefits consulting firm, also based in Chicago, where he was a compensation consultant. In 1979, his first marriage was ending and he decided it was time to make his move to California for a fresh start. Kochis joined Bank of America in San Francisco, where he was in charge of the Executive Financial Counseling Group. Those were the days when everyone was thinking big and planning for the financial supermarkets they expected to build at Sears/Dean Witter, for example, or Shearson/American Express.

Kochis was part of that wave, supervising forty-six people at Bank of America. One of them, a junior staff member named Linda Fitz, had been in the first graduating class of the UCLA financial planning certificate program that Kochis had helped to establish at the University of California.

Then in 1985, Bank of America decided it had had its fill of executive counseling and that it was time to bail out of the business. "Several of us started shopping ourselves around to the large accounting firms," Kochis says. Kochis and Fitz joined the Deloitte, Haskins & Sells office in San Francisco. "We formed the nucleus of the personal financial planning practice at Deloitte," Kochis says, and he was named national director of personal financial planning. Over the course of six years, they built the business and designed the tools and software they needed for it. "We brought a whole degree of energy and sophistication that had not been there before," says Kochis.

By 1991 it became clear that it would be very difficult to have the kind of personal financial planning practice Kochis wanted at what was first and foremost an accounting firm. "They were so focused on their mainline business that it was impossible for a small business like ours to get any traction," he says. When Deloitte merged with Touche Ross to become Deloitte & Touche, Kochis was named national director of financial planning for both firms, but, he says, "it became obvious that we wouldn't get the resources we needed to build our business. I decided to quit beating my head against the wall and start my own practice." Fitz joined him.

Kochis's experience and his law background served him well in getting things started. He and Fitz made an offer to give Deloitte a small royalty on any business they took with them in exchange for Deloitte's agreement not to object. The new firm, Kochis Fitz, also got right of first refusal on any business Deloitte planned to do using help from outside the firm. "That was an important message for us to send clients," Kochis says, "that we were leaving on good terms." Kochis also arranged to take all the software and collateral materials that he'd helped develop for Deloitte in exchange for a token payment.

"It showed how they little they valued the practice," Kochis says. "For me, it was important to be able to carry all this stuff with us that we'd developed, and I think they were just as happy to see it go."

Kochis and Fitz launched the firm with just the two principals and a secretary. "All decisions were made by the two of us, and we were successful right out of the box because we brought the clients with us and had good referrals," says Kochis. And Kochis Fitz knew it wanted to be in the discretionary investment management business. Clients at Deloitte had been asking Kochis for years to take over their investments, but he couldn't do it at the accounting firm. "Now we wanted the ability to charge investment management fees," Kochis says. The two acquired a small investment management firm and with it a registered investment adviser, giving the principal a share in their business. But after a year or so, Kochis Fitz bought out the former owner.

The firm also needed more help. Kochis knew people from Deloitte whose work he admired. But his agreement included the provision that he wouldn't poach any of its employees for one year. He went to Deloitte and was able to get approval to hire Tom Tracy, a tax accountant at Deloitte who had worked with Kochis's financial planning team.

Kochis Fitz was formed as a C corporation and then became an S corporation, with shares of stock that could be bought and sold. From the beginning, Kochis and Fitz wanted to create the opportunity for new partners to buy into the firm as soon as they came on board. Both Kochis and Fitz are in their early fifties; neither has children. "So we didn't have the same kind of motivations that some other planning firms have to pass the business on to children," he says. "Our child was the business, and we put the viability of the business first so we wanted to make it easy for talented people to come on and have a long-term stake. We went out of the way to create a business where the big payoff was not in the short term but where new partners could build equity in the firm." Kacy Gott and Michael Fitzhugh joined Kochis from Deloitte as well, and in 1998 the firm became Kochis Fitz Tracy Fitzhugh & Gott.

Whatever Kochis's plans may have been starting out, one of the industry's top planners is a fair enough description of who he is now. What's more, his broad experience working for both large institutional firms and as an independent adviser has given him a very different view of the future of the business of financial planning than the one held by Mark Hurley at Undiscovered Managers. Kochis dismisses Hurley's idea that in ten years a small group of very large firms will dominate the industry. "I think five or ten years from now, we will still see mostly small, independent firms," he says. "I've heard this one-stop shopping idea over and over again. The idea is meritorious, but it doesn't happen," he says. Big companies have lots of resources. "But they have short attention spans," Kochis says. "They have a bad quarter or two and all bets are off. They don't consistently and reliably apply their resources." What's more, he says, wealthy individuals expect the "best of breed" for providing what they need. They want independent advisers who don't put together or sell proprietary products and who are willing to customize plans for them. From the start, Kochis was confident he could do that.

So it doesn't surprise me that when Kochis decided to set up shop in 1991, he created a white-shoe firm, where 80 percent of the clients are corporate executives, and that he did it in San Francisco, his favorite city. Like other successful planners, Kochis has combined his skills and passions to create the type of practice that suits him. Kochis Fitz manages $700 million for 260 clients with a staff of twenty-three and the services of a subcontractor for bookkeeping. The firm's goal is to provide unparalleled service to clients of high net worth and to create a firm big enough to provide value for the present owners and to create value for the next generation of owners. The firm emulates an accounting or a law firm as its model for a business that will continue to serve clients when one generation exits and another takes its place.

To achieve those goals for value and service, the firm must continue to grow, and that's happening on schedule, despite the difficult market in these early years of the twenty-first century. The average client has a portfolio of about $3 million, and the firm picked up several new clients in 2002, each with a portfolio of $10 million or more. So Kochis says he's confident that the firm can meet its goals without being acquired or acquiring other firms. That said, Kochis has been approached by companies with a wide range of proposals: some want to buy the firm; others, to invest in it; still others hoped he'd consider joining in to help form a national consortium. "I think everyone is keeping all his options open," he says. "We're still talking to people about various possibilities, but we're passive and responsive. We think we can be as successful as we want to be without combining with anyone."

Because Kochis Fitz has a depth of knowledge in restricted stock and employee stock options, the firm is often hired by corporations to serve its top executives, as well as by individuals. And Kochis acknowledges that some client firms with executives around the country might find a national firm a more attractive choice for financial planning. But he's not convinced it's necessary for success. "The affluent market demands a customized approach," he says." If a national firm permits customization, it immediately runs into quality-control problems." Kochis says his competition is Northern Trust, Bessemer Trust, and U.S. Trust. And he feels confident that his firm can compete with them. "We're local and local only," he says. "We're owned by people who operate the firm and small enough to be extremely responsive."

But the firm's responsiveness has its limits—namely when it comes to life planning and personal services. The firm does not babysit its clients, says Kochis. "Our clients are not whiney. They don't say, 'How come you don't get me tickets to the opera?'" Kochis thinks financial advisory firms that get that personally involved with clients diffuse their energy and lose their financial optimization and ability to focus on the most important issues. "It's clearly not our style," he says. "If a client were in a jam and wanted us to arrange for someone to pick him up at the airport because his arrangements fell through, we'd probably do that," Kochis says. "But our clients don't feel they need that kind of help from us."

When it comes to addressing clients' financial issues, however, few problems are out of bounds. "Many of our clients change career positions frequently," says Kochis, "and we help them make transitions and negotiate contract terms with their attorneys." The firm also works with clients' children to help them deal with the money they will inherit. "But we have not made a distinct practice area out of that," he says. One benefit that has resulted from keeping personal involvement to a minimum is that the firm tends to retain clients even in situations as sensitive as divorce. Kochis tells both partners, "We're happy to continue to work with both of you and make the best of this situation." In every case, both partners have remained clients of the firm.

Given Kochis Fitz's acknowledged strengths, some would say that it's a niche firm, specializing in executive financial planning and executive compensation. But it fits equally well into the regional category because 90 percent of its clients are in the Bay Area, where the firm has such a high profile with local corporations. Definitions aside, the important question is how well the business works. Kochis's perspective on models comes from having worked as a financial adviser for so many large companies that no longer offer financial advice. And he's betting that his firm's model—a top-notch regional firm that has a specialty in executive compensation and is willing to customize planning for each client—is a good long-term strategy.

The approach has worked well so far, but Kochis Fitz doesn't take the future for granted. The firm hired a full-time director to develop a marketing strategy. The marketing director has been working to develop relationships with attorneys who take companies public, spreading the word that Kochis Fitz is the place for their clients to get financial advice. "If we're not your first call," the director tells the attorneys he visits, "we should be."

— ❧ ❧ ❧ —

Peggy Ruhlin: Tight Ships and Smooth Sailing

JIM BUDROS IS PASSIONATE about cooking. His culinary skills have earned him a number of awards, and he often appears on television, one time to prepare an original lobster and scallop recipe with the late Craig Claiborne, who was then food editor of the *New York Times*. Budros brings the same zest to financial planning that he does to cooking, armed with similarly top-notch skills in interacting with clients. In the recipe for his firm's professional success, though, the key ingredient has been Peggy Ruhlin, a CPA with a knack for running a business. The two teamed up back in 1987.

Budros & Ruhlin, in Columbus, Ohio, gets kudos from all types of management consultants for being one of the best-managed financial advisory firms in the country. Certainly, it's one of the most organized and efficient, managing, as of 2003, $475 million for 287 clients in central Ohio. The firm operates out of one office and has four principals, two senior planners, and five planners—all of whom have earned the certified financial planner designation. Each client is assigned to one of the seven planners, so that each planner has 30 to 45 clients. Each time a client comes in, he meets with the same planner, and one of the four principals—a different one each time—sits in on the meeting. The firm also employs four assistant planners, so that each of the senior planners has an assistant of his own and the five planners on the next level share the other two. The firm has a four-person data-management team; an office manager; a receptionist; an executive assistant, who does typing and dictation for the principals; a client-services coordinator, who schedules client meetings; and an investment specialist.

The firm's efficiency was evident when I called Ruhlin for a scheduled telephone interview. Budros was spending a couple of weeks in France and one of the other principals was out with a sick child, so Ruhlin was pinch-hitting on client meetings for the two absent principals as well as running the show. But she still found time for a leisurely phone conversation about the firm's roots. Indeed, whenever I call Budros & Ruhlin, I get the impression that everyone there is very busy but never in a frenzy.

Ruhlin says the precedent for how smoothly the organization runs was set early on. The partners started off with all their paperwork in place from day one and then carefully built an infrastructure and standardized procedures so that no one person would be indispensable. Indeed, every step in the evolution of Budros & Ruhlin seems to have been taken with care.

Budros spent the early part of his career working in the trust department of a bank, after which he set up a fee-only planning firm with a partner in the early 1980s. Ruhlin, a CPA, was doing business and retirement planning for a small accounting firm that specialized in health care professionals, mainly dentists. Budros's firm was doing the financial planning for many of Ruhlin's clients. Ruhlin was intrigued by financial planning and wrote to the College of Financial Planning in Denver, asking for information. When she received it, she felt it was just what she'd been looking for all her life: She could help people plan their future, meet goals, and achieve success. Accounting had become dissatisfying to her because it was about looking back. "I tried to focus on tax planning and make it more forward looking," she says, "but it was always historical." Financial planning, she thought, would satisfy her appetite for number crunching and, in addition, she'd be able to "dream and scheme and help make things happen for people."

Ruhlin got her CFP designation, and Budros asked if she would consider joining his firm. At the time, Ruhlin's husband had been named chief executive officer of a company in Akron. Their daughter was in high school in Columbus, and Ruhlin and her daughter had decided not to relocate for two years until the girl finished. But Ruhlin told Budros and his partner that her future was up in the air. Before she joined the firm, she requested a business plan and a buy-out agreement. By touching these bases, Ruhlin says, her relationship with the firm started off on a solid, professional footing. They put together a buy/sell agreement. Ruhlin negotiated from the perspective of a partner who might be leaving in two years, whereas Budros and his partner negotiated from the perspective of partners who would be staying on, which, Ruhlin says, made it a fair deal. She became a one-third owner. "It worked so well," Ruhlin says. "It was a textbook case."

As it turned out, Ruhlin's husband wasn't happy in Akron and he moved back to Columbus. Ruhlin, though, was happy at the new firm. But Budros's original partner wasn't. He ended up leaving, but his departure was made easy by the buy/sell agreement already in place. In 1991, the firm became Budros & Ruhlin. "I consider myself so lucky to have found this profession when I did," Ruhlin says. "Accounting was starting to go down the drain, and I got in on the ground floor of the financial planning boom."

Budros and Ruhlin, who are members of the National Association of Personal Financial Advisors (NAPFA), knew from the beginning that they didn't want theirs to be the small, cozy type of firm that many NAPFA members choose to run out of their homes. "We wanted to be large because we get a lot of pleasure out of training new financial planners," says Ruhlin, "and because we wanted to work with bigger clients." The two also wanted to have a life outside the office. Ruhlin says she never takes work home or comes in on weekends. In fact, when the principals of the firm met recently with the Boston Consulting Group, the BCG consultants said they were surprised to see what balanced and well-rounded lives the principals lived.

Like most firms, Budros & Ruhlin has evolved over the past decade. Initially the fee-only firm did almost no investment management. When it first began managing assets, it decided to charge a fee only on the assets it managed and not, for example, on money held in a 401(k) plan. But they realized that assets that were not under the firm's direct management could be more troublesome than those that were. So they began basing their fees on total assets.

The firm has two types of clients. The first—about 25 percent of the clientele—uses Budros & Ruhlin only for investment management. Some of these clients are private foundations; others are longtime clients who don't meet the firm's minimum for assets under management. All of the clients in this group pay fees based on assets under management. The remaining 75 percent of the firm's clients pay for both financial planning and investment management. "We charge this group a onetime financial planning fee, and then every asset, including 401(k) money, is included in tallying the separate asset management fee, which has a $10,000 minimum," Ruhlin says.

The financial planning fee is a lump-sum charge that's billed over the first two years. So a client with a $15,000 fee will be billed $7,500 each year for the first two years. In the third year, the client pays only the assets-under-management fee.

Crucial to the firm's growth has been the recruitment of new planners. When I talked to Ruhlin about recruitment a couple of years ago, she told me how difficult it was to find good candidates. The firm has largely solved that by recruiting planners right out of college financial planning programs, typically Ohio State's, and then training them at the firm. "Anybody we get in here we're going to have to teach and train anyway," Ruhlin says. "So we're looking for someone who's got enough brains to pick this up but also some personality and the right outlook." Ruhlin says she wants people with a "concierge attitude," who look for things they can do to help the clients and the planners they work with.

Hiring still presents challenges, Ruhlin says. She would often call a professor in the financial planning department at Ohio State to inquire about candidates, until she learned that he gives everyone the same great recommendation. Now, she has started using a screen called the Kolbe Index, which bears some resemblance to the Meyers-Briggs Type Indicator. The Kolbe measures analytical and creative skills. Ruhlin asked her best assistant planner to take the test and then used her score as "the profile of a great assistant planner."

Budros & Ruhlin did manage to double the number of principals in the firm smoothly enough, although there have been a few bumps along the way. In the early 1990s, a planner telephoned Ruhlin "out of the blue," saying he remembered her from financial planning courses and wanted to join the firm. "We weren't looking to add a principal, but we hired him and the clients accepted him," Ruhlin says. "At the end of two years, we told him it was time to talk about a buy-in and explained our formula and gave him an offering letter." But he wasn't interested. "He started his own company," Ruhlin says. "I was heartbroken when he left the firm; I thought we'd never again find someone we liked."

Soon after, Dan Roe, a planner from Cincinnati, called and inquired about joining the firm. Ruhlin knew him from IAFP, where she had been president, and she liked him. Ruhlin and Budros hired him in April 1996 and had Mark Tibergien appraise the firm, so that they could work out a five-year phase-in of Roe's compensation. In year one, he would get a certain percentage of what Budros and Ruhlin got, and that percentage would increase yearly thereafter until his compensation was on a par with theirs. Ruhlin says they encouraged him to get his own attorney and appraiser, but he was happy with the deal proposed. He became a one-third owner under their buy-sell agreement in January 1999.

Having three principals changed the balance in the firm, Ruhlin says. "Jim and I agreed on every major thing. That is not to say we never argued, but before Dan came, we hardly ever disagreed. When Dan became a partner, the dynamic definitely changed, because it was often two against one." Fortunately, it was not always the same two on one side, Ruhlin says. But resolutions required more compromise.

Two years ago, the firm hired a fourth principal, John Schuman, an attorney and CPA, who had been doing high-level estate and tax planning for business owners at Deloitte & Touche. The firm also has an investment specialist, who takes care of all the investment-only clients. From the start, the principals have made a point of taking turns meeting with all the clients. "We did it to institutionalize the business," Ruhlin says. Some clients don't like it. Some women prefer Ruhlin; some older clients prefer Budros; and some younger people like Roe. "But the clients don't get the benefit of all we have to offer if they meet with only one of us," Ruhlin says. "We each have different strengths."

And when it comes to strengths, Ruhlin is nothing if not organized. Although she insists that the other partners are "the big, wild thinkers," one can't help but sense that she holds things together. One of her innovations was to hire a consultant, Leigh H. Bailey, founder of the Bailey Consulting Group in Minneapolis, Minnesota, to meet with the principals off-site three times a year. Ruhlin had gotten to know Bailey when she was president of the IAFP and the group was competing with the Institute of Certified Financial Planners (ICFP) to attract members. Ruhlin was impressed with the way Bailey worked with the IAFP and wanted to hire him to help Budros & Ruhlin with its strategic planning. "We knew we couldn't have strategic-planning meetings on our own because we wouldn't get anything done," Ruhlin says. Bailey helps them set goals and develop a five-year plan and then makes sure that they're progressing toward the goals, that they're crossing things off the list.

Three years ago, as Budros, Ruhlin, and Roe prepared for one of those meetings, they felt they had a problem in managing the operations of the firm, and one of the items on the meeting agenda was the possibility of hiring a chief operating officer. "No one was minding the store and making decisions," Ruhlin says. "Jim and Dan are total extroverts. They hate the mundane stuff of running a business. All they want to do is meet with clients all day long."

So the three talked at the meeting about hiring a COO. But that, Roe finally told them, would happen "over his dead body," Ruhlin says. "He refused to hire someone he didn't know and pay them $200,000 a year." Instead, Roe suggested that Ruhlin do it. She agreed to sleep on it but came back the next day and turned them down. Undeterred, the others persuaded her to give it a try. "I said I would commit only for two years, and I made them sign an agreement," she says. If Ruhlin were to operate as managing partner, the firm needed a fourth principal, and Schuman was hired in June 2001. Ruhlin became the administrator that October, with a two-year commitment through October 2003. During those two years, she has been responsible for hiring people, keeping marketing materials up to date, overseeing compliance, and implementing strategic planning. Early in 2003, she spent time on the audit the Securities and Exchange Commission was conducting.

In February 2003, when I talked with Ruhlin, she was eager to get back into client rotation but trying to keep an open mind. She agrees that they've "gotten a lot of things marked off the to-do list," and there's a good chance she may be signing on for another term as COO.

Negotiations aside, one can't help but notice the remarkable teamwork at Budros & Ruhlin. Hiring an objective "referee" has certainly made it even stronger. "Working with Leigh [Bailey] is expensive, and we have to ask each other if it's worth it," Ruhlin says. The answer so far has been yes. Building a firm requires a set of tools altogether different from the skills in play in financial planning. Budros & Ruhlin is one firm that's managed to acquire both.

— ✿ ✿ ✿ —

C h a p t e r **9** *N i n e*

The Sole Practitioner

THE PLAN OF CHOICE for most businesses is to start small and grow big, the way Hewlett-Packard outgrew its California garage. That's the accepted model of success. The idea of staying small smacks of failure, and certainly the notion of a sole practitioner juggling all the balls in any kind of practice appears as dated as the country doctor making his rounds. These assumptions are just as widely held among financial advisers. Financial planning conferences repeatedly focus educational sessions on how to grow your practice, recruit and train people, and plan for succession, because these are the generally recognized hallmarks of a successful planning practice.

But some planners have no intention of giving their attention to anything associated with expansion plans or bigger staffs. They've built a firm that suits their lifestyle and provides satisfying work. They don't want to manage people; they want to work with clients. They don't want to delegate responsibilities for taking care of the client; they want to take care of the client themselves. Their business model has more in common with a psychologist's or therapist's practice than with any corporation. But for some reason, the idea of being a sole practitioner is a controversial one at financial planning get-togethers. Indeed, among planners who've built larger businesses, there are some who argue that sole practitioners have overlooked their biggest responsibility: Taking care of clients. How can such a planner claim to be taking care of clients, they point out, when the clients would be out in the cold if the adviser were to get hit by a truck or to retire. What's more, a planner who doesn't build his business will have no value to take from it later on.

These arguments seem to make sense. But I don't buy them. Most people who set up shop for themselves do so because they don't like bureaucracy and inefficiency and buck passing. They want a successful business, but they define success largely in terms of how well the business matches their personal style. Why should a practitioner who chooses an independent lifestyle and wants to do his own work be pressed into the business-building mold?

I relate to sole practitioners in terms of the satisfaction of doing things your own way and keeping a healthy distance from red tape and routine. I spent a decade working on newspaper staffs as a reporter. Each time I was asked to become business editor or desk chief, I moved on to another newspaper. I didn't want to supervise people who'd be doing the reporting and writing, partly because I'd be a terrible supervisor and partly because I wanted to report and write. Finally, I went to a magazine, reasoning that a magazine wouldn't be similarly inclined to "promote" good writers into bad supervisors. Of course, I was wrong, and I saw that the only way I could remain a writer was to work for myself, which I did, beginning in 1984.

But the same question comes up again from time to time. When I turn down assignments because I'm too busy, people often press me to take them on anyway. "Why don't you just hire some junior people to research and write?" I'm asked. "Then you could put your name on it and build a business. You would make more money and have something to sell."

Well, that's exactly what I don't want. I don't want to build a business. I don't want to hire people or train people or supervise them or teach them how to report and write. I also reserve the right to occasionally indulge my impatient and cranky moods, and to do that guilt-free, I have to work for myself.

Of course, I realize that my situation is different from that of a financial planner. If I got hit by a truck someday, my clients wouldn't suffer. They certainly wouldn't lose a key person in their lives who watches over all their critical financial details. But potential losses must be weighed against real ones. And I would argue that my clients would lose something now if I hired recent college grads to report and write the stories I'm assigned. The reason I'm asked to write these stories has a lot to do with the fact that I have many years of experience. What kind of a story would I be delivering if it were written by someone whose historical perspective on business goes back about as far as the Clinton Administration?

I'm not suggesting that financial planners who decide to build a business by recruiting and training people are giving their clients short shrift. But people tend to build the type of business that suits them and then attract the type of clients who are in turn comfortable with that business model. Financial advisers often bring much creative energy to acquiring and developing talented new planners. In the long run, clients reap the benefits of that creativity, no matter who ultimately conducts the meeting or puts the plan together. But the relationship the sole practitioner builds with each client is much like that of a psychotherapist and patient. Stand-ins won't work. Clients who don't like dealing with the possibility of such a critical relationship ending one day had best sign up with a different kind of planning firm. But I'll bet some clients would rather have a great planner for a dozen years than do business with one who never quite makes a connection or with a firm where they never meet the same players twice.

Choosing the sole-practitioner model is certainly not the easiest way out for an adviser. The challenges are different from those faced by planners heading up corporations, but they're just as difficult. You must be able to occasionally say no if you want to have time left over for a life. You need vacations and holidays to recharge, and you can't allow yourself to feel guilty about taking them. Also, this model may be the wrong fit for micromanagers: You're going to need help, whether it's in the office or in the form of outsourcing. You'll have to be realistic about your strengths and limitations as you assess your situation and set up a system that works for both you and your clients. The ingenuity required to address these challenges is the mark of a truly creative planner.

Still, some critics believe the sole practitioner business model lacks sophistication. That's hardly the case. A planning business that keeps its client list short doesn't necessarily mean it's one that operates out of a back bedroom or a converted garage. It's just owned by a planner who happens to prefer to operate a business model that suits his own objectives rather than those of others in the industry. Some sole practitioners, in fact, are among the most elite planners in the country.

Unconvinced? Meet Judy Shine.

— ❋ ❋ ❋ —

Judy Shine: Singular Sensation

NO MATTER HOW SMALL the group of planners that might gather for a brainstorming session, Judy Shine always seems to be among them. Her firm, Shine Investment Advisory Services in Englewood, Colorado, is an example of just how successful a sole practitioner can be.

Shine is modest about her success but vocal about her beliefs. As competition in the planning profession has grown and many planners have decided that the logical way to keep up is to grow their practices, she has consistently argued that bigger is not necessarily better. Indeed, she believes growth often turns out badly. Partnering can be dicey. Shine knows because she's tried it. "All you have to do is get a few drinks in people, and they'll tell you how much they hate their partners," she says. What's more, she points out, top professionals in many businesses practice alone. When you look at a chiropractor and he doesn't have three partners, you don't assume he's a loser, she says.

But what does it take to succeed as a sole practitioner? In Shine's case, my impression is she loves the mental gymnastics required of someone who manages large amounts of money for a large group of clients. She's plenty smart and enjoys grappling with new wrinkles in estate planning and new provisions in the tax code or even figuring out how an Internal Revenue Service private letter ruling might affect one of her clients. She's now using a traditional 60/40 ratio of equity to debt for most clients' portfolios, and for those in the highest income tax bracket, she uses real estate, the Merger Fund, bonds, PIMCO Hard Assets, and high-yield Treasury inflation-indexed securities (TIPs). In the bear market, she's kept innovations to a minimum, but she does use exchange funds, which pool stocks from different investors in order to diversify. The investors must leave the stocks in the fund for seven years. For example, she had a client put $1 million of Sun Microsystems stock into the fund, and other investors put in their own undiversified stocks. At one point, the exchange fund was down by 40 percent, but Sun was down by 95 percent.

Most important, though, Shine is a hard worker and probably someone who's convinced that no one else could take care of her clients quite the way she does. Her dedication to her clients' welfare makes her willing to go out on a limb. At the start of 2000, for instance, she told clients, "If you want to get more conservative about investing, do it now." Indeed, a sole practitioner shoulders a huge responsibility for each client's welfare. That burden is not for everyone, but Shine's good at carrying it, and such involvement offers certain satisfactions that have nothing to do with building a business. It's not surprising that Shine would seek them out, since she has at least one toe in the waters where heart meets mind. In fact, the only other profession I remember Shine expressing interest in is psychotherapy, and she continues to enjoy theology classes.

Shine got into financial planning in 1984, when she was pregnant with her son, Connor. "I started at the kitchen table back in New Jersey, working on my CFP," she says. In 1985, she and her husband moved to Denver, and Shine began writing financial plans for the New England Group when that company decided to offer financial planning. Once she gained some experience, she set up a practice with a partner, and when the partnership didn't work out, she built her own firm.

She now manages $350 million for 175 clients. A new client must have a minimum of $1 million in assets. The fee for the first million is a $10,000 retainer, which covers financial planning. She has a staff of seven support people. One is a certified financial planner; another, Shine's closest friend, works with the CFP. An office manager manages projects for her top ten clients; a "tech head" works on Centerpiece, the firm's portfolio-design software; one staffer writes financial plans; and another is an administrator. Shine also does some outsourcing, using separate-account managers and exchange-traded funds, Charles Schwab, and SEI Investments for small accounts.

Critical to her firm's success, says Shine, is how selective she has been about the clients she takes on. "I turn down a lot of business," Shine says. A sure sign of trouble is when a prospective client acts as if he can do his own planning. That's when she suggests, "It sounds as if this is something you think you can do on your own, and maybe you'd enjoy it. If it doesn't work out, come back." About half of them do. What she looks for is someone who really needs the firm, like a client who has $1 million and is clueless about what to do with it. Just before I spoke with her, in fact, Shine had met with a forty-nine-year-old woman, newly divorced and full of hurt, who had a $1.3 million settlement. "This is a perfect person for my office because she'll be safe here," Shine says.

But no matter how picky Shine is, caring for clients takes time and she has to use hers wisely. Shine's time is spent on clients and their needs rather than on staff meetings or plan writing or portfolio design. She'll tell her staff, "Here are ten people I'd like to see next week," and they'll take care of setting up appointments and doing the necessary research, thereby allowing Shine to target her own efforts more efficiently. Shine still has all of her original clients, who require only regular maintenance: She meets with clients only once or twice a year; few want or require more than that. Many prefer to communicate by e-mail. She sends performance reports once a year.

Is Shine caring for clients at the expense of building value for her firm? "Mark Hurley tells me," Shine says, "that if I get hit by a car, I've left incredible assets with no value." Shine doesn't see it that way. "I've got $1.2 million in revenues. Isn't it easier to do business the way I want and get a $1 million term policy for my kids?" She has a buy/sell agreement with another planner in Denver, who would come in and help her clients through a transition if she suddenly had to retire, she says.

But Shine doesn't see retirement coming soon; nor does she want it to. "You don't talk to a lot of people who love being retired," she says. "Really smart people get bored with being retired." Shine's view of retirement is that you "just kind of fall apart. Not only do you fail to contribute, but you become critical of everyone else."

Shine says it would be wonderful to work full throttle for perhaps another decade and then have the luxury of cutting down to four days a week and then three days a week. "Isn't that everyone's dream," she says, "to do something you love and then gradually make more time for yourself and for volunteer work and other things you want to do?" Shine says it was never her goal to become rich as a planner. "It's not a gold mine," she says. "But you can have a comfortable life and solve people's problems."

I pointed out to Shine that a study by the Financial Planning Association (FPA) in 2001 seemed to bolster Hurley's idea that firms have to get big to keep from getting poor. The study found that assets under management rose by 16.7 percent in 2001 at the typical advisory firm but that overhead expenses were up 32 percent, operating profit was down 28 percent, and net profit was down 33.5 percent. These numbers seemed to reinforce Hurley's notion that small planning firms were under intense margin pressure.

Shine disagrees. "Those are bear market numbers," she says, noting the layoffs on Wall Street. "Schwab's stock is down 80 percent and Merrill's is down 68 percent," she says. "These are supposed to be our competitors. Have you seen any of us folding?" Shine says her revenues are down. But "I'm not firing anybody. I don't know anyone in the investment advisory business who's laying people off, but firms like Janus, Schwab, and JP Morgan have gone through rounds of layoffs," she says. "If you had a personal investment adviser at one of the big Wall Street firms, chances are he's gone now." A client with a million bucks is better off going to an independent adviser who's owned his firm for twenty years than to a big Wall Street brokerage, no matter what it calls itself, Shine says.

Like Tim Kochis at Kochis Fitz, Shine doesn't believe Wall Street offers much competition to individual planners. "Corporate America is so diseased that it could never take away our business," she says. If a planner like Judy Lau or Roger Gibson or Dave Diesslin moved in next door, Shine says, she'd be worried. But competition from the big banks and brokers will never cause her to lose sleep.

Shine brushes aside the idea that sole practitioners are an endangered species. Trends come and go in the planning business, she says, but in the end, "the one-decision-maker model is a very good one when you're trying to get something done." It's the future of brokerages, she adds, that should be cause for concern. "I don't know how the brokerages are going to go on," she says. "They're going to implode." Shine cites the story of a friend of hers—let's call her Jane—who took her half-million-dollar account to Merrill Lynch. Jane liked the Merrill Lynch adviser who helped her set up her portfolio. But that adviser soon got an assistant, and because Jane was considered a client of low net worth, she was passed off to the assistant, whom she didn't like. Jane finally decided to move her money out of Merrill Lynch, but thanks to exit fees, it's costing her $18,000 to do it. "How can this be considered competition?" Shine says. "That's insulting."

Shine points out that a financial planner needs knowledge and skills in estate planning, executive compensation, and investment management. She doesn't believe that planners at any brokerage will be able to offer the depth and breadth of experience that many independent planners have acquired over twenty to thirty years. What's more, she believes the financial motivation of brokers is entirely different from that of sole practitioners like herself. In response to Hurley's argument that brokerage firms will capture clients by offering planning at a much-reduced price, Shine quips, "If I'm charging $10,000, they'd have to charge $10 to make it more attractive." That's the difference in value. And that value has Shine convinced that the sole practitioner model will play a major role in the future of financial planning.

The market crash of 2000–2002 has given investors a new perspective. They've learned a lot about whom they can't trust and they're looking now for someone they can trust. Planners like Shine, who are willing to take on risks, are sure to be found.

— 🌺 🌺 🌺 —

Chapter 10 *Ten*

The Maverick

IN ORGANIZING THE material for a book about the business models of the most successful financial planning firms in the industry, the left brain wants to convince you that you can categorize, delineate, separate, or otherwise neatly arrange these practices into mutually exclusive camps. The reality is a lot blurrier than that. Of course, some firms—like Sheryl Garrett's hourly model or Janet Briaud's niche—fit comfortably into the mold you have in mind for them. Other firms fit more than one.

Kochis Fitz, for example, landed in our chapter on regional firms and BBR Partners wound up among our large firms, even though both would probably think of themselves as "best of breed" practices, offering services clients will find nowhere else. Similarly challenging was the choice of where to put the singular firm Mark Spangler has created. Spangler calls it a multiclient family office and that's where we placed it, even though, strictly speaking, it's not. His clients are not necessarily in the same family, but they are related to one another by their common interest in technology. Spangler's practice could just as easily have been included among the mavericks, especially considering that he's allowed his certified financial planner designation to lapse.

Certainly, the book's goal starting out was to present successful approaches to shaping a business model, which other planners could adapt to their own use. But it quickly became clear that the categories were elastic; no two practices followed exactly the same path. We've left some of the industry's best planners out of the book entirely, simply because of the space it would take to include so many examples. And some of the most successful and well-run practices defy definition altogether. Examples of such one-of-a-kind planners deserve mention here:

➤ **Ross Levin.** Past chairman of the International Association for Financial Planning (IAFP) and a frequent—and very entertaining—speaker at financial planning conferences, Levin is one of the big names in planning. He and Wil Heupel—his partner at Accredited Investors, a financial advisory firm in Minneapolis, Minnesota—developed a process to help planners quantify the nebulous business of financial planning. In his book, *The Wealth Management Index,* Levin lays out the method he uses to categorize client goals such as asset protection, disability and income protection, debt management, investment and cash flow planning, and estate planning. Within the categories, Levin has developed a series of targeted questions and subcategories. His intention is to quantify the client's goals so that he can measure progress over each year and use it as a basis for ongoing discussion.

This might make Levin sound like a bean counter, who believes that only tangible financial goals are relevant. Quite the opposite. Levin is one of the most perceptive, insightful people I've run into in the business. With a series of questions, he can change the direction of someone's life. That's what he did with mine one December morning midway through a telephone conversation about bonds. I was worried about some major surgery I was about to undergo the following month, and it showed. He asked permission to do some soul searching with me and the advice that followed his probing and very personal questions was tremendously helpful.

Levin uses similarly probing questions to get to know prospective clients. It's a process he describes as a minuet, with both partners dancing carefully around certain issues. His purpose is to determine whether they'd work well together. Armed with the results of his inquiries, Levin puts clients into one of four categories: Relationship clients are those who are looking to form a bond with someone they trust. Fear-based clients have little—or negative—experience with finances and must overcome their fears. Curious clients want to work with you; they know something about investing and financial planning but don't have enough time to do it the way it should be done. So they want to look over your shoulder and be involved. Greedy clients are looking for the person who can get them the best investment return. Levin acknowledges that clients are often a mix of these types, but the greedy clients, he says, are never worth the trouble. No matter how one tries to coddle them, they'll never be loyal, because they believe they might be missing out on a higher return somewhere else. Every time he's taken on a greedy client, he's regretted it.

➤ **Cynthia Meyers.** A decade ago, when many planners prided themselves on making the leap from commissions to fees, I got to know Meyers, owner of Cynthia Meyers CFP/Foothill Securities, a financial planning firm in Sacramento, California. She did comprehensive financial planning and used the efficient, low-load American funds because she believed it was cheaper for the clients she served to pay the load for advice rather than an annual fee based on assets under management.

At that time Meyers, along with George Kinder, was one of the only planners doing what we now call life planning, using a process that she developed for clients based on her own values and beliefs about what's involved in making a good life. Meyers is a musician, and when I think of her life-planning efforts, I think of the phrase "composing a life." Meyers moved way beyond what the typical planner was doing in this area. Some planners considered it "butting in"; many still do. For instance, when a forty-year-old client insisted on buying a piece of real estate because she didn't want to miss the opportunity, Meyers guessed—rightly—that the opportunity she truly worried about missing was to have a child. Meyers helped her research single parenthood to determine whether it would be right for her. In the end, the woman decided not to have a child on her own and was grateful to Meyers for bringing the issue into the open so she could resolve it.

➤ **David Diesslin.** Sometimes it's difficult to put your finger on just what a planner does. Diesslin, president of Diesslin & Associates in Fort Worth, Texas, is a sole practitioner who serves 250 clients in seventy families, with a staff of fifteen. He provides customized services to each client with the goal of bringing corporate efficiencies to families while maintaining individual service. He begins client service with what he calls an "insight session" that looks at the hierarchy of needs: survival, safety, belonging, achievement, and self-actualization. The goal is to get clients to talk about their own vision for their lives so that Diesslin can develop a plan to help them attain it.

➤ **Barry Freedman.** Of course, even maverick planners are always looking for ways to standardize procedures—but not so much so that they lose the specialness that gives them their edge. As a planner's business evolves and he introduces better ways to manage clients' expectations or to allay their fears, the practice takes on his own personality and grows in the ways that suit the firm. Freedman, owner of Freedman Financial Associates in Peabody, Massachusetts, solved his succession problem by bringing in his son, Marc. The two also worked out a hybrid system whereby Marc would bring in younger clients and work with them on a commission basis—if that structure proved more economical for the client—and Barry would work with larger clients, charging them fees based on assets under management. The Freedmans set up a second office in Florida, and Barry began to spend stretches of his time there, realizing a dream of many planners: to stay active in the business and still achieve his own vision and find balance in his own life as well.

So in an industry with no shortage of mavericks, I applaud the many who've found a way to stand out from the crowd. And I delight—hoping you will too—in taking a closer look at a few who manage to earn recognition even among the vanguard: After all, how many planners build a practice in Maui and teach Zen Buddhism on the side? But George Kinder does. And how many walk through deserted oil fields looking for alternative investments the way Richie Lee does? Or become general partner of a client's failed partnership and work out the kinks as Bob Willard has?

Such terrain may seem far afield, but in exploring it, mavericks show that for the creative adviser, no innovations that can serve clients' needs are really out of the way.

— 🐝 🐝 🐝 —

George Kinder: Zen and the Art of Financial Planning

WHEN A GROUP OF financial advisers held a retreat in Traverse City, Michigan, in July 1996, George Kinder was the only attendee wearing a Hawaiian shirt, which was a stroke of luck for me, because I was trying to pick him out from the rest. Kinder is the man who coined the term "life planning" back in the early 1990s in an interview with Bob Veres. I'd talked with Kinder on the phone several times before the Traverse City retreat but hadn't had a chance to meet him. As it turned out, Kinder and I sat together at a presentation by Dr. William R. Nixon Jr., a psychoanalyst from Birmingham, Michigan, which was fitting because Nixon's lecture marked the beginning for me of an understanding of how a planner might assist a client with more than just his financial life. And that's what Kinder was already doing.

Nixon's presentation was doubly interesting because he was an outsider to planning, a psychologist who had done some research about what planners do and how they could do it better. Oftentimes, presentations at these conferences are off the mark because the presenters don't fully understand the work of advisers. They'll address the group as if planners were salespeople trying to sneak their hands into someone's back pocket. They talk about loopholes and exceptions and ways to help clients cheat the Internal Revenue Service. In other words, they insult planners by underestimating their goals and intentions. Nixon was just the opposite. He talked to these advisers as if they were among the most important professionals in the country.

What's more, he invited them to look at their clients from the point of view of a psychologist. The relationship between a person and his money is complex, mysterious, and often secretive, Nixon told the planners. Many people erect intricate barriers around money issues and wall off entire areas of their lives. Nixon told the planners it was their job to delicately break down those barriers and persuade a client to outline his dreams and his fears and the role that money plays in them. "Working with a financial planner means delving into the most volatile of human conflicts," Nixon said. A planner's ultimate success or failure will have more to do with how he handles this challenge than with any other aspect of the planning process.

Kinder already knew this. Indeed, he had worked through his own life plan and, like many of us, fell at first into the job of least resistance. But soon he began to mold the job to fit his needs and desires. When he graduated from Harvard University in 1971, Kinder and his wife made a deal that each would take a turn working to support the other person's passion. His wife worked the first two-year shift, while Kinder explored theology and philosophy, spending hours each day studying the world's major religions. He read and wrote and painted and delved into the study of the human experience. When the two years were up, Kinder was unwilling to leave his pursuits behind. He had to go to work. But how do you live the life of the mind when someone else buys your brain from nine to five?

Kinder, who had scored a perfect 800 in math on the college boards, decided that doing something with his math talent would be the most efficient way to make money without eating up too much of his time. The field of accounting, Kinder reasoned, would allow him to work hard and make good money during the tax season and take the rest of the year off. He went to Northeastern University in Boston to study accounting and got the third-highest score in the state on his CPA exam.

Even back when he was a tax accountant, Kinder was asking clients questions about their lives. To be a good tax preparer for his clients, who were professors, artists, writers, and other professionals, he felt he had to know a good deal about their lives. Who did they spend time with? Who did they eat with? Where did they travel and why? Getting adequate travel and meal deductions depended on knowing who the person was, he says. So "right from the beginning I was exploring: Who is this person?" As a result of digging deeper, he got many more deductions for clients than another tax accountant might have.

What he later discovered, though, was that his clients needed far more than accounting advice. They had no objective place to go for financial planning help. Kinder would offer suggestions, but when the clients returned the following year, he discovered they had either done nothing to follow up or they'd been taken advantage of by unscrupulous salespeople. So he started to do financial planning in the late 1970s, got his certified financial planner designation in the early 1980s, and joined the National Association of Personal Financial Advisors (NAPFA) in 1984. "I already had this inclination to find out who the person was and what he wanted out of life," says Kinder. So by the early 1980s, he was already asking the clients who came to what was then Kinder Financial Planning his three famous questions. Still, in 1984, he was specializing in money management as many planners did then. Although he asked the questions and helped people mold their lives, money management was what people started coming to him for. Today, people come to him for the life planning because he's so well known for it.

That's because in 1999, Kinder wrote *The Seven Stages of Money Maturity,* in which he outlined the ways people approach money, beginning with innocence—the period before we understand that we have to work to earn a living and that money is one determinant of who we will be—and ending with "aloha," which Kinder defines as giving money and ourselves out of pure joy with no strings attached, no expectations, no thought of money as a marker.

Early on, he says, "people who came to see me were astounded that I was asking those questions, yet they were excited and happy about it." He recalls one person out of ten would balk at the questions, but he suspects that the resistance had as much to do with him as with them. About one couple in their early sixties who came to see him, he says, "I sensed their New England reserve and so I backed off and went to the traditional model with them." When his book came out fifteen years later, he sent a copy to each client. This couple responded immediately, telling him how much they liked the book and asking why he hadn't asked them such questions. Kinder believes he read them wrong because he was young and a bit intimidated.

Although very involved in his financial planning practice, Kinder was not about to give up his own spiritual journey. That journey took him to Maui. He had always longed to take a trip to Hawaii, and once he visited the tropical rain forests, he was determined to make Maui part of his life's plan. His goal was not to grow rich but to arrange his life to accommodate those things that were essential to him. One of them was to spend a chunk of time each year in Maui. He managed to arrange that by building a planning practice there and gradually increasing the amount of time he spent in Maui each year. Kinder also developed his practice of Zen Buddhism, finally becoming a Zen Buddhist teacher. He saw that the various parts of his life were actually forming a circle, the need to study theology and the human experience, to help people with money issues, to practice Zen.

I visited Kinder at his home outside Concord, Massachusetts, the day after Easter in 1999 to talk about the book and his plans for it. To reach Kinder's place, you must pass through what he calls Dante's inferno. The approach isn't quite as bad as that; still, it's not a route for a Sunday driver. The house is hidden from the highway. A sharp hairpin turn takes you onto a bumpy dirt road that passes under a high-voltage line and over the railroad tracks at an unmarked crossing before you pull up to Kinder's house on a quiet lake. It was a beautiful April morning, and I followed Kinder down a stone path out to a narrow spit of land banked by water to a cabin made chiefly of glass that he built for writing, reading, and meditation. Here and in his other home on Maui, where he spends four months a year, Kinder works out his own aspirations. "If we are willing to learn the hard lessons, to go inside ourselves and see what is there, then I think we have a wisdom that we can bring to clients that will make a difference," Kinder says.

Kinder's own search has shaped the way he works with clients. "What a shame that human beings feel constrained to work a job in quiet desperation rather than figuring out: 'Why am I here? What do I want to accomplish?'" Kinder argues in his book that each of us faces some type of suffering around money. Perhaps we don't have enough of it to accomplish our goals. Or maybe we have so much that we've lost the excitement and enthusiasm earned from a creative day's work. Kinder believes that it's the job of a financial planner to guide clients through this morass, to help them identify their aspirations and figure out how to work toward them. "These aspirations and ideals are what financial planning is really about," Kinder says. "We need to help our clients lead the most fulfilling lives they can and make the greatest possible contribution to the planet."

Finding out about aspirations—about what freedom means to that particular person—is Kinder's first order of business when he meets a new client, a task he compares to a Chinese doctor taking the pulse of a new patient. "Sometimes they'll take the pulse for half an hour," he says, "and they're not counting, but they're reading off your entire system, and they can tell you about your kidneys, your internal organs, whether you have cancer."

Indeed, as Kinder's practice evolved, he discovered that finding the right financial life plan for the client and helping him execute it was what was most satisfying to him. For instance, a client might say he wants to live a life that has more integrity or more spirit or more creativity and he wants to know how he can afford to do that. That's the type of challenge Kinder loves. "Implementing the plan is helping the person live a more vital or fulfilling life," he says. "That's become more of a focus for me because I see how clients block themselves."

Kinder uses a series of exercises to take a client's financial pulse and dislodge those blocks, sometimes suggesting that the client write a financial autobiography to help focus on the role money plays in his life: "Do you feel that dealing with money intrudes on the real purpose of your life? What is that purpose? Does your conflict with money involve some sacrifice of integrity? Do you feel you are giving up a piece of yourself in exchange for a dollar? List all the ways this happens. Then choose a few of them to do differently in the future."

To help clients clarify their goals, he asks these three questions:

1   You have plenty of money. How will you live the rest of your life?
2   Your doctor tells you that you have five to ten years to live. You will not be in pain. But you will die suddenly, without warning. What changes will you make now?
3   You have just twenty-four hours to live. What regrets do you have?

Kinder, of course, has plenty of background experience to draw on for this approach. Planners hoping to use it effectively, he suggests, need to do some self-examination, perhaps with a counselor or therapist, and also to take some courses in counseling and listening skills. "Without a willingness to examine your own life and someone to listen to your struggles, to the things you're ashamed of and wouldn't want to share with most people, how can you create that environment for others?" he asks.

Indeed, to create the environment he wanted for his own life, Kinder decided to get out of the money management and administrative aspects of planning and focus strictly on helping clients design and implement a financial life plan. In 1999, he sold his money management business to Sherman Financial in Philadelphia. With the business went about seventy-five clients who had used Kinder as a money manager as well as a financial planner. In addition to a payout for that business, Kinder is paid as a part-time employee by Sherman Financial. He sits on the firm's investment policy board, where he believes his long investment experience—including the 1973–74 stock market crash and his studies of the stock market from 1929 to 1933—bring valuable perspective. He's also available to meet with the clients he transferred to Sherman Financial, some of whom are in Hawaii and some in Cambridge, Massachusetts. These clients contact Kinder only for the big picture, not for details on their investment portfolios or insurance policies. "I am not the primary contact for any of those clients," he says. "I'm a life planner, and I'm available to talk about whether they're moving in the right direction with their lives."

That arrangement has freed Kinder to do what he loves to do. "I no longer have the managerial, bureaucratic, or administration responsibilities of running a firm," he says. In addition to his duties for Sherman Financial, he takes on life-planning clients with his own firm—Kinder and Co.—and charges an hourly fee of $300. He has about seventy-five of these clients, most of whom he's picked up since he sold his old firm. About 20 percent of them are in Hawaii, 50 percent are in Cambridge, and 30 percent are scattered over the rest of the country. Kinder prefers to meet with clients in person "because the body language is so important," but he does have a handful of clients whom he has never met and works with over the phone. Because he charges by the hour, Kinder doesn't necessarily target wealthy clients. "I work with people who don't have a pot to piss in as well as those who are very affluent," he says.

Kinder has a permanent part-time assistant in Cambridge and a part-time assistant in Maui for the four months he spends there. Clients contact him by phone, e-mail, or through his assistants. The nature of the life-planning process is such that it is intense during the first two years—when clients might come every ten days for the first several months. Later, some clients feel they're on course and don't need to come back; others may come back for a quarterly or annual checkup. Of course, Kinder also looks at a client's pension, insurance, and investment portfolio and identifies areas where they need to do some work. But he refers them to someone who can do that work for them.

About half of Kinder's time is spent serving his own clients and the clients he works with for Sherman Financial. The other half he spends on his workshops. When his book came out in 1999, many planners received it enthusiastically, and Kinder began a series of Seven Stages of Money Maturity seminars for planners interested in using the process in their own practices. A two-day workshop, which is taken by both financial planners and nonprofessionals, takes participants through the life-planning process and helps them identify the money issues in their lives. They explore their attitudes toward money and do some goal-setting exercises. A separate, five-day program trains people to do life planning. "It's soup to nuts on how you create the business," says Kinder, "how you work with couples that have very different ideas and notions about money, how you deal with people with a mall mentality, how you identify resistance to certain money issues." Yet another, six-day, workshop trains planners to conduct the workshops themselves. In November 2002, Kinder set up the Kinder Institute of Life Planning to organize the Seven Stages workshops. Susan Galvan in Orinda, California, is executive director of the institute. Seven Stages workshops have been conducted in the United States, Canada, Great Britain, and Australia.

Kinder also teaches Buddhism once a week in Cambridge or Maui and conducts five week-long Buddhist seminars each year.

How's that for planning a life?

— 🐝 🐝 🐝 —

Richie Lee: Human Capital, the Ultimate Alternative

MANY PLANNERS AROUND the country look to Richie Lee, president of Lee Financial in Dallas, as a mentor, someone who's been in the business for thirty years and has never been afraid to innovate or to take a risk, particularly in exploring the role of the planner and in investing in alternative asset classes. Although by the standards of a young industry, Lee is a grand old man in the profession, the most refreshing thing about him is the novel perspective he brings to nearly every issue, one that allows for unexpected possibilities. "One of the most wonderful things about this business is that there are one hundred thousand people out there, each trying to do the job in different ways," he says.

Lee brushes aside the idea of dividing the planning business into a handful of models. "We can't stop innovating now because we don't know which things will work well and grow. A genius who can execute a plan at one level may have difficulty taking it to the next." He cites the example of a talented money manager who develops a stock-picking process that clicks; he seems to have the magic touch. "But it might be an intuitive capability," Lee says. "Then the money rolls in and he has to hire more people to handle the business, and pretty soon he's morphed into a manager of people, which isn't what he's good at." So it's not just about the strategy, but whether the strategy can be executed at another level.

Nor does Lee see much to be gained in searching for a perfect model and then trying to replicate it. "The experimentation is just starting. The industry is in its youth," he says. "It's no good to have people trying to build someone else's model rather than going through the experience itself. All these little seeds have been planted out there, and people are creating phenomenal business ideas right and left." Lee applauds Sheryl Garrett's hourly model, for example, and the steps she's taken to franchise her business. "It shows that you don't need an enormous amount of capital to create great business ideas and execute them," he says. You learn how to build your business by doing, by making mistakes, and then trying something else. "You don't learn by strategizing."

Experimentation has also led to people developing ideas and services that support the industry, Lee says. "Someone will discover that they're not really good at planning but that they love creating planning software. And there are planners like Dave Drucker, who shows everyone how to outsource," Lee says. Innovation and exceptional service are the fruits of independence.

Indeed, according to Lee, independent planners got their start because individual investors weren't being served by Wall Street. "Wall Street originally existed for the corporations and for private financings and equity," he says. "The retail broker who takes care of the individuals was a subset of that, but the most important client—the corporation—got the service." Those conflicts on Wall Street created an opening for the independent planner. "In the late sixties and early seventies," Lee says, "it was a question of acquiring the tools to penetrate the retail market; eventually those tools became a profession. And the individual is the centerpiece of our profession rather than the corporation." All the talk about conflict of interest, he says, means more opportunity for independent planners. "This army of independent planners has invested enormous amounts in human capital. No one would have allocated funds to do that. We've done it ourselves."

The job of a financial planner is to think, Lee says. "That is the most important thing we can do, because the people we represent don't have the time to do that. They're so completely caught up in their business and career and family that they don't have time to think about the big-picture issues that will influence their lives."

Perhaps the most distinctive of Lee's many qualities is his curiosity. After he earned his CFP designation in 1974, he decided he needed to learn more about investments, so he went to graduate school at Southern Methodist University to get an M.B.A. Soon after, he earned his CFA. "There was a very small group of guys back then who were beginning to do that," Lee says. "We sort of found each other through the financial planning organizations and formed a study group: the Society of Independent Financial Advisors (SIFA). The group experimented with as many approaches to the planning business—and to compensation—as they could think of. They tried hourly fees, which didn't work out and were difficult to keep track of, then went to retainer fees, and later a retainer plus a percentage of assets under management. "We still experiment all the time," Lee says. "Sometimes we take the assets and multiply by 30 basis points. Those kinds of things are becoming more possible."

When Lee started in the planning business in 1972, clients were looking only for the basics: a plan for reducing taxes, educating their kids, saving for retirement, and estate planning. Then tax lawyers began to create limited partnerships with the promise of lowering taxes. The products were poorly designed and carried high fees; many of them went into the tank. From the beginning, Lee made direct investments for clients in things like energy, coal mining, and rail cars. But he didn't use the prepackaged partnerships the lawyers proffered. He did his own due diligence and put together his own deals. "We did a lot of that kind of stuff, and our investments came out very well," he says. "What propelled us as a firm is that we took the responsibility and time to work things out and even took some of [the companies] over when they were failing." In one partnership, for example, Lee and his clients owned and leased offshore barges. The partnership fell apart, and Lee sued the general partner for fraud and got a judgment against him. Then Lee took over as general partner and turned the thing around. "The only reason we ever become general partner," Lee says, "is when the general partner doesn't do his job."

Lee compares what his firm does to Warren Buffett's buying Fruit of the Loom in bankruptcy. "There are a lot of broken and bankrupt companies out there, and a few of them are a good chance to buy something inexpensive," he says. "When things get really, really bad, you can buy something for cash in an amount that would normally serve only as a down payment." For example, Lee was once given the opportunity to buy four offshore oil rigs that cost $150 to $200 million to build. The partnership he participated in bought all four for $4 million and sold them within a year for $16 million. Optimism and pessimism are often the most important factors in pricing, Lee says. But it's not easy to talk clients into buying an asset that's out of favor.

Today, stocks make up the core of Lee's client portfolios, but he uses hedge funds, private debt, private equity, and private real estate as well as real assets. "We charge the same fee for what we do as [other planners] charge for using mutual funds," he says. "We have a whole team of analytical people." They function not so much to garner greater returns but to manage the risk and calm the standard deviation of the returns. The efficiency in the private markets is very low, Lee says, so it's possible for a knowledgeable investor to get good returns with lower risk.

Lee Financial manages $600 million for eighty to one hundred clients. The staff totals thirty-four, half professional and half support. The chief financial officer is a CPA, and the firm has eight financial planners, each with certified financial planner (CFP) designations, and eight investment people, most of whom have earned or are working toward their chartered financial analyst (CFA) designation. The planners and investment people are equally important to the firm because the investments are so complex. Running a firm that uses alternative investment strategies requires much more financial and technological expertise from its staff.

The person who oversees technology for the firm has run a couple of small companies on his own. Lee also has a professional programmer and someone with a master's degree in records management, who is head of knowledge management. "He looks at the way we acquire, use, and distribute information," Lee says. Lee is one of four principals and owners of the firm, although he owns the largest share. He also brings in most of the clients, although he doesn't work with the newer clients.

Lee claims that he hires the most talented people he can find and lets things fall into place in terms of who does what. He says he's not good at organization, administration, or management but that the other partners are. "Everybody takes a little piece of what he's good at and does it," Lee says. "A lot of people don't want to get involved in being a manager. They enjoy what they do and they want to keep doing that. It gradually evolves, and you find that people enjoy doing the things they do well. If you can get the round pegs into the round holes, it works extremely well. "One thing that's made us successful is that we're consistent in the delivery of the process," says Lee. "We take a very holistic approach and deliver both a comprehensive financial planning process and a comprehensive investment management process and weave the two together."

Lee doesn't follow trends. "You pick up a magazine and one of the things everyone has nested on is life planning. This was an egg that was discovered thirty years ago," he says. "It's not just about asking the right questions and listening and building a relationship with people; it's about going through the emotional ups and downs that come with the changes in the economy and in their lives. You speak the same language. Each of you understands what the other one means. You have to really know your people. For example, if you plan to invest in something extremely volatile and your client is a real estate broker, you don't want to pick something that has a high correlation with real estate."

Lee has deliberately chosen to work with a broad cross-section of clients rather than establish a niche, because he values the knowledge he gets from interacting with so many professions and industries. "We get ideas working with widows and divorcees that we can use for entrepreneurs," he says. "It's such a great cross-pollination benefit." He also values the diversification. "There's a cycle of ups and downs in different groups of clients," he says. "We train our people to understand the problems associated with all of these groups."

That's why Lee likes his role as a generalist. "I'm not all that crazy about specialization," he says. "I think you have to be a very broad generalist to offer the most value." The model his firm is developing is one that helps clients maximize the value they can get out of life—a tall order that touches on human capital, psychological capital, the return on investing in your mind, and spiritual and lifestyle decisions.

Not surprisingly, Lee has a keen interest in people. When planners describe Lee's strengths, they mention both his expertise in alternative investments and his focus on human capital—the strengths, talents, guts, and adaptability that people bring to a changing situation. Lee believes the key job of his planners is to develop a client's human capital, which is a unique skill, he says. "Our job is to think, and when we discover that some fundamental change is going on [that affects our clients]—in their industry, for example—we have to prepare them." For that reason, human capital is the biggest balance sheet item, he says, bigger than hard assets or financial capital.

Today, for example, a golfer like Tiger Woods has an image with enormous value separate from his value as an athlete. That value must be managed. Although not everyone can be a Tiger Woods, Lee argues that a planner can help any client achieve something meaningful if his human capital is fully invested. Take Janet Briaud, for example. She may have college professors who could create names for themselves. "The crowning accomplishment for Janet is that four or five of those guys are going to get patents," he says. "Given the right help, a college professor can become a Bill Gates."

But the road to realized potential can be long and difficult. When Lee went to his daughter's college orientation recently, the students were told that by the age of thirty-four, they will have had nine jobs, and over the course of their careers, four different major occupations. "How do you put the working capital together to move from one career to another?" Lee asks. "This is the main task we have with our clients."

To achieve it, a planner should help clients avoid putting all their human and financial capital into the same basket. "We meet every single quarter with our people like a board of directors," he says. "We ask them about their experience and whether their life vision has changed." If a client says he's thinking of starting his own business, Lee and his staff ask, What are the risks involved? How do you prepare? What does your family need to do?

"The perfect example of [the need to cultivate] human capital is what's going on in technology," Lee says. "People lost jobs they'd had for fifteen years, with portfolios full of stock options from Cisco or Oracle." So if a client wants to go back and get retrained and retooled for another career, where does the money come from? Clearly the biggest value in anyone's portfolio—maybe 60 to 70 percent of it—is the human capital, he says, and how you manage that is so much more important and so much more creative than anything an adviser can do with stocks and bonds.

Lee values the richness in the independent financial planning business more than anyone I know. He talks about the various threads of the profession: life planning from George Kinder; asset allocation and investment management from Roger Gibson of Gibson Capital Management Ltd. in Pittsburgh, who wrote a breakthrough book on asset allocation; and coaches like Sherry Hazan-Cohen of Dream Achieve in Plano, Texas, to whom Lee refers clients for life-planning and coaching services. "In my business," Lee says, "we try to make use of everything that everyone's doing, evolving and adapting to the ever-changing environment of what's necessary to make our people successful."

Lee, who was one of the organizers of the 1999 workshop with a futurist that top planners attended in Dallas, says that the pace of change is one of the most dominant characteristics of the financial planning business right now. "We have to be students of the future," he says, "if we're going to deal with the issues coming along today."

— ❧ ❧ ❧ —

Robert Willard: Taking Care of Business

ROBERT WILLARD, OWNER OF Willard & Co. in Colorado Springs, Colorado, is one of those rare birds, a financial planner who knew what he wanted to do right from the start, but no business model existed for what he had in mind. So he made one up. Willard wanted a fee-only business—a cross between a family office and a venture-capital firm—with a limited number of clients whom he would serve as a personal chief financial officer. He would be involved in all parts of their businesses, learning as he went along. What's more, his involvement would lead to business opportunities that benefited both him and the client.

Twenty years ago, when he started out, Willard was warned that fee-only compensation wouldn't work in financial planning, that a practice with so few clients was too risky, and that the role he intended to play in his clients' lives would mean shouldering too much liability. He didn't listen; instead, he built the firm he wanted. In fact, the only thing that's changed over the years I've known him is the number of clients he considers ideal for his practice. A half-dozen years ago, he thought twenty-four was the magic number. Today, he has eighteen, but ideally he'd like to have just three or four.

As we've seen with so many successful planners, Willard's background paved the way for the kind of practice he would develop. His father was a senior military officer, and Willard spent his childhood in Japan, Greece, and Belgium. He, too, planned to make the military his career. But when he was passed over for major in 1979, he decided to call it quits. He went to work for Texas Instruments but soon after was diagnosed with cancer. The tumor, a malignant melanoma, was successfully removed in 1980 and hasn't recurred. But the disease put his life and his goals into sharper focus. He realized he didn't want to spend his life working for somebody else, so he started collecting his securities licenses and developing a financial planning practice on the side. As he mulled over the opportunities in planning and how he wanted to pursue them, "I came to the conclusion that the average person needs a financial bodyguard," he says. "They need someone to represent them in all their financial tasks."

Although Willard knew the model he wanted for his business, happenstance dictated his niche in ophthalmology. In 1984, Willard landed a large client, an ophthalmologist who later became one of the world's top surgeons in his specialty. The doctor and Willard clicked immediately. "We are a lot alike in our lifestyle," Willard says. "We have strong, Midwestern family values." From the start, Willard was at the wheel. Now that his client is a famous surgeon, he says, "people want to have their names attached to the doctor, as if he were a sports figure." Willard acts as his agent as well as his financial adviser, sitting in on all the doctor's business deals. "It's interesting how planners evolve in their business," he says. "Your clients take you in a certain direction." First comes setting a business objective for your clients. "But then you end up taking a path and developing a specialty in an area that you might have known nothing about."

To serve clients well, planner Richie Lee stresses the importance of investing in human capital. Willard stresses the need for the planner to invest in himself. "The key is to ask yourself what you do best," he says. Willard's strong suit is his shrewdness, his ability to gauge people's strengths accurately and evaluate business deals. "You begin to get involved in business activities, helping them with corporate planning, interviewing employees, helping with transitions." He has guided his clients in taking their companies public and helped others take public companies private.

Willard gets so involved in the lives of his clients that he's frequently invited to participate in their other business projects—ventures that are far more lucrative than the modest asset-based fees he sets. One client, for example, invested in two-family property deals put together by his brother. When the brother committed suicide, the client stood to lose all of the $300,000 he'd invested in the venture to date. Willard went to Phoenix to clean up the situation. He was made general partner of the project, and for two years he worked practically full time on bailing out the properties. When he managed to turn the project around and sell it, Willard collected a half-million dollars. "It started out as doing a job for nothing, just taking care of a client," he says. This deal isn't atypical for Willard. Because he often gets in on the ground floor and he's comfortable with taking big risks, his own net worth has escalated along with his clients'. In fact, Willard sees himself more as an entrepreneur than a professional. "The way to make money is by taking risks and solving problems," he says. "Professionals make money. But the real money is made by entrepreneurs."

When it comes to investing for his clients, Willard's more comfortable buying real estate and making direct loans for clients than investing in technology stocks or mutual funds, which he prefers not to use. Willard's specialty is direct investments for first-generation entrepreneurs. These deals benefit both him and his clients. One of his areas of expertise is direct mortgage loans. He puts together a pool of money from his clients and makes direct loans just the way a bank would. He does the due diligence on the borrowers. Willard is skilled in setting them up and he's had no defaults. The loans are a great investment for his clients. They were getting 11.5 percent returns in 2002, although returns dropped to 9.5 percent a year later, with the drop in interest rates. Still, that 9.5 percent comes as regular income every month. It's great for retirees, and it's more investment income than they'll find anywhere else.

Willard invests in the loans himself. In fact, he's been asked to start a mutual fund for direct mortgage loans but he doesn't have that kind of quantity. They're just for his clients. In any case, Willard is far more interested in serving his clients. The work of providing custom financial services for a small client base keeps him continually challenged and engaged. The job of a traditional financial planner would bore him, he says. He leaves the firm's routine financial planning work and dealing with issues like 529 plans to his team of two: Larry Voreadis, a certified financial planner, and an office manager/bookkeeper. Voreadis takes care of administration and much of the interaction with clients as well as running the loan program and executing the investments. "Larry does all the grinding detail work and all the implementation," says Willard.

The firm charges a retainer, which, according to Willard's Form ADV (application for investment advisor registration) is a negotiated fee between 40 and 80 basis points of a client's investment net worth. "It's a negotiated fee based on my assessment of how much handholding they'll need and the complexity of their situation," he says, noting that it's typically 70 basis points. He has five additional clients who participate only in the direct loans he sets up. But the financial planning is a loss leader, he says. "The payoff comes in the long-term relationship and growing with the clients."

To keep the long-term odds on his side, Willard doesn't accept clients who aren't suited to the firm. "I would never be a good planner for widows and orphans," Willard says. "It would be so easy that I would find it professionally boring and I would be embarrassed taking money for it." He looks instead for clients with more complicated needs. When he does accept a client, he agrees to do everything except legal and accounting work. "I do whatever needs to be done," he says. "When the client starts a new company, I end up being the one to do the work." He negotiates partnership buyouts and helps clients raise money for spin-off businesses. He has helped put together initial public offerings. And he has helped evaluate businesses that a client wants to buy into, chiefly by doing primary research, that is, going to the company and talking to management. He also uses a private detective to do additional research.

If a client is planning an acquisition or has an offer to be acquired, Willard attends all business meetings with him. "You can tell whether it's a good deal," he says. "You don't have to know about medical technology. You can tell if there's an energy in the company and a respect for the boss." Willard says his job is to determine whether the business makes sense for his client's goals and strategies. "You get involved in the pulse of that person's business."

Sometimes when Willard assists in setting up a new company, he asks for equity in the business rather than a fee. For instance, he asked for $30,000 equity, about 2 percent, to set up a company that he estimated would grow to be worth $50 million. On another occasion, a client asked Willard to visit a company with him. Willard liked what he saw and told the client it was a good investment. The client invested $200,000 and made $3 million. "I've got a knack for bringing people together and structuring something for a common goal," he says.

That knack has been tested under pressure. Willard had two partners until 1998, when he got involved in a deal that scared them to death. He loaned $4 million of client money to an outfit to buy 210 acres of "environmentally challenged land" in the middle of Colorado Springs. The land, which had been abandoned for fifty years, was the site of an old gold mine. The land had more than 11 million tons of gold-mining tailings, or residue, and the folks who bought it planned to reprocess the tailings, pull out the gold, and sell it at $300 an ounce. Willard's partners were convinced he would lose every penny of his clients' money and that he'd be sued for every penny of his own. Willard would not back away. He left the firm, taking his name, his clients, his planner, and his office manager, with him.

But the project did run into trouble: The land had a special environmental designation and investors would be required to move the gold tailings somewhere else to reprocess them. In the end, the problem was enough to cause the plan to fall apart, and Willard—along with his clients—ended up with a lot of land on their hands. To pull the deal out of the fire, he had to refinance the land for $3 million and that meant asking his clients to invest additional money. Twenty minutes before the closing, he was still a quarter of a million dollars short. The rescuer Willard called on turned up in time with a $250,000 cashier's check. He and his clients are now in it to the tune of $7 million.

To salvage the investment, Willard had to do extensive research to figure out what kind of development might be possible on the land. He has spent four years on the project and come up with a developer who's agreed to buy the land for $14 million and build an ambitious residential and commercial project. Willard's clients may either take their money out or continue to invest in the development project, which will include 1,000 homes, an apartment complex, and a shopping center. Willard plans to stay with the deal and expects to get a nice return on both his investment and for the time and work he's put in on the project. Because of the way the deal is structured, however, he will have to drop out of NAPFA. According to NAPFA's rules—which Willard helped to write—a member can receive compensation only from a client. This development project is more complex than that, and he will be compensated in other ways for the work he's doing.

Willard's view of the role of the financial adviser is unconventional, to say the least. He describes the role as akin to those played by people like Mark Spangler, who created a technology network; Richie Lee, a master dealmaker; and Roberta Smith, owner of Matrix Planning, who specializes in alternative investments "for artists, fruits, and flakes in California." Willard has created a network from a core client base of ophthalmologists. The commonality among these advisers is the willingness to go out on a limb, to take risks and do something different for clients. Willard says he once stopped by an oil derrick graveyard in Oklahoma with Richie Lee and Roberta Smith to do due diligence. Willard later heard that Lee bought a bunch of the equipment, and before long, oil prices turned around. "We love the deals," he says. "All four of us love the deals. So much so that they're part of a network of planners who get together to discuss private investments. "Richie Lee is the primary mentor," he says.

Willard's emphasis on business deals doesn't mean he isn't interested in life planning. "I do a lot of life planning even though I didn't always know I was doing it," he says. Still, addressing life-planning issues isn't where Willard really shines. He prefers clients who can profit from his analytical skills. "I look at every investment as if it were a business," he says. "It has a return and overhead and what is left over will be your profit. As an adviser, you're overhead to your client. You have to perform for your client. Keep them on track for their stated objectives."

In the early days, Willard says he sometimes got slightly derailed and made some mistakes. "I paid for them and so did my clients," he says. "When you're younger, you believe some of the stuff people tell you. Then you learn to trust but verify everything."

Willard doesn't give a hoot that he is not creating a business with value he can sell when he retires. What's important to him is to get satisfaction and enjoyment out of his work now. To do that, the work's got to be challenging and different every day. Willard's clients want his advice on whether they're doing the right thing by building a new office complex or investing in expensive medical equipment. And he readily gives it. "I've got enough confidence to know I'm good at this," Willard says. His largest client pays him $3,000 a month; indeed, an accountant told Willard he had a $1,000-an-hour skill and he was giving it away. But Willard is pleased with the arrangement. He believes that charging fees based on assets under management is a conflict of interest and that planners who charge a fee for picking mutual funds should be worried about reports like Mark Hurley's because picking mutual funds is a commodity business that can be done just as well by a broker.

Willard values lifestyle and satisfaction from his work over compensation. "My clients and I stick together," he says. "I have four clients whose combined fees come to $80,000 a year. I could live on that in retirement." He doesn't mind that he won't have anything to sell. "The transportability of your business is different from the transferability of your business," he says. "When I retire I'm going to take the key clients with me. My clients are my age, and I'm not taking on any new ones." And he doesn't believe that many planners would be willing to do what he does for clients, flying around the world if necessary to analyze business deals. (Willard flies and maintains his own plane.)

Willard doesn't think it's easy to get into financial planning, especially the kind he does. But he believes someone with talent and determination can find his own niche. "Most financial planners bring a history of where they came from," he says. "People from accounting or a legal background or a commission background will bring their own perspectives to it."

Willard's perspective is that financial planning is a wonderful life, helping a small group of successful people to try new things and do them well—and have them become your friends to boot, he says. "There are not many people who can help them the way I do."

True enough. But thanks to the success of Willard's model, others may be willing to step up and give it a try.

— ❀ ❀ ❀ —

Chapter Eleven

The Virtual Office

A COUPLE OF YEARS AGO, when the Internet seemed to have claimed the future, it looked as if Web-based financial planning services like Financial Engines and myCFO stood a chance of nibbling away at the financial advisory business. Financial Engines is the brainchild of Bill Sharpe, Nobel laureate in economics and co-parent with Harry Markowitz of modern portfolio theory. Having started out offering 401(k) advice, Financial Engines planned to move on to provide advice on taxable portfolios, mortgages, loans, and just about any financial service a Middle American might need.

Then came the tech crash. In 2002, myCFO was absorbed into Harris wealth management group, a division of the Bank of Montreal. Around the same time, Financial Engines admitted that clients need hand holding; that they weren't willing to accept advice from a machine. Sharpe appeared at the T.D. Waterhouse conference in Orlando that year to announce an alliance with Waterhouse brokers. I did some research in late 2002 on consumer websites as well and found that they didn't pass muster because too many users' individual quirks can fall through the cracks. For example, I was told on one site that the limit for my IRA-SEP was the same as the limit for a 401(k) plan, which was not true.

Does this mean that the Web doesn't work as a way to deliver financial planning services? Throughout this book, I've been talking about the importance of high-touch, customized service and the importance of each planner finding a way to merge his own passion with the needs of a group of clients to create a distinctive practice. I think the troubles faced by myCFO and Financial Engines and other Web-based enterprises illustrate the difficulties of trying to standardize the delivery of financial planning services. Nonetheless, a handful of planners have proved that they can offer personalized service online and that there is a group of clients who clearly prefer to do business that way.

Indeed, nearly all planners—even those based in brick and mortar—are moving as best they can to a paperless office. Many of them are devouring *Virtual-Office Tools for a High-Margin Practice: How Client-Centered Financial Advisers Can Cut Paperwork, Overhead, and Wasted Hours* (Bloomberg Press) by David J. Drucker and Joel P. Bruckenstein. Drucker's business, Sunset Financial Management in Albuquerque, New Mexico, is an excellent example of how a practice can be revolutionized. When I first met Drucker in the mid-1990s, he was part of a successful partnership called Malgoire Drucker, Inc., in Bethesda, Maryland, with plans to continue to grow the firm to provide top-level, comprehensive, fee-only planning. But the birth of his daughter, Gracey, when he was forty-two years old, led Drucker to explore other possibilities.

In his book, he explains that because he didn't want to ship her off to day care, he set up shop in a spare bedroom where he could be with her and work at the same time. I can relate. I decided even before I had my daughter, Krista, who was born in 1986, that I wanted to work at home. So I set up my own business and have her to thank for the timing, because I might have put off the decision. I wrote a column every week for six years for the *New York Times* and went into the *Times'* newsroom on four occasions. The additional advantage came in discovering that the freedom from dealing with office politics made me so much happier and so much more productive.

Something similar happened to Drucker. First off, he discovered that he was one of those people who get energized by working on their own. Second, he found that larger planning firms don't really generate economies of scale and that a firm with under $150,000 in revenues has about the same profit margin—56 percent—as a firm with more than $1 million in revenues. "If the numbers suggest any trend at all, it might be that advisory firms experience diseconomies of scale as they grow," Drucker writes.

Drucker's experiment with working from home gave him the courage to try a bigger experiment. He was growing tired of the Washington, D.C. area and longed to live life on a smaller scale. In September 1996, he and his wife bought a house in Albuquerque simply because that's where they wanted to live. Drucker and Malgoire then spent eighteen months unwinding their partnership, and Drucker made plans to work with his clients from Albuquerque. But he quickly discovered that because he would no longer be able to split overhead costs, his net compensation would take a big hit.

He decided to set up a one-man shop, outsourcing all the administrative work that he could. He serves forty-five high-net-worth clients throughout the country, with about $60 million in assets under management. What's more, he finds time to write magazine columns and books. And he has become the master of outsourcing, someone whom planners across the country look to for tips on how to create virtual working partnerships to handle administrative chores rather than hiring employees.

Drucker came to find the perfect model for his firm by a combination of happenstance, luck, and the willingness to take a big risk. Although he's the first to say that the virtual office isn't for everyone, he's quick to add that creating a paperless office and outsourcing bits of administrative work can make any practice more efficient.

When I began looking into virtual planning, I was prepared to be put off by the lack of handholding and personal contact. But then I realized I'm not really all that keen on handholding and personal contact. I'd probably be an ideal virtual client. I also discovered that a virtual planner spends no less time on each client. The process is simply handled more efficiently. For some clients—and planners—it comes close to being the perfect model.

— ❧ ❧ ❧ —

Dave Yeske: The Pared-Down Practice

A DOZEN YEARS AGO, Dave Yeske was the planner who never refused. His practice in San Francisco offered what he calls a Chinese menu of financial planning services that covered portfolio analysis, comprehensive plans, and money management. Even his fees were a smorgasbord: hourly, fixed, a percentage of assets under management. The client made the call. "I have trouble with boundaries," Yeske admits. That's putting it mildly. He was in a tizzy. "I couldn't say no, and I became so pressed for time that I couldn't operate." Yeske had to make some decisions about what business model he would use going forward. Unfortunately, Yeske's business had grown pretty nearly out of control before he started looking for an alternative.

Yeske had worked as managing general partner of a limited partnership investing in agricultural products as well as on the options trading floor of the Pacific Stock Exchange. The first time he met a certified financial planner, Yeske knew that was what he wanted to become—to "work with individuals as a consultant," he calls it. "The goal was so clear to me that I got my CFP and opened my door in 1990 without a single client."

Like most young planners, Yeske did a little bit of this and a little bit of that to get by. "I started out doing everything," he says. "I would do stand-alone plans, give investment advice, manage assets, use retainer fees—whatever they wanted." Yeske quickly found himself engaged in many diverse projects. In 1996, he even accepted a seat on the board of the Institute of Certified Financial Planners (ICFP). "All of a sudden, I was behind all the time. Someone would come in and have an initial interview and if I was hired, I would be depressed and in a funk, thinking, 'Here's another person who's going to hate me in six months because I don't have time to get to this.'"

Yeske had clients in all stages of development, usually six to eight who were working through comprehensive plans. "I remember one morning sitting on the side of the bed and thinking, I wish my client Karen would fire me today. I got to the office and the phone rang and it was Karen, firing me. Am I psychic? I wondered." Not really. Actually he had been waking up every morning for ten months wishing that Karen would fire him that day. "Some clients become psychic vampires," he says. "They call you up constantly and suck everything out of you, just suck you dry so you don't have enough left for other clients."

At one point, Yeske got so buried in work that he decided he had to hire an associate planner. Before long, "she got hired away and I was glad to see her go," he says. Managing her work had become just one more job to do. That's when he finally began to focus on determining what type of business would suit him and what kind of clients he could best serve. The result was Yeske & Company, a scrupulously pared-down operation that allows him to give very personal attention to a hand-picked group of ninety-five clients. "The change was driven by my desire to operate on a small scale without a lot of staff and associate planners," he says. For Yeske, virtual planning was the only way to get the job done and enjoy life at the same time.

"I add clients only very occasionally," says Yeske. He accepts perhaps one in fifty of those who ask for his services. "I've gotten so much better at spotting clients who will not be a good fit and won't stick around, those who soak up emotional energy and time," he says. "I don't take them on and things run much more smoothly." Of his ninety-five clients, fifty are what he calls core clients and thirty or forty are carryovers from the early days. "So there are fifty clients the firm is really focusing on, and we have continual quality contact without spending stupendous amounts of time." Yeske says he's happy with ninety-five clients and that he can't imagine having more than 110 or 120 and still managing to have his own diversified portfolio of activities. "If I have under one hundred clients, I can know them, know about their families, know what they look like," he says.

He realizes that some planners' biggest kick comes from building a business; once it's running smoothly, they hire associates to carry on. That isn't a fit for Yeske. He doesn't want to supervise people. His website (www.yeske.com) is the focal point for his clients. Under "Dave's Travel Schedule," clients can find out where Yeske will be on any given day. "We use the publicly accessible website as well as private pages with individual access," he says. "This becomes the portal through which we can share information." When Yeske signs up a new client, he sets up a private page for him. The home page of the client's private site contains an action list for that client. So the first thing the client sees when he signs on is that action list. It might say: See an estate planning attorney. Get a $2 million umbrella liability policy. Reallocate your 401(k) money. Beside each item, Yeske indicates whether it's something he will do or something the client should take care of himself. If it's the client's responsibility, Yeske uses a hot link to show him how to reach the attorney he needs to talk with or the insurance carrier he should use for his insurance policy. If he needs to reallocate his 401(k) money, Yeske provides the instructions. If the client is systematically liquidating employee options, Yeske attaches a hot link with the schedule for doing so.

"As we update financial plans, we post those along with the latest tax analysis," says Yeske. Clients e-mail him with their questions. "Half of the e-mails I get from clients come from the private pages," he says. Yeske also uses the private pages to provide monthly portfolio updates. Within three days of the end of the month, the client gets a current statement showing year-to-date returns, the month's returns, the internal rate of return for the year to date, and the return since inception. In a month, perhaps half of his clients visit their home pages. "I insert little checkmarks indicating what I've done and what they've done, and the next time we touch base, we start with a fresh list and clear off the old items and add new ones. So it's an ongoing process," says Yeske. Sometimes he talks with a client on the phone while each views the action page on the screen. "That's why I like using the Web. The richer the spectrum of alternatives, the richer the communication can be." The site allows him to be in continual dialogue with clients, relieving the pressure of having an annual or semiannual meeting.

Every client now starts with a comprehensive plan. To be accepted as clients, they must believe in taking a holistic approach to planning and making integrated decisions. And they must have a compatible investment strategy, which means passive management. Yeske constructs passive portfolios with exchange-traded funds and Dimensional Fund Advisors (DFA) index funds and trades only to rebalance and to harvest tax losses. "If a prospect has even the seeds of the hot stock belief, I root it out or I don't take him on," says Yeske. The investment strategy is a low priority. "People make a big deal about the investment piece because you can make it into something mysterious and complex," he says. "But it's really pretty boring. Clients don't do it on their own, just like people don't floss all the time. But as financial planners, it's the least important and least time consuming thing we do. The high-leverage stuff is making the right tax selections and insurance selections and updating estate plans."

Yeske manages assets for clients with a minimum portfolio of $1 million. He does not hesitate to turn away people who don't want financial planning or who don't want to pay an asset-based fee. His fee is 1 percent on the first $500,000, 75 basis points for up to $1 million, 50 basis points when assets exceed $1 million, and 25 basis points for assets over $2 million.

Setting up these conditions for working with a client was a real breakthrough for him. Something always propels a client through the door. They've inherited some money or they've gotten burned by a sleazy salesman. But Yeske says it's a mistake to take on clients and try to help them in a vacuum. "I say, tell me about your life, your job, your second home, talk to me about dreams and goals and what you want to do for retirement." Yeske prefers it when his clients are compatible with his personal style and share some of his interests. For example, he recently read a review about a book called *The Highwayman*, devoted to some black artists in Florida. He ordered the book, and reading it reminded him of one of his clients so he ordered one for her as well.

Yeske's business model reflects both his background and desire for diversity. He can become easily bored and needs a variety of activities in his life to feed his imagination and his work. He's finished an M.A. in economics and is now working on a doctoral program in finance, which he says enriches his relationship with clients. He also teaches classes, takes on leadership roles in the financial planning industry, and writes columns for various magazines. "I'm at my best working with a diversified portfolio of personal activities," he says.

Yeske uses Schwab Institutional as a custodian. Schwab debits client accounts and cuts Yeske a check. Yeske, like all financial planners, is required to send clients a statement or an invoice to disclose the fee. The Schwab boilerplate language states how investment management services are calculated. Yeske considered using retainers or minimum fees but found they were more difficult for clients to understand. "I use what works for me," he says. "When it stops working, I'll change." He thinks asset-based fees are more fair to clients in a bear market because the adviser shares the pain. "Our fees are decreasing as assets decrease so we're sharing the burden," he says. "Clients who pay retainers are stuck with bull market fees in a bear market."

Yeske argues that technology can make a financial planner much more efficient, enabling him to work with a larger number of clients. That's different from technology replacing advisers. "I'm not talking about technology replacing a planner but about technology enriching the relationship," he says. "Human beings make decisions in a social context. Even people who are intelligent, well educated, and articulate need someone who is good to think with."

He doesn't worry about not building intrinsic value in his practice. "An alternative is to be as cost efficient as you can be and put $40,000 a year in retirement and $40,000 a year in savings and in a couple years, you'll have a couple of million dollars," he says. "It doesn't matter if your practice has no intrinsic value."

As for the refrain in the financial planning industry that any planner who doesn't have a succession plan is cheating his clients, Yeske tosses that aside, too. "I have trouble seeing the problem," he says. "My clients have a financial plan and everything is documented. They'd be able to go to a new planner and show why their affairs are arranged as they are. The virtue of financial planning is that it prepares clients for the unexpected," he says. "The day I get run over by a bus is not a crisis for clients. It doesn't mean they need to make any changes."

Like many other planners, Yeske rejects Mark Hurley's ideas of what the future of planning will be. "Hurley has this deterministic view about what planning will look like ten years from now," Yeske says, noting that a good planner would never allow a client to make a projection of what his life will look like in a decade. Instead, a planner does a Monte Carlo simulation to show the range of possibilities for what might happen in a client's lifetime. If the planner himself put all his resources into one model, he would be going against his own advice, Yeske says. "My approach to planning is to recognize its limitations," he says. "We talk a lot about the future and that's an unknowable beast. Financial planning is not an exercise in Newtonian physics. It's more like orienteering. You take a compass and you plan to go straight, but you see an obstacle or a cliff or a mountain or a lion's den. You have to stop and take another bearing."

And sometimes the new direction gets you exactly where you need to be.

— 🌺 🌺 🌺 —

 Ben Utley: Have Keyboard Will Plan

IN AN ARTICLE FOR Morningstar Advisor.com in February 2002, David Drucker suggests that there exists a new breed of advisers—a group in their twenties and early thirties—who are far more comfortable with technology than are those of Drucker's generation. For that reason, these younger planners are more apt to become sole practitioners with a computer as a staff. As an example, he points to Ben Utley of Utley & Associates in Eugene, Oregon, who has had a paperless office for two years and can work from anywhere as long as he has his laptop.

I called Utley to find out how he became attracted to financial planning and how this new breed ticks. Utley, thirty-three, says the computer connection was a natural. He's been a techie since he started writing software when he was ten. Of course, an affinity for technology need not lead to a gift for planning. For Utley, it led first to chemistry, which is what he was studying in graduate school at the University of Oregon in 1992, working in a pharmaceutical lab, when he became interested in investing. He thought he might be able to put what he knew about medicine to use in picking stocks, so he did some research on Merck and Cyanamide and bought both. Stock research fascinated him.

"I found myself hopelessly drawn to finances," he says. "I was so powerfully attracted that I started looking at it in terms of my own family." What he saw was that his family didn't have adequate insurance; they didn't have a financial plan; and they didn't have financial goals. But Utley didn't know where to turn for advice on how to pursue this line of work. He tried talking to the stockbroker he'd used for his stock purchases. "I'd like to do what you do," he told the stockbroker and asked where he could go for training. The wisecracking broker advised him to get experience by selling used cars. Instead, Utley took a job selling mutual funds for Waddell & Reed, a broker-dealer and mutual fund manager. But he found he didn't have any appetite for selling a fund with a 4 percent yield and a 4 percent commission. So he got his certified financial planner (CFP) designation, filed his Form ADV (application for investment advisor registration) with the SEC, indicating the fees he would charge, and contracted with Charles Schwab & Co. to serve as custodian for his clients. He bought a desk for five bucks, a chair for three, and set up shop with the help of an old computer given to him by a friend.

Like most planners, Utley had to feel his way along. But it didn't take him too much time to figure out that picking investments for clients was not enough—not what was most important for the client or for the planner. "Where the client really gets value is in the strategic plan," he says. "And the planning model is what ties clients to the firm when investments go bad." Indeed, investing may be the easiest thing to outsource, he says, noting that Richard A. Ferry, a chartered financial analyst (CFA) and president of Portfolio Solutions in Troy, Michigan (www.psinvest.com), will set up a passive portfolio of DFA and Vanguard funds for a planner's clients for about 20 basis points. "He does a lot of outsourcing for advisers," Utley says. "In a perfect world, I would do just the planning, goal setting, and develop the strategy and tactics."

In determining how best to serve clients, Utley had only to recall how things were for him back in graduate school, when he knew he needed financial planning help and had nowhere to turn. "I wondered who had my best interests at heart," Utley says. "Nobody did." That's why he believes that what serves up the most value for a client is a good relationship that lets him tap into the planner's problem-solving skills.

When Utley and his wife moved into a three-bedroom home three years ago, he figured it was time to retire his recycled desk and chair and spruce up his workplace. He set up a room near the front door as an office, with track lighting, a large aquarium, ergonomically designed office furniture, and a brand new computer. He hung his master's degree in chemistry on the wall. One of Utley's reasons for working out of his home is the desire to keep balance in his life and spend time with his wife and young daughter. But when a client comes for a meeting, Utley's family is nowhere in evidence. Although Utley's client work is not generally done face to face, most clients want to see him in person for the first meeting. After that, they work on the Web.

Utley does not charge for that initial goal-setting meeting. To do a follow-up financial plan, he charges a flat fee, which varies based on the client's ability to pay and the complexity of the plan. The fee ranges from $750 to $3,000, averaging $1,500. "I can deliver a plan attached to a pdf file," he says. Once he's completed the plan, the client is free to take it wherever he likes. If he wants to continue to work with Utley for wealth accumulation, management, or distribution, Utley charges a retainer of $250 to $1,000 a month.

Most of Utley's clients are doctors. He finds that his chemistry background, his fluency with numbers, his training in Latin, and his understanding of science and the human body all help him to relate better with doctors than other planners might. He speaks their language. Although he wouldn't tell me how many clients he has or his total assets under management, Drucker reported in February 2002 that Utley had twelve core clients, with a goal of acquiring a total of three-dozen high-net-worth clients, primarily doctors.

Utley says his office is completely paperless. "I don't have any file cabinets in my office," he says. "The paper that comes in gets scanned and then returned or shredded." Utley says the paperless office described in Drucker's book can drastically reduce costs for planners. It also reduces clutter and distraction. "Doctors who come in say, 'I really like your house. It's so peaceful and calm.'"

Although Utley works alone, he formed a virtual study group in 2003 with other planners from the National Association of Personal Financial Advisors (NAPFA). "I polled the seven hundred members of NAPFA to see if anyone else worked the way I do," he says. He ended up with a group of a dozen advisers who now exchange ideas and information on practice-management issues for virtual planners.

Utley designed and set up his own website (www.utleyassociates. com), something many advisers would be reluctant to do. On the site, Utley stresses his firm's independence, comparing its fee-only structure to one a doctor, lawyer, or accountant might use. The site does a nice job summing up his press mentions and also tells us that in December 2002, *Medical Economics* magazine named him as one of the 150 best advisers for doctors.

Because they're very much on their own, virtual planners are more likely than other planners to outsource work, Utley says. In addition to Ferry at Portfolio Solutions, who does investment work,

Utley says Patricia Jennerjohn, a former music teacher who became a financial planner when she set up Focused Finances in Oakland, California (www.focusedfinances.com), writes financial plans for other planners. Sherry Hazan-Cohen at www.dreamachieve.com does outsourced life-planning work, with the help of a psychologist in California. All of the people Utley relies on for outsourcing were recommended to him by members of his NAPFA network.

Utley says he may outsource more of his work in the future as his business grows. His own strength, he says, comes from remembering what it was like back in graduate school, when he realized his family was financially at sea and he didn't know where to find someone to trust. "I always try to put myself in my client's shoes," he says. He uses the same credit card, the same attorney, the same investments, and the same insurance broker he recommends to clients. "I walk my talk."

Virtually, that is.

— ❀ ❀ ❀ —

Part Three

New Findings

C h a p t e r **12** *T w e l v e*

Life Planning:
Whose Job Is It Anyway?

B Y THE TIME the twenty-first century got under way, life planning—the ill-defined area of financial planning that has more
to do with a client's hopes and dreams than with his trusts
and taxes—had become the most controversial topic in the financial
advisory world. Planners couldn't even agree on what the term "life
planning" was supposed to mean. Most planners who venture into
the territory say that it means getting involved in a client's life decisions, those that go beyond the obvious challenges of investments and
retirement and estate planning. Some advisers, like Janet Briaud in
Bryan, Texas, see this work as a natural outgrowth of financial planning, but the skills it requires come only after mastering the tools of
planning. "To make a difference in someone's life is the highest level
of planning," Briaud says; her involvement in her clients' lives has
become part of her own life journey. She's willing, for example, to
go out on a limb and tell a client that he's allowing money details to
prevent him from making a personal commitment.

Such involvement doesn't necessarily mean getting involved in
spiritual matters, but it can. That's why planners like Tom Connelly
in Phoenix, Arizona, bristle at the notion of life planning. It's not that
Connelly isn't interested in spirituality. I've had conversations with
him about reading the likes of Thomas Merton and the desert monks.

It's just that he doesn't think that this kind of conversation has a place in a business relationship. "My clients are Buddhists and Hindus and Muslims and Christians and Jews," he says. "They're not asking me what I think of their religion."

Maybe not. But advisers are going to have to decide how important life planning will be to their practice. We don't know yet what the future of life planning will be, but one thing is clear: It's not going away. Bob Veres, for one, thinks it's the natural evolution of the profession and that life planning will become the "top of the menu offering" for planners in the new decade. I disagree. I think 2003—or maybe even 2002—marked the zenith of this idea, or at least the idea of building a practice around it. Like other aspects of financial planning, life planning is sure to find its place in each practice. How much attention it gets will largely depend on the adviser. For Briaud, financial planning wouldn't engage her were it not for the risks she takes to change people's outlook about their lives and their money. For Connelly, the idea of life planning is little more than a blip on his radar screen.

So when did life planning first appear on the screen anyway? Throughout the 1990s, as planners honed their skills and grew their practices, they began to realize—in various ways—that clients were turning to them for advice on more than just dollars and cents. They were talking about the troubles they had with their teens or how unhappy they felt at their jobs or what a difficult time they were having dealing with grief or retirement. Planners listened. I suspect most of them responded with warmth. Some no doubt felt uncomfortable; others started to tiptoe into the "soft" areas that seemed only indirectly related to planning. Some were even raising questions clients hadn't asked. Before long, a vast underground "service" began to develop in the planning profession, a service that no one really talked about because they didn't have a name for it and perhaps, too, because it felt sort of scary to talk about what came dangerously close to meddling in people's private lives.

But in the early 1990s, at least two planners were practicing what they called life planning, or life-stages planning. One was Cynthia Meyers, who had developed her own unique practice in Sacramento, California, and the other was George Kinder in Cambridge, Massachusetts. Many planners considered both of them oddballs of a sort, a little far out, on the fringes of planning. Then at the Institute of Certified Financial Planners (ICFP) retreat in 1994, Kinder and Dick Wagner—who left his successful planning practice in Denver in 2000 to set up a company called WorthLiving, which helps clients find balance in their lives and seek their own vision—made a presentation on "the soul of money." The topic generated enough interest to prompt the two to invite three dozen planners to a follow-up retreat in 1995 at a YMCA in the Rocky Mountains. This marked the beginning of the Nazrudin Project, a group of roughly one hundred planners who get together for a retreat once a year to discuss the emotional and psychological issues tied to money. Actually, they call themselves a nongroup because there's no leader and no formal organization. "Whoever is supposed to be there should come" for talk and meditation, according to the nongroup's website. Kinder's book *The Seven Stages of Money Maturity* came out of this think tank as did Susan Bradley's *Sudden Money*. The name Nazrudin is a reference to the Mullah Nazrudin, who had a knack for coming up with unconventional solutions to problems.

My introduction to life planning came the following year. As part of the research for *Best Practices for Financial Advisors,* I went to the ICFP retreat in Traverse City, Michigan, in July 1996. The presentation on the program that interested me most was one by Dr. William R. Nixon Jr., a psychologist, who planned to talk about the psychology of money. Nixon, who has a therapy practice, was an outsider to planning. But he'd done an impressive amount of legwork—coming to the convention early and talking to advisers in the hallways, over meals, on the elevator—to get a solid take on what was important to them.

Writers are warned away from talking about epiphanies; they're almost invariably a hackneyed way of describing something that, at its core, is probably not that far from ordinary. Still, for me, Nixon's speech was an epiphany. Before then, I thought of advisers as experts in the financial arena. If I could figure out how much life insurance to buy, how much to put away for retirement and so forth, I didn't need one. But Nixon's talk put planners in an entirely different light. Money, he said, is the area where people are most dysfunctional. He told the planners that when a new client comes to them, he has a whole raft of problems that are tied to money and emotions, which he simply can't sort through. Nixon talked about his own experiences with family and money issues and how both had shamed him, making him dysfunctional, even neurotic, in certain ways. The picture Nixon painted of a new financial planning client—a soul adrift in a sea of emotions he can't even put a name to—touched a nerve. What a new client is really saying to a planner, Nixon said, is, "Help me. My life is a mess. I don't make enough money or I have too much or I feel guilty about the way I spend it or I'm hurt that I was disinherited or I'm traumatized by divorce or my wife doesn't think I work hard enough." Whatever the emotional issues, rarely can they be unbraided from the money issues. Nixon said something else that I'll never forget: Most people never accomplish what they could have in life, never achieve what's within their reach. But it's not from lack of money. It's from a lack of knowing what they want their money to do.

I saw Nixon's speech as a turning point not only for me but for many others in the room and indeed for the profession as a whole. The place was packed, and many planners stayed behind for an impromptu session. They wanted to know how they could address these issues, how they could help clients with them. I suspect lots of planners had been craving just such a session; no doubt the issue was becoming an important one in their practices.

As I went over my notes and tapes for the book, I saw that what most planners liked best about their work was not managing money but working with clients. They performed due diligence and executed their fiduciary responsibilities, of course, but they did it out of dedication and commitment to clients. What planners loved to do, what made them really enthusiastic, was getting to know people, learning about their lives, and finding ways to help enrich them. Ask any planner for his favorite story and it will have something to do with a client who got the courage to do what he had long wanted to do. Katharine McGee, a financial planner in Davenport, Iowa, counseled a divorced woman, who was worried about her future, to sell off everything and move to Santa Fe, New Mexico, so she could get involved in the arts, which had always been her passion. Meyers attended auditions with a retired client who developed a second career as a singer. Kinder helped a client discover that one of her dreams was to live on the water; within a year, she was living on a lake. The sad truth is that most of us never get around to articulating what we want to do or even dare to dream about it until someone asks us the right questions. Nixon told these planners that they were in the perfect position to ask about these things, to help people discover and realize their dreams.

Nixon's talk so impressed me that I made it a key part of the *Best Practices* book. In the spring of 1999, when I was asked to speak at the National Association of Personal Financial Advisors (NAPFA) national conference in Washington D.C., I focused on these unheralded services planners provide, the way they stick their necks out to offer guidance or to warn a client that he might be making a mistake. I urged planners to be willing to take the risk that life planning entailed. In a follow-up session, the room was packed with planners who wanted to share their stories of both success and failure and to network with other planners, to find out how they were handling this new challenge and opportunity.

Life planning had become a movement. Bob Veres, a longtime observer of what goes on in the profession, enthusiastically embraced it, which should not surprise anyone who knows him. The real surprise is that Veres didn't invent it. He's a guy who's never lost the idealism of the 1960s and lives life the way he wants to, no matter where the chips fall. Veres has managed to work as a respected figure in the financial services world for more than twenty years, all the while wearing a full beard and long curly hair that make him look like a modern-day Moses—minus only the long, flowing robe. He'll often show up at conferences wearing his dinosaur shirt, a white t-shirt with various species of dinosaurs labeled with the names of wire houses like Merrill Lynch, Dean Witter, and Paine Webber. Veres believes that one person can change the world—or at least a part of it. He's certainly testament to that, because when he throws his weight on the side of some financial planning trend—say charging fees rather than commissions—he brings a good deal of influence to bear. We're at a unique point in history, Veres says, where technology has increased productivity so that many people will be able to work wherever they like, doing whatever they please. All they need is a financial planner to guide them to perfect happiness.

I think that order is even taller than it seems. I emerged from the 1960s with far less idealism than Veres did. I may have a darker view of human nature and be less optimistic about progress. I've seen any number of people who are able to keep a great distance between themselves and happiness, and I don't know how a financial planner—however well intentioned—is going to be able to bridge the gap for such people.

Still, Veres, a member of the Nazrudin Project, believes that life planning is the latest—and most progressive—evolution of financial planning. He thinks of financial planning as a menu of services. Investment management, once the service at the top of the menu, has now become a commodity, and life planning is moving to the top of the list for financial planners, he says.

I don't agree. The notion of life planning predates the Nazrudin Project by a long stretch. I remember talking to planners like Carol Caruthers when she was head of the personal financial planning practice for Price Waterhouse back in the early 1990s. One would expect the planners at a Big Eight firm to conservatively stick to the numbers. Caruthers certainly didn't. She and her husband had adopted two children and they had the same kind of child-rearing issues as the rest of us. Caruthers was always willing to share her own experiences with clients and to provide homey advice. Caruthers is plenty smart—she taught operations research at the college level—but when I talk to her on the phone, I picture her wearing an apron. Before I'm stoned as a sexist, let me say I mean that as a compliment to Carol. Not only does she know every nook and cranny of the tax code, ERISA, and estate law, but she also manages to make you feel as if she's giving you advice at the kitchen table over hot apple pie à la mode. Caruthers went on to become chief executive of Fiduciary Counseling in St. Paul, Minnesota, the family office of the Weyerhauser family. I suspect this blend of hard-headed efficiency in money matters and shrewd judgments on how best to help clients in their personal lives is what got her the job. Caruthers doesn't get involved in counseling, but she's willing to use material from her own life, to talk about the mistakes she's made and help clients try to avoid repeating them. That's something many planners could do.

Over the past couple of years, I've talked to several industry groups about life planning. "Life Crafting," my editor called it, and I like that term much better. That's what this rediscovered trend in planning might be called. In September 2000, I spoke at the annual national convention of the Institute of Financial Planning in the UK, and the feedback was interesting. Planners lined up to discuss the idea. Most of them were intrigued, but some were skeptical. The general consensus was that the British aren't quite so chummy with clients as the Americans are. Still, they were eager to know what they could do to build better relationships with clients. One of the key things I learned in writing about practice models is that a successful planner creates a practice to fit his own needs, needs he feels passionate about. Every planner has a relationship with each of his clients and advises them on a list of issues, or a menu, as Veres calls it. I don't think life planning will ever be the top-of-the-menu item for all planners. But they all probably form a continuum in terms of the intimacy they develop with clients.

That's the case for the planners I've featured in this book. George Kinder is certainly at the far end of that continuum. Finding out what people really want in life is what his work has been about. Even as a tax accountant, Kinder was always poking into clients' personal lives. This interest in people led him into financial planning and from there into life planning and writing a book on people's money hang-ups, and finally to offering a series of workshops to help people work through them. Kinder's interest all along has been in helping clients identify and execute a plan for their lives that can bring them joy. Many of the members of the Nazrudin Project believe, as Kinder does, that life planning is the key to financial planning, that there's no point in trying to help someone with financial issues unless you uncover the obstacles he has to dealing with money and help him find the life of his dreams.

Elissa Buie, president of Financial Planning Group in Falls Church, Virginia, is one of the many planners who've attended one of Kinder's Seven Stages workshops. The experience led to her own soul-searching, a divorce, and a restructured life. When Buie appeared on a panel discussion at the T.D. Waterhouse conference in Orlando, Florida, in February 2002, she said she believed there are two things a planner must do if he wants to do financial life planning: Care about his clients, and lead a fulfilling life himself. Buie said she didn't realize that she wasn't living a fulfilling life until she took the workshop. "Now I have faith in the process that helps clients get to the deep-down stuff of defining a fulfilling life," Buie says. She embraced the tools Kinder uses in his workshop including the three primary questions. It was, in fact, the question on what you would most regret if you had just twenty-four hours to live that turned Buie's life around.

What she would most regret, she realized, was not finding her soul mate. Buie also realized, this time in working with a business consultant, that her best clients were the ones she knew the most about. So the consultant helped her create a process whereby she would get to know clients first, before she signed them on, thereby starting to build the relationship long before she started the financial plan.

Richie Lee in Dallas looks at life planning a bit differently. He believes the biggest asset each client has is his human capital and that a planner adds the most value by helping him achieve his potential. "The management of human capital is the future of our business," Lee says, noting that in his business the biggest growth has come not from more assets under management but from figuring out how to help clients better manage their business lives and careers. Lee has distilled the approach to a formula that looks something like this: net worth = human capital + financial capital (stocks, bonds, etc.) + psychological capital (house, cars, living expense, jewelry, available assets) - social capital (taxes and charitable giving, for example).

Although Lee considers this process the most important part of his practice, he actually outsources other aspects of life planning to Sherry Hazan-Cohen, a financial planner in Plano, Texas, who calls her coaching business Dream Achieve. Dana Pingenot, a planner in Lee's office, says that Lee Financial works with all aspects of a client's financial life and career. The firm gets involved with kids and parents and spending and all the uses of human capital. But once a client demonstrates the need for a psychologist or psychiatrist, he's referred to an outside member of Lee's team, which includes Hazan-Cohen as well as psychiatrists. "When we're working with a client and see that we're crossing a line, where, for example, the client is in denial or is manic-depressive, then we go outside to get help," Pingenot says.

Hazan-Cohen describes what she does as financial planning and coaching. "I hate the term 'life planning,'" she says. Hazan-Cohen took an introduction to coaching class from the College of Executive Coaching and then met James Gottsurcht, a psychologist in Los Angeles, through the Nazrudin Project online. She took a second course from him on coaching skills and practice development. Hazan-Cohen says she's learned how to help clients push to the next step and also learned when to tell a client that he needs to see a therapist.

Hazan-Cohen offers clients a choice of financial planning only, coaching only, or both. The financial planning and coaching combination carries a minimum annual fee of $4,000. For those who want à la carte services, Hazan-Cohen's hourly fee is $200. When she works with Lee's clients, she offers the coaching sessions only, which involve a three-month program of thirty-minute meetings every other week. The price is $200 a month for an individual and $350 a month for a couple. Sometimes a member of Lee's staff, like Pingenot, sits in on the sessions.

At the other end of the life-planning continuum, it seems to me, are the firms I've included as regional firms. They're the ones most likely to keep their relationships with clients at arm's length. This is not surprising, since firms like Sullivan, Bruyette; Kochis Fitz; and Budros & Ruhlin have worked hard to create a standardized structure and to recruit and train new planners. They obviously don't want a junior planner exploring issues related to a client's divorce. These firms seem to be the most "professional," but in this case, that's a subjective term. Perhaps "methodical" describes them better.

Peggy Ruhlin at Budros & Ruhlin says, "When we first heard about life planning, we knew we didn't want anything to do with it." Yet Ruhlin's partner, Jim Budros, a gourmet cook, has been known to stop in at holiday time to make lunch for a newly widowed client. But the point of the visit is to lift her spirits, not to provide counseling or help her get started in a new career.

Eleanor Blayney at Sullivan, Bruyette also sees life planning as a turnoff. Yet, Blayney has told me that when she goes to a conference, she always learns more if she can relate the material to a particular client. "I learn best when I can get the emotional flavor of an event," she says. "That takes knowing a client, seeing him eye to eye. I do a better job that way." So Blayney wants to know her clients and their financial problems; she wants to feel as if she's been in their shoes. But she doesn't want to help them decide whether to change from high heels to sneakers.

Tim Kochis says much the same thing, "We're not baby-sitters, and our clients are not babies." Kochis and his partners are experts in executive compensation, so much so that employers often hire them to work with employees. That's hardly the type of situation where a planner would be likely to enquire whether all's well on the home front.

One of the planners whom I would have considered highly unlikely to embrace life planning is Charles Haines in Birmingham, Alabama. He admits to being a tech head and not particularly adept at spotting when someone has something on his mind. But Haines decided that life planning and family succession planning issues are so important to his high-net-worth clients that he has hired psychologists and social workers on retainer. He now has a full-time social worker, Marty Carter, who specializes in money issues for wealthy families. In fact, he's always on the lookout for problems that are common among these families. So when five of his clients were victims of theft or embezzlement, with total losses of $5 million stolen by secretaries or business managers, Haines hired a security firm to check out all the people his clients work with. He also arranged to have clients learn defensive driving techniques and ways to avoid being kidnapped.

For other planners, community building is their way of helping clients with life issues. Mark Spangler created a nifty practice in Seattle, made up mostly of rich, young retirees from high-tech companies. They're looking for the next step, the next deal. His firm links these clients together into a community, which includes marketers, developers, and researchers who put together deals. I can't imagine Spangler trying to get touchy-feely, but he most certainly affects clients' lives with his ability to make the right associations for them. For example, when a lawyer expressed interest in joining his group, Spangler plugged him into the network. That lawyer now structures the group's legal services. Spangler also saw that some of his wealthy clients were concerned about teaching their children about money. So he hired someone to come in and give a workshop on the subject.

Judy Shine, in Englewood, Colorado, doesn't embrace the idea of life planning yet, either. Still, she tells a similar story about community. Shine had three couples as clients who had important things in common. Each had started a family foundation with $1 million and each had kids in their twenties. Although she was a bit hesitant about the issue of client confidentiality, Shine took the risk and asked each of them if they'd like to meet the others. They all agreed and Shine took the group out to dinner. "They've become good friends, and they've all gained something from it," Shine says.

By the time this book is published, I'm guessing that the life-crafting movement will have peaked, albeit after greatly enriching the profession. What we're likely to continue to see are planners building on their strengths and outsourcing what they don't feel comfortable doing themselves.

Every adviser with longtime clients serves as a counselor from time to time. Some planners embrace the role and move it to the top of the menu. But financial life planning doesn't have to be all or nothing. "I believe there's a continuum of how much of a relationship a planner is interested in having with clients," says Buie. "There's no good or bad end to that spectrum, but anywhere on it, you're getting to know the client and figuring out what will create a fulfilling life for him before you move on to the money."

Money? You know. The stuff you can't take with you from this life into the next, no matter how well you plan it.

— 🌾 🌾 🌾 —

Chapter *Thirteen*

The Fuss About Fees

S TAY ON VACATION too long and you might miss the latest trend in the way planners set fees. In fact, one of the most exciting things going on in financial planning is the rapid pace of change in how advisers structure their compensation. Five years ago, the trend in fees was clear: Elite planners were moving from commission-based products that they "sold" to charging fees for services, a move that allowed them to sit on the client's side of the table the way accountants and lawyers do. The key difference was that lawyers and accountants charge by the hour, whereas fee-only planners would charge a percentage—typically 1 percent—of the assets under management (AUM).

Throughout the 1990s, moving to fees, or transitioning to "fee-only" planning, became the most important way to distinguish oneself from someone who sold products—or so the press and consumers thought. At planning conventions, every adviser wanted to be able to say he was "fee only," and the National Association of Personal Financial Advisors (NAPFA), which had worked so hard to make the "fee-only" label distinctive, decided to copyright the moniker, making it a registered trademark of that group.

But the popularity of the fee-only model—that is, charging a percentage of assets under management—has lost ground in recent years. In April 2003, Bob Veres wrote a eulogy for the AUM business model in his monthly newsletter, *Inside Information*. Veres acknowledged that the AUM fee structure was initially a breath of fresh air in a business that had been dominated by commissions cloaked in secrecy. The AUM concept was a breakthrough devised by idealistic planners who wanted to disclose all the fees clients paid as well as give them a clear picture of how their portfolios were performing, by using a benchmark such as the S&P 500 Index, Veres says. "It was as if bright shafts of sunlight had broken through the investing clouds," he says, adding that fee-only advisers were free to spend time developing better portfolios that took into account the efficient frontier, correlation coefficients, asset classes, risk tolerance, indexing, and expense control. Clients benefited. And the AUM structure provided a huge competitive advantage for the planners who used it, Veres says, because clients welcomed the portfolio transparency that came with it. But all that is history. Today, he says, "pretty much everybody—even the bigger brokerage firms—are offering top-down transparent and scientific portfolios," and AUM has lost its marketing advantage. "AUM planners reformed the marketplace and made the world a better place, but that, alas, doesn't mean their business model will remain competitive."

The AUM model has other problems as well. For one thing, although planners typically charge 1 percent of assets, what a client gets for that 1 percent varies greatly. At Lee Financial, he gets comprehensive financial planning as well as creative management of alternative asset classes and ideas on how to make the most of his human capital. At other shops, the service isn't quite that interesting. Yet during the 1990s bull market, some advisers decided to drop planning altogether and charge 1 percent just for money management—working with a group of mutual funds, each with its own expense structure. Some argue that planners using the AUM model earned more than they were worth during that market. Others planners say they're offering more services than ever in the bear market and getting paid less. Many advisers point out that AUM is too expensive for the truly wealthy, who are better served by retainers. Many planners set a sliding scale, so that the percentage going to fees goes down as the assets go up. Other planners complain that charging fees based on assets presents them with a conflict of interest. If they advise a client to pay off debt or pay down the mortgage, that leaves less money under the adviser's management, which translates into a lower fee. Moreover, there's never been widespread agreement on which assets should be counted. Some advisers include money in a 401(k) plan; others won't do that, arguing that those assets are not under their management.

Indeed, I was surprised as I interviewed planners for this book at the variety of methods they use for charging fees. Sharon Rich and Sheryl Garrett offer à la carte planning based on an hourly fee. Their model is a good one for beginners. But hourly fees also work well for certain specialists, like George Kinder. Kinder doesn't want to manage money or a staff. He wants his time free to work with clients on life planning and on the Kinder Life Planning Institute and his Seven Stages of Money Maturity workshops. So Kinder charges clients an hourly fee of $300 and focuses on making and executing a financial life plan for his clients.

More and more planners—like Tom Connelly in Phoenix, Arizona, and Myra Salzer in Boulder, Colorado—are moving to retainer fees, reasoning that if a client pays an annual retainer, it frees up the planner to make more objective decisions. Another advantage in moving away from the AUM model is that it frees planners to charge for what they do. Few planners believe that investing a client's portfolio is the most important service they provide. Many have moved to using exchange-traded funds and index funds and other forms of passive management. Charging a client based on AUM gives the impression that he's paying for a planner's investment expertise. In fact, setting up a portfolio of index funds is not that tough. And many planners are beginning to tell clients just that. Financial planning contains layers and layers of complexity. Investments are not necessarily one of them, particularly for middle-market clients. I've long been telling investors that a balanced portfolio set up by a financial planner, which typically splits into 60 percent in equity and 40 percent in bonds, should turn in a performance similar to Vanguard's STAR Fund, a mutual fund made up of a number of underlying Vanguard funds that invest in domestic and international stocks and bonds. I was delighted to see in Veres's newsletter that Susan Kimmel, a planner in Short Hills, New Jersey, recommends STAR to her clients. "I know Vanguard is overseeing the managers, the cost structure is good, and I don't believe in paying huge fees for management," she says.

Of course, the assets under management model is still used in many practices, particularly the more structured firms like Budros & Ruhlin. Ruhlin says that 25 percent of the firm's clients require only money management. Some of them are institutions, and some are smaller investors who don't meet the firm's new minimums. This group pays only an AUM fee. The other 75 percent pay the AUM fee as well as a onetime financial planning fee. I suspect it's not difficult for Budros & Ruhlin to show clients what they're getting for their money, because the firm is highly structured and the partners meet regularly with clients to talk about their financial planning needs. "We'll charge on AUM until God comes back to Earth," says Judy Shine in Englewood, Colorado, because she believes it's the only way to get paid for what she's doing.

But for a planner who uses expensive mutual funds to put together a client portfolio, the AUM model can be tricky. Suppose, for example, that a planner charges 1 percent of AUM and puts a client's money into in eight mutual funds, with an average expense ratio of 1.25 percent. That setup drains 2.25 percent from that client's return every year. Planners in that situation, Veres suggests, should base their fees on the value they add. For some planners, that value is obvious. Kinder offers life planning, and his hourly fee makes sense. Lee's clients get alternative investments managed by his staff for the same price that another planner might charge to put his clients in the Vanguard 500 Index.

The differences in strengths among planners are becoming more apparent, and it seems that planners have two choices: Focus your fees on the value you bring to clients, or look for ways to cut fees to the bone. Some planners choose to look at the total cost paid by the client—including mutual fund expenses, life insurance commissions, and financial planning—and place a cap on what the client will pay. It's interesting that while mutual fund companies seem to have lost their way—raising fees and treating shareholders with arrogance—many planners have begun looking for ways to keep the total cost to their clients at 1 percent. That's why clients of a planner like Patti Houlihan, president of Houlihan Financial in Fairfax, Virginia, pay much less for a complete financial plan, including insurance and investment management, than they might pay if they put together a mutual fund portfolio on their own and bought their own life insurance policy. That's impressive.

I talked with Houlihan in the spring of 2003 to find out how she does it. She uses index funds and exchange-traded funds with very low expenses and puts together the large-cap stock portfolios herself. She simply doesn't charge as much as many other planners, partly because she has very high-net-worth clients. These folks are getting a bargain. Houlihan does all their financial planning and investments and even arranges insurance policies for them, all for 1 percent of assets, which includes the funds' expenses.

Including the insurance policies is a bit of a stretch on my part because Houlihan doesn't get compensated for them. But that gives her extra points in my book. In fact, planners could add a lot of value and save clients a lot of money by helping with insurance if they weren't afraid to get their hands dirty. Insurance is the most arcane of the financial products that most Americans must buy. A cash-value policy, for example, is obscure, counterintuitive, and nearly impossible to evaluate. For those reasons, thousands of consumers are ripped off each year when they buy policies that are totally inappropriate or even unnecessary.

To learn something about how insurance worked, Houlihan taught a certified financial planner review course on insurance for five years. Like other planners, she didn't want to get an insurance license because she didn't want to take commissions. She wanted to remain a fee-only planner. But she also wanted to help her clients find the right insurance.

In 2003, Houlihan found a way to do both. She began working with Brian Peterson, senior insurance consultant at Teachers Insurance and Annuity Association–College Retirement Equities Fund (TIAA-CREF), which offers no-load insurance. The idea of no-load insurance has long appealed to advisers. But there are obstacles. Some of the companies that offer it do not offer top-rated products; others don't have an infrastructure to assist advisers in finding the right policy. TIAA-CREF has both. The company is one of the handful with a top rating from all four agencies: Fitch, A.M. Best Co., Standard & Poor's, and Moody's Investors Service. Peterson, who joined TIAA-CREF in August 2002 to build an infrastructure for TIAA-CREF Life Insurance Co., says he believes its no-load insurance is the best deal offered for fee-only planners. Rather than referring clients to a commissioned agent, a planner can refer them to TIAA-CREF for a no-load product. The adviser can participate in a conference call with the client and TIAA-CREF if he likes. Or he can turn it over to TIAA-CREF entirely.

Peterson says much of the work he's been doing with advisers has to do with replacement policies. A planner might ask if the client's policy is the best one for him. TIAA-CREF does not always have a better product, Peterson says. But Houlihan can't find enough good things to say about working with TIAA-CREF. "I felt like I'd died and gone to heaven," she says. "They're really on the side of the consumer."

The objection to offering insurance I hear most frequently from planners is that selling a commissioned insurance product would sully their fee-only label. That hasn't happened to Houlihan. She doesn't gain anything from the money that goes into a life insurance product because she's not managing it and she doesn't get paid anything for helping to evaluate insurance needs and hooking the client up with TIAA-CREF. At least she doesn't get paid anything extra. Part of Houlihan's job, as she sees it, is to reduce the expenses for her clients while increasing her value to them. "Every year I ask, 'What has the client paid me and have I provided value for him?'" she says. Houlihan gives advice on 401(k) plans, but she doesn't include that money in total assets under management. "I'm fairly compensated," she says.

Harold Evensky and Deena Katz also plan to offer insurance to clients of the Evensky Group, the new firm they're planning to build. It's a tough decision, Evensky says, because the firm has long prided itself on being fee-only. But they polled their clients about this issue, and the clients told them that the firm's self-righteousness on this matter was costing them a lot of money.

Overall, planners are now ready to be much more flexible in structuring fees. Keats, Connelly, for instance, one of the first firms to move to retainers, is still willing to charge a percentage of assets under management for certain clients. They even do some business based on hourly fees. The generation of planners that reached maturity in the 1990s feels more self-confident in loosening up about fee structure. They worry less about occasionally stepping outside the fee-only label.

Not surprising. None of them seems to have much use for labels anyway.

— ❦ ❦ ❦ —

C h a p t e r 14 *F o u r t e e n*

Outsourcing:
Only What Comes Naturally

I F I HAD TO NAME the one thing that's done the most to change the face of financial planning, it would have to be outsourcing. Five years ago, for example, it was almost unthinkable for a planner not to be in charge of clients' investments. The only planners mentioned in my book *Best Practices* who didn't manage money were Stuart Kessler, senior tax partner at Goldstein, Golub, Kessler & Co. in New York, and Sharon Rich, an hourly planner in Belmont, Massachusetts. When I wrote about Rich, I got some cranky letters from other planners telling me that she wasn't really a planner because she didn't manage investments. In preparation for this book, I came across many advisers who don't invest money and even more who are planning to leave that work behind. How can this be?

Outsourcing. It's the biggest news in financial planning because it allows planners to create the practice and the lifestyle they want. How different each planning firm is now. So much about planning has changed. Five years ago, elite planners seemed to all be moving in the same direction, toward creating excellence in their practices, finding the very best ways to work with clients, do due diligence, carry out their fiduciary responsibilities, and offer the best in basic services.

Now financial planning looks more like a pastiche, a potpourri of services, each chosen by the individual planner as he determines where his practice will go. Will he focus on life planning? Alternative investments? Coaching? Executive compensation? Comprehensive planning? A niche? On Amazon.com, the book on outsourcing by David J. Drucker and Joel P. Bruckenstein called *Virtual-Office Tools for a High-Margin Practice* gets rave reviews from planners. "This book is a must-read for all advisers," one planner writes. "Get this book if you're looking for a way to live your life the way you want to," writes another.

Indeed, Drucker practices what he preaches. He left a partner and a thriving business in Maryland and moved to Albuquerque, New Mexico, bringing along some clients and adding others. But he has pared down, letting some clients go, to create the life he wants. In fact, once he moved to the Southwest, interesting things began to happen. Drucker had for years written a column for the National Association of Personal Financial Advisors (NAPFA) newsletter. But soon after the move he became a columnist for *Morningstar Advisor* and a regular contributor to *Bloomberg Wealth Manager* magazine. He discovered an interest in helping other planners improve the way they do business, and out of that grew his book on outsourcing.

Everyone has various skills and strengths that haven't yet been developed. Financial planning seems to be a good place for such people to be right now, because it offers the choice of such a variety of lifestyles and practices. You need look no further than the firms described in this book to see how outsourcing has been employed to shape practices that are virtual declarations of independence. But such approaches are relatively new. Go back a little ways—OK, a long way, maybe fifteen years—and you'll find that two services were introduced that became essential for independent financial advisers: Morningstar began providing independent research and data on mutual funds in 1985, enabling advisers to do their own research, and Charles Schwab provided a back office for planners, which would clear their trades and draw up detailed statements for each client. These are the two legs independent financial planning was built on.

It's not surprising then that back in the mid- and late 1980s, the most valuable service many advisers could perform for clients was to cut through the mystery and deceit surrounding mutual funds and help clients put together a portfolio of low-cost, stable funds to suit their needs. The accounts could be set up at Schwab, where the adviser could manage them. Many clients felt comfortable, no doubt for the first time, that they were getting sound and objective investment advice.

Today, though, it's no secret that managing investments has become a commodity. We hear as much from Don Philips, managing director at Morningstar, and Mark Hurley of Undiscovered Managers, and from planners themselves. Mutual funds are getting more and more expensive. Many advisers are responding by going to passive management with DFA funds or exchange-traded funds on the American Stock Exchange. Others are outsourcing investment altogether with companies like SEI Investments, which provides a turnkey operation for advisers who don't want to handle the investing. Look around. A whole new vista has opened up in planning; investing is not necessarily the horse that pulls the wagon anymore.

The options available are limited only by the imagination. Mark Spangler in Seattle has made venture capital investing the core of his practice, turning a group of techies who retired in middle age on stock options into something of a business incubator for start-ups. Again, it's an example of an adviser identifying his strength and finding a way to capitalize on it. A planner like Richie Lee in Dallas, who's built a staff of analysts and created a reputation for finding assets that are out-of-favor but perhaps poised for a turnaround, is clearly not going to outsource investing. Investing in alternative assets is one of the values that Lee Financial offers clients. But, as Lee points out, his clients pay the same fee to get these direct investments in real estate and oil equipment and other hard assets that a client might pay another financial planner to pick a portfolio of index funds.

And that's the problem.

It seems to me that each planner had better figure out what skill has earned him bragging rights. He's going to have to look at where he's adding value and then build his practice around that. Many advisers are moving to passive management. George Kinder, who had been an active investor since 1971, says he once believed in tactical asset allocation. Now he's a loyal convert to passive management. Ditto for Judy Shine, who picked individual stocks for clients "for years and years and years," and now uses mostly passive index funds, with an active fund here and there so that the client won't get bored.

From one coast to the other, I find advisers farming out investment management. Sharon Rich and Sheryl Garrett and other hourly financial planners will help a client research mutual funds on Morningstar's Principia Mutual Funds Advanced. But they don't manage money. Hourly planners, of course, are not likely to have clients complaining they're not getting their money's worth because their investments are down. Investing is not what they're paying for. They're paying to see if they can afford to buy a house or retire or for a portfolio checkup or advice on insurance.

On the other end of the service spectrum, BBR Partners in New York is perhaps the fastest-growing wealth management firm in the country, and guess what? It outsources investments. The three partners have Wharton M.B.A.s, and they all served their time at Goldman Sachs. But they believe that managing client money would be a conflict of interest and that clients come to them because the firm has no proprietary investment products and no interest in selling any particular product to a client. So these planners use their considerable money management skills to find the best managers they can find around the world.

Cicily Maton in Chicago feels free to focus on divorce and, more recently, on life planning for clients in transition. Investing is a very small part of what she does, setting up passive portfolios for her clients. Maton says that if something were to happen to her, the other members of the firm say that the first thing they'd outsource is the money management. Nancy Langdon Jones assigned her investment management duties to a young planner in a different part of the country. Another adviser I talked to simply recommends Vanguard's STAR Fund, which is good competition for any balanced portfolio devised—however complicated the means.

Some advisers believe their calling is life planning and hope to build a practice based on it. They're encouraged by Kinder's success and by the buzz around the Nazrudin Project and the life-planning sessions that have become all but mandatory at conferences. Bob Veres, for one, believes that life planning will become highly sought after by clients. I'm not so sure. I think planners must address life planning and decide how they will integrate it into their practices. But, in the end, it's just another service they'll have to decide whether or not to outsource, which is what Richie Lee does with it.

Many planners scoff at life planning and at anyone who's counting on making a living at it. They say it's just part of the job. It seems to me there's merit in that view. Shine says that people don't want to pay for life planning. It's like going to a therapist, she says. Maybe you know you need the treatment, but you're looking forward to the day when it's over and you don't have to pay anymore.

Kinder is worth studying in this respect. He's undoubtedly the best-known name in life planning. And he has managed to execute his plan for a life that allows him to practice it. But not too many advisers will be able to follow his model. Structuring it took a great deal of work—and risk. And the rewards of those risks are what support his choices now. He's been in the financial services business for thirty years, doing tax accounting and investing and all the other pieces of financial planning. He first built his own planning firm and then sold it to another firm. He continues to get a payout on that as well as a salary for advising the firm on investments and for keeping up client relationships. Kinder charges $300 an hour for life planning and is sufficiently well-known to get clients. Still, he diversifies by offering the Seven Stages workshops. There doesn't seem to be room for thousands of advisers in that niche.

Running parallel to planners' new preference for outsourcing the parts of the business that don't suit them is a trend to offer clients more and more services. Case in point is Charlie Haines at Charles D. Haines, LLC, in Birmingham, Alabama, who does it all and then some. Haines has built a multifamily office model that includes everything from a trust company to a social worker who specializes in family wealth issues, as well as security services and bookkeeping. Of course, he doesn't have people on the payroll to do all of these things. But he offers the services to clients in a single package, competing with firms like Bessemer Trust and U.S. Trust. Harold Evensky and Deena Katz, too, are looking at creating an all-in-one model that would include counseling services, medical insurance, mortgages, insurance, and assistance with car buying or leasing. Evensky and Katz hope to create a high-volume business and then contract with specialists to do many of these chores, because they're inefficient uses of a planner's time. The regional firms, too, seem to intend to do it all. In the case of Budros & Ruhlin, that includes tax preparation. Of course, with Ruhlin's background as a CPA, doing taxes is a natural.

Although the possibilities in outsourcing have not yet been fully explored, what seems clear so far about outsourcing is this: What a firm decides to outsource will determine its identity. So think about it carefully. That's because one thing hasn't changed in all the years I've been writing about financial planning: the relationship between planner and client is the glue that holds everything together. When experts talk of the planner's demise, of the takeover by Wall Street firms and big insurers, they overlook this all-important relationship. It will serve as the planners' moat during the siege on the castle. Advisers who've succeeded in the industry have done so by building a relationship of trust with clients. Take Shine, for example. When I asked her how she defines the client who's right for her firm, she describes him as someone who would be taken advantage of somewhere else. Her clients are safe at her firm. Every planner has similar things to say about their clients.

As I write these pages, Hewitt Associates is setting up a referral group of financial planners. Hewitt, a top-drawer employee-benefits firm in Chicago, says that the most common request they get from clients is for someone to help with personal financial planning. Hewitt has grown tired of telling people: Call the Financial Planning Association (FPA). Call the National Association for Personal Financial Advisors (NAPFA). So it decided to pick eighty-five planners from across the country and bring them to Chicago for a training session. Once the preparation is complete, Hewitt will refer clients to these eighty-five people—the best of breed, each one an adviser who's become known for the way he builds trusting relationships.

That brings us back to where we started, when I said that there's no magic way to identify good planners. Still, certain names are getting around. When Hewitt wanted to put together a list, they knew where to find them. The top planners are those who have built relationships of trust with their clients, who have created a safe haven where a client need not worry that anyone will take advantage of him. That's what's at the core of the best financial planning. The fees you charge, how you handle life planning, what you decide to outsource, and the way you build on and market your strengths must all come from that relationship. That's what will define what you have to offer and what you create in the world.

— 🐝 🐝 🐝 —

Index

About Bloomberg

Bloomberg L.P., founded in 1981, is a global information services, news, and media company. Headquartered in New York, the company has nine sales offices, two data centers, and 87 news bureaus worldwide.

Bloomberg, serving customers in 126 countries around the world, holds a unique position within the financial services industry by providing an unparalleled range of features in a single package known as the BLOOMBERG PROFESSIONAL™ service. By addressing the demand for investment performance and efficiency through an exceptional combination of information, analytic, electronic trading, and Straight Through Processing tools, Bloomberg has built a worldwide customer base of corporations, issuers, financial intermediaries, and institutional investors.

BLOOMBERG NEWS®, founded in 1990, provides stories and columns on business, general news, politics, and sports to leading newspapers and magazines throughout the world. BLOOMBERG TELEVISION®, a 24-hour business and financial news network, is produced and distributed globally in seven different languages. BLOOMBERG RADIO℠ is an international radio network anchored by flagship station BLOOMBERG® 1130 (WBBR-AM) in New York.

In addition to the BLOOMBERG PRESS® line of books, Bloomberg publishes *BLOOMBERG® MARKETS* and *BLOOMBERG® WEALTH MANAGER*. To learn more about Bloomberg, call a sales representative at:

Frankfurt:	49-69-92041-280	São Paulo:	5511-3048-4500
Hong Kong:	852-2977-6900	Singapore:	65-6212-1100
London:	44-20-7330-7500	Sydney:	612-9777-8686
New York:	1-212-318-2200	Tokyo:	813-3201-8910
San Francisco:	1-415-912-2970		

FOR IN-DEPTH MARKET INFORMATION and news, visit the Bloomberg website at **www.bloomberg.com**, which draws from the news and power of the BLOOMBERG PROFESSIONAL® service and Bloomberg's host of media products to provide high-quality news and information in multiple languages on stocks, bonds, currencies, and commodities.

About the Author

Mary Rowland has been covering business and investing news for more than twenty-five years, six of them as personal finance columnist for the Sunday *New York Times*. She writes a monthly column for financial planners in *Bloomberg Wealth Manager* magazine. Her articles have also appeared in *Fortune, Business Week, Worth, Institutional Investor, USA Today, Money, Ladies' Home Journal, Woman's Day, Self, More, Family Circle* and many other publications.

She is the author of four books—*The Fidelity Guide to Mutual Funds* (Simon & Schuster, 1990), *Best Practices for Financial Advisors* (Bloomberg Press, 1997), *A Commonsense Guide to Your 401(k)* (Bloomberg Press, 1997), and *The New Commonsense Guide to Mutual Funds* (Bloomberg Press, 1998)—and speaks frequently to business and consumer groups and financial planners.